PIRATES

BY THE NUMBERS

PIRATES

BY THE NUMBERS

A Complete Team History of the
Bucs by Uniform Number

David Finoli

SPORTS
PUBLISHING

Sports Publishing books may be purchased in bulk at special discounts for sales promotion, corporate gifts, fund-raising, or educational purposes. Special editions can also be created to specifications. For details, contact the Special Sales Department, Sports Publishing, 307 West 36th Street, 11th Floor, New York, NY 10018 or sportspubbooks@skyhorsepublishing.com.

Sports Publishing® is a registered trademark of Skyhorse Publishing, Inc.®, a Delaware corporation.

Visit our website at www.sportspubbooks.com.

10 9 8 7 6 5 4 3 2 1

Library of Congress Cataloging-in-Publication Data is available on file.

Cover design by Tom Lau
Cover photo credits: Courtesy of the Pittsburgh Pirates

ISBN: 978-1-61321-923-2
Ebook ISBN: 978-1-61321-924-9

Printed in the United States of America

To my Uncle Tom Aikens Sr., my Uncle Paul
Lonigro, my wife Vivian, as well as the great
Pittsburgh sportswriters of my youth, including
Myron Cope, Phil Musick, Al Abrams, Roy
Mc Hugh, and Bill Christine, just to name a few.
All were incredible inspirations without whom
my dreams of writing these books would never
have become a reality.

CONTENTS

INTRODUCTION

As sports fans we take for granted the numbers players wear on their uniforms today. We identify the players by the digits they wear so proudly. Mention the number 21 to any Pittsburgh Pirates fans, and before you have finished your question they quickly shout out "Roberto Clemente." It would seem difficult to follow the game without players' numbers, but almost ninety years ago that's exactly how the game was played.

It would be comparable to being at the ballpark during Jackie Robinson Day, when all players wear the number 42 to honor one of the greatest personalities the game has ever known. As wonderful and deserved an honor as it is, it also can be difficult to identify the players, since they all have the same numbers.

It's incredible to believe that not only were there no numbers in the early part of the twentieth century, but there was debate by the owners about ever using them, especially in the National League. Numbers had been worn on a temporary basis by the Cleveland Indians and the St. Louis Cardinals, but it wasn't until 1929 that the New York Yankees became the first team to don them on a permanent basis. They did so based on the position of the player in the batting order; therefore, the number 3 will always mean Babe Ruth, and the cleanup hitter, the legendary Lou Gehrig, was number 4.

Two years later, numbers were the rule on uniforms in the American League as every team now used them; the National League was another story. The Boston Braves began the 1932 season with numbers on their backs, but as the year went on the debate continued among owners as to whether or not to use them by all teams. It wasn't until an owners meeting on June 22, 1932, when they finally decided to make the change, following what was described as a "spirited" debate. It was deemed that as soon as teams could get them sewn on numbers would be the rule in the National League as well. For the Pirates it would be eight days later, on June 30, when they joined the modern era debuting player numbers in a 9–6 victory against the Cardinals.

It was a moment that opened up the future we take for granted. It's such a simple yet important part of the game. For the teams that fought against it for so long, the ultimate honor they give players in the modern game is to retire their numbers. Numbers become the identity of the players we root for, and they tell the story of a franchise that will be brought to life in the pages of this book.

(NOTE: While the official number list of franchises varies from the different baseball websites on the internet, the numbers used in this book are from the official list provided by the franchise itself.)

THE BEGINNING

It was a funny way to usher in an iconic moment, the first time a Pittsburgh Pirate team would don numbers on its uniforms. Ironically, despite its historic importance, and how long it took for the National League and the Pirates to adopt this initiative, the main selling point of the game against the St. Louis Cardinals on June 30, 1932 at Forbes Field was the fact that it was the first Ladies Day at Forbes Field.

While it was a different era, things seemed relatively comparable to today's team owners as they dragged their feet on issues of change, this one being that numbers on a uniform would be good for the game and the fans. In an article on the Baseball Hall of Fame website written by Matt Rothenberg, the author quoted *The Sporting News* referencing an editorial on November 26, 1931, when discussing this issue. "The big leagues have always been slow about adopting innovations. The magnates hemmed and hawed for a long time before they put into effect the foul-strike rule, and one circuit delayed a year or two after the other had adopted this boon to modern baseball. It is proper that the powers that be in baseball should jealously guard the game's traditions, but there is such a thing as bending over backward in refusing to adopt improvements, the value of which can hardly be denied."

After the American League had completely adopted it by the 1931 season, only the Boston Braves of the National League had decided to utilize numbers at the beginning of the 1932 campaign. The owners in the senior circuit still "hemmed and hawed" when it came to this subject. Finally, in a meeting on June 22 they overcame a heated debate to come to the conclusion that numbers made sense on a uniform. It was deemed that as soon as the teams could get them on the back of their jerseys, numbers would be the rule of the land in the entire world of Major League Baseball.

For the Pittsburgh Pirates that time period would be exactly eight days later, June 30. Instead of touting this as a new adventure to make the game easier for fans to follow, numbers became an afterthought; the main event was Ladies Day. It was not proclaimed that "We will have numbers and you will revel in them . . . FOREVER!!!" *The Pittsburgh Press* said simply, "Congratulations to Pirate management for their courtesy to the fair fans . . . every Thursday when the team is at home, Miss and Mrs. fan are invited to be guests of our pennant aspiring Pirates." The huge cartoon they put on the front page of the sports section went on to mention Ladies Day four other times, and the first-time numbers were used exactly *zero* times! The game-altering decision to wear numbers received a secondary mention in the game article in the *Pittsburgh Post-Gazette.* After talking about Ladies Day first, the paper said simply, "Also it will be the first time the local athletes have worn numbers upon their uniforms to enable spectators to identify them by glancing at the corresponding numerals on the score cards." Not certainly announcing this with trumpets blaring, but sometimes it's the simple things that can be life altering.

In the game, every Pirates starter except the pitchers got a hit, as Pie Traynor collected four and Earl Grace knocked in two with Pittsburgh defeating St. Louis 9–6. It's not the game that was memorable, or the fact the team and the paper got it wrong. In the long run, it was the numbers that changed everything and would be the everlasting legacy that came out of this affair. Below is a list of the Pirates who played that day and the numbers they donned for their curious fans.

NO	POS	PLAYER
24	1B	GUS SUHR
22	2B	TONY PIET
21	SS	ARKY VAUGHAN
20	3B	PIE TRAYNOR
11	RF	PAUL WANER
10	CF	LLOYD WANER
14	LF	DAVE BARBEE
30	C	EARL GRACE
41	SP	HEINIE MEINE
45	RP	BILL SWIFT

FIRST BATTER WITH A UNIFORM NUMBER FOR THE PIRATES: LLOYD WANER- HE FLEW OUT.

#0– 00: NOTHIN' FROM NOTHIN'

#0

ALL TIME NO. 0 ROSTER	YEAR
Junior Ortiz	(1989)

#00

ALL TIME NO. 00 ROSTER	YEAR
Joe Page	(1954)
Rick White	(2005)

NUMBER RETIRED: None

HALL OF FAMERS TO WEAR THE NUMBER: None

FIRST PERFORMANCE WITH EITHER NUMBER

9/18/1954- Joe Page tossed two innings of relief in a 7–1 loss to the Philadelphia Phillies. He gave up a hit and a walk, allowing no runs in the game.

FIRST HOME RUN WITH EITHER NUMBER

7/30/1989- Junior Ortiz had a double and a home run in an 8–6 loss against the Philadelphia Phillies. It was Ortiz's only home run of the season, a fourth-inning line drive over the left-field fence scoring Andy Van Slyke ahead of him that gave the Bucs a temporary 5–0 lead.

FIRST VICTORY BY A PITCHER WITH EITHER NUMBER

5/3/2005- Rick White tosses 1 2/3 innings in a 7–4 victory against the Houston Astros to pick up the victory, allowing a hit and striking out one.

BEST PIRATES TO WEAR THE NUMBER: (HR-RBI-AVE) (W-L-ERA)
Junior Ortiz- (1–22-.217)

He only wore it for a short time period, one season to be exact, but for a number that only three people in franchise history wore, Junior Ortiz wins the battle for the best Pirates player ever to wear a number lower than 1.

More famous for being the backstop against whom Rickey Henderson swiped the base to become the all-time major league stolen base

5

king, Ortiz was never anything more than a back-up catcher over his thirteen-year major league career. He hit .256 with the Pirates, Mets, Twins, Indians, and Rangers.

While he did have two exceptional seasons at the plate — hitting .336 in 1986 for the Bucs and a .335 average with the 1990 Twins — 1989 was not one of them. A .217 hitter that year for Pittsburgh, '89 proved to be exceptional for one reason for the Pirate catcher; it began his love affair with the number zero. After wearing 36, 24, and 26 between 1982 and 1988, Ortiz would don this special number for the remaining six seasons of his career; the reason: his name began with an O.

Rick White (10–15–4.03)

If there was a co-zero MVP it would be Rick White. Like Ortiz, White was in his second tour of duty with the Pirates when he donned the special number. In 2005 the Springfield, Ohio, native was in his tenth season when he signed a free agent contract with the Bucs. He was an effective middle reliever who would accumulate only 16 saves in his 613 appearances. With the Pirates, White was 4–7 with a decent 3.72 ERA, but his indecent 1.587 record of Walks and Hits per Innings Pitched (WHIP) probably told the true story of an aging reliever with a bad team. Pittsburgh released him following the season; White went on to play for four more teams in three seasons, collecting more than 1/3 of his 11 major league hats worn over 12 seasons.

WORST PIRATE TO WEAR THE NUMBER: (W-L-ERA)
Joe Page (0–0-11.17)

At one point in time, Joe Page was the best reliever in the game, making the odds that he would be included in this book as the worst Pittsburgh Pirate ever to wear the number 00 long indeed. Born in Cherry Hills, PA, Page grew up in Springdale, near the city where he would end his major league career in such a miserable manner. He began with the New York Yankees in 1944 and led the junior circuit in saves with 17 in 1947 before accumulating what was then a major league record 27 two years later. The year 1949 would also see Page win one and save one in the World Series, being awarded the initial Babe Ruth Award as the first MVP in the fall classic.

With everything looking up, Page felt a pop in his hip, then hurt his arm, leaving him out of the majors from 1950 until 1954, when a new-found sinker ball led him back into the majors with the Pirates. When he made the team that season he wanted the number

Junior Ortiz (photo courtesy of the Pittsburgh Pirates)

11, which was taken by catcher Toby Atwell, so instead he chose the double number nearest to 11; not 22, which most would have assumed from that reasoning, but 00. All looked well for the man they called the "Fireman," or the "Gay Reliever," as he began the season with five scoreless innings of relief. Eventually, he would have his modest scoreless streak ended; four appearances later he allowed seven runs in an inning of work and was quickly out of the majors, never to return again. After Page retired he stayed close to home running two bars: first, the Bullpen in Irwin, then Page's Rocky Lodge in nearby Laughlintown. Later in life, he was involved in a situation with Dick Schaap and *Sport Magazine* when Schaap ran into a heavy drinker in a bar who claimed to be Page. Schaap wrote a story from the conversation insinuating that the former hurler was a heavy drinker himself. Page sued for $1.5 million, finally settling for $25,000 winning a case of mistaken identity.

OTHER NOTABLE PIRATES TO WEAR THE NUMBER

There were only three to wear the number; they have all been described above . . . and all were pretty damn interesting!

#1: NICE GUYS FINISH FIRST

ALL TIME NO. 1 ROSTER	YEAR
Dixie Howell	(1947)
Bill Salkeld	(1945–1947)
Bill Baker	(1941–1943)
MANAGERS	
Billy Meyer	(1948–1952)

NUMBER RETIRED

BILLY MEYER, Manager (1954)

HALL OF FAMERS TO WEAR

THE NUMBER: None

FIRST PERFORMANCE WITH THE NUMBER

5/13/1941- After playing two games with the Cincinnati Reds to start the 1941 campaign, catcher Bill Baker was purchased by the Pittsburgh Pirates and played his first game in a Pirates uniform with the number 1 on his back. Baker started the game and had no official at bat in his first appearance, coming up twice with a walk and a sacrifice bunt while scoring a run in the Bucs' 6–3 victory over Philadelphia. He would be pinch-hit for by Spud Davis, and wouldn't get his official first at bat until the next day.

Billy Meyer (right): (Photo courtesy of the Pittsburgh Pirates)

FIRST HOME RUN WITH THE NUMBER

7/30/1943- Going two-and-a-half seasons without a major league home run, Bill Baker finally ended his streak of futility on July 30, 1943, against the New York Giants, doing so in an impressive manner. With the bases full and the Bucs down 12–2 in the sixth, Baker pinch-hit for Al Lopez and ripped a grand slam to cut the Giants' lead in half at 12–6. While the Pirates went on to lose 13–7, it was still a memorable day for the North Carolina native.

FIRST VICTORY BY A PITCHER WITH THE NUMBER

No pitcher ever wore number 1 for the Pirates.

BEST PIRATETO WEAR THE NUMBER: (HR-RBI-AVE)
Bill Salkeld (18–79-.293)

There are not many places you would see catcher Bill Salkeld listed as the best of anything, but in a field that includes three he is the king of the mountain indeed when it comes to players for the Pirates who wore the number 1.

Born in Pocatello, Idaho, Salkeld had a long, painful trip to the major leagues. Signing with the Sacramento Senators of the Pacific Coast League at only seventeen years of age in 1934, the young catcher played two seasons in the state capital before moving to the San Francisco Seals in 1936. It was there that his career and life took a detour when he was spiked in the right knee, causing an infection so severe they considered amputating his leg; his playing days were thought to be over.

Three years later he returned to the game, first with Tucson of the Arizona-Texas League, then back with the Seals. He signed with the San Diego Padres in 1940 and stayed there for five seasons, until he finally realized his major league dream when the Pirates purchased him late in 1944.

He made the team as a twenty-eight-year-old rookie in 1945, and took advantage of the opportunity with 15 home runs his rookie year, the last of the World War II seasons, with a .314 average, higher than he had hit in any minor league season he had played in to that point. It was a miracle that he was still playing the game, much less having so much success with the Bucs.

Salkeld spent two more seasons in Pittsburgh, hitting .294 and .213 respectively, before being dealt to the Boston Braves after the 1947 campaign together with Al Lyons and Jim Russell in exchange for Johnny Hopp and future managerial legend Danny Murtaugh.

WORST PIRATE TO WEAR THE NUMBER: (HR-RBI-AVE)

Bill Baker (2–42-.247)

He was the first and the worst number 1 in the history of the franchise. Bill Baker came to the Steel City in his second major league season, in 1941, after playing in only two games with the Cincinnati Reds, and backed up Al Lopez for three seasons for the Bucs.

He had little power in those seasons, hitting his first and only long ball of the time period making the most of the moment as the home run was a grand slam. While 1943 was his best year, hitting .273 in 172 at bats, it would prove to be his last wearing number 1 in a Pirates uniform. He entered the navy in 1944 and didn't return to the team until two seasons later, in 1946, when he became number 44; Bill Salkeld was wearing his former number 1. It was Baker's last season in Pittsburgh, as he went to the minors in 1947 before hooking on with the Cardinals, where he stayed two seasons before ending his major league career in 1949.

OTHER NOTABLE PIRATES TO WEAR THE NUMBER

Billy Meyer, Manager

Between 1946 and 1957 the Pittsburgh Pirates had only one winning season, 1948. Other than that, their teams were among the worst, not only in franchise history, but some would claim the worst ever to play the game. Manager Billy Meyer began his tenure with the Bucs during that surprising 1948 campaign. In 1948, when the Pirates needed a manager to fix the team, they looked toward the fifty-six-year-old minor league manager to change their fortunes. Finally making it to the big leagues, Meyer did not disappoint. As Bill James said in his book, *The Bill James Guide to Baseball Managers,* the 1947 team was flawed. "They had no left-handed hitting, no speed, and a group of old pitchers who couldn't throw strikes." Meyer added left-handed hitting and some speed, and the team finished 83–71. The beginning of a winning tenure in the Steel City was only a mirage, however, as the majority of his time with the Bucs found him managing incredibly bad teams.

Apparently, he was a nice guy because, while he had a less than stellar 317–452 mark with the team in five seasons, that included a .273 winning percentage in his last year, 1952, Billy Meyer being a nice guy seems to be the only reason that, in his honor, the number 1 was the second number ever retired by the team. Meyer had some health issues after leaving the team, suffering a stroke in 1955, and two years later he passed away. While he was not a success in his major league career, Billy Meyer was loved by fans and the press alike. When he died the local reporters were all glowing in their assessment of the man. In his hometown of Knoxville, they named their baseball stadium after him.

His mark in Pirates history is that his number was retired officially in 1954, and no player had worn it since he resigned two years earlier. It's a date that has no concrete basis. In fact there was a report in the *Pittsburgh Press* on February 7, 1958, that the team had made number 1 the second number retired in franchise history in honor of Meyer, next to number 33 that the great Honus Wagner wore as a coach. With no reasonable explanation as to why the number was retired except that he was a nice guy, it remains probably the most confusing retired number in the history of the sport, maybe in the history of all sports.

#2: AND A BROADCASTER SHALL LEAD THEM

ALL TIME NO. 2 ROSTER	YEAR
Brandon Inge	(2013)
Marlon Byrd	(2013)
Brock Holt	(2012)
Brandon Wood	(2011)
Bobby Crosby	(2010)
Jack Wilson	(2003–2009)
Pat Meares	(1999–2001)
Kevin Polcovich	(1997–1998)
Angelo Encarnacion	(1995–1996)
Lonnie Smith	(1993)
Gary Redus	(1990–1992)
Orestes Destrade	(1989)
Mackey Sasser	(1987)
Jim Morrison	(1982–1987)
Vance Law	(1981–1982)
Bernie Carbo	(1980)
Gary Hargis	(1979)
Jackie Hernandez	(1971–1973)
Freddie Patek	(1968–1970)
Chuck Hiller	(1968)
Hal Smith	(1965)
Dave Wissman	(1964)
Ted Savage	(1963–1964)
Elmo Plaskett	(1962–1963)
Don Leppert	(1961–1962)
Bob Oldis	(1960–1961)
Joe Garagiola	(1951–1952)
Hank Schenz	(1950–1951)
Les Fleming	(1949)
Jimmy Bloodworth	(1947)
Bill Salkeld	(1947)
Jimmy Brown	(1946)
Tony Ordenana	(1943)
Ripper Collins	(1941)
MANAGERS	
Bobby Bragan	(1956–1957)
Fred Haney	(1953–1955)
COACHES	
Hal Smith	(1965–1967)
Jose Pagan	(1974–1978)
Jeff Branson	(2014–2015)

NUMBER RETIRED: None

HALL OF FAMERS TO WEAR THE NUMBER

JOE GARAGIOLA (1991 Ford Frick Award winner)

FIRST PERFORMANCE WITH THE NUMBER

4/19/1941- After a three-year layoff from the major leagues, the former star of the famed Gashouse Gang with the St. Louis Cardinals, Rip Collins, returned to the majors with the Pittsburgh Pirates. His former manager and teammate with the Cards, Frankie Frisch, was now at the helm of the Bucs and hoped to get whatever talent Collins had left. The thirty-seven-year-old Altoona native struck out after pinch-hitting for Frankie Gustine.

FIRST HOME RUN WITH THE NUMBER

7/6/1947- In the first game of a double-header against the Chicago Cubs, Jimmy Bloodworth, an eight-year veteran who had been purchased by the Bucs from Detroit in the off-season, had a three-hit game that included the first home run a number 2 would ever hit. It was in the sixth inning with the great Hank Green-

Joe Garagiola (photo courtesy of the Pittsburgh Pirates)

berg aboard, giving the Bucs a 3–1 lead in a game the team would eventually win, 6–2.

FIRST VICTORY BY A PITCHER WITH THE NUMBER

No pitcher won a game wearing the number 2 for the Pirates.

BEST PIRATES TO WEAR THE NUMBER: (HR-RBI-AVE)

Jack Wilson (60–389-.269)

After wearing Terry Bradshaw's number for the first two seasons he was with the Pirates, following his acquisition from the St. Louis Cardinals in 2000 for reliever Jeff Christiansen, slick-fielding shortstop Jack Wilson donned the number 2 for the first time in 2003, the beginning of his ascension as one of the top at his position in the National League, and one of the soon to be most popular faces of the then moribund franchise.

A year later, Wilson broke the .300 plateau for his first time in the majors with a .308 average, capturing the league's Silver Slugger Award, and was selected to play in the only All-Star game of his twelve-year career. By the time he left Pittsburgh in mid-season of 2009, while the team was trying to rebuild once again, Wilson had made himself the best number 2 in franchise history.

Jim Morrison (57–241-.274)

Obtained from the Chicago White Sox in June of 1982, Jim Morrison was a good hitting utility player for the Pirates his first three-and-a-half seasons with the team, until he had the chance to take over the starting nod at third in 1986. He then blossomed into one of the most powerful at his position in the senior circuit.

Morrison finished in the top ten in the NL in slugging percentage, home runs, doubles, extra base hits and RBIs, hitting 23 homers and knocking in 88 runs. By making himself such an effective player, Morrison became a prime candidate to be traded by the rebuilding Bucs, which they did, sending him to the Tigers for Darnell Coles and Morris Madden in August of 1987. While he hit .400 in the 1987 ALCS with Detroit, it proved to be a good move for Pittsburgh; Morrison was out of the majors a year later, following two mostly unproductive seasons with the Tigers and Braves.

Jack Wilson (photo courtesy of author)

Gary Redus (24–96–.255)

A top prospect for the Cincinnati Reds in the late 1970s and early 1980s, where he hit over .300 with 93 homers in five seasons, Gary Redus came to the majors in an impressive fashion, hitting 17 home runs his official rookie campaign in 1983. But he was unable to repeat his success, and after time spent with the Phillies and White Sox, Redus was dealt to the Pirates in August of 1988 for Mike Diaz.

Even though Redus never was a starter for the Bucs, he was an indispensable utility outfielder and bench player for the three-time eastern division champions between 1990 and 1992.

After hitting .255 in his five seasons in a Pirates uniform, he was signed as a free agent by Texas in 1993, where he ended his major league career after the 1994 campaign.

WORST PIRATES TO WEAR THE NUMBER: (HR-RBI-AVE)
Bob Oldis (0–1–.160)

After spending four seasons in the minor leagues following three very sporadic seasons with the Washington Senators, Bob Oldis was picked up by the Pirates in the Rule V draft following the 1959 campaign. What the Bucs got for their efforts was a funny man who was good defensively. On offense, though, he made people forget another famous Pirate: Mario Mendoza.

While spending the entire 1960 season on the roster, Oldis came to the plate exactly 21 times, reaching the Mendoza line on the button with a .200 average. He achieved exactly two things that season: keeping his teammates laughing with his sense of humor and earning himself a World Series ring while keeping the bench warm.

Oldis was hitless in five at bats in 1961, ending his Pirates career by nose-diving below the famed Mendoza line, finishing his Pirates career with a .160 average, a mark worthy of the worst number 2 in Pirates history.

Brandon Inge (1–7-.181)

Brandon Inge was a slugging third baseman for the Detroit Tigers in the first decade of the twenty-first century, twice hitting 27 home runs in a season. The Pirates had just finished their twentieth consecutive losing season, in 2012, when they inked the thirty-six-year-old former slugger, and he did flex his muscle with the Bucs, hitting home runs at an impressive rate comparable to another legendary slugger with the team, Luke Walker. Inge did nothing that Pirates management hoped he would, smacking exactly one long ball in 105 at bats while coming in with a "scintillating" .181 average. Before August was four days old he was released, never to play in the majors again.

Vance Law (0–6-.184)

A thirty-ninth round draft pick out of Brigham Young University, Vance Law was the son of former Cy Young Award winner Vern Law, and in 1980 hoped to team up with another son of a baseball legend, Dale Berra, to keep the Pirates' winning ways afloat. Instead, what we got was the son of Yogi in trouble off the field on several occasions while not causing trouble for Pirates opponents on it. As for Law, he was not as much of an embarrassment to the franchise as Berra had been in some of his exploits, but he was his equal on the diamond, hitting a mere .184 over two seasons.

Although he did not lift the Pirates to the heights his father did, Vance Law's career did improve after he left the Steel City, finishing his eleven-year career with a .256 average with the Expos, White Sox, Cubs, and A's.

Special mention in number 2s goes in a negative way to Gary Hargis and the other Hal Smith, who were hitless with the Pirates, and with applause to the great Bobby Bragan and his .397 winning percentage.

OTHER NOTABLE PIRATES TO WEAR THE NUMBER

Tony Ordenana

Born in Guanabacoa, Cuba, Tony Ordenana was truly a one-game wonder, playing in his lone major league game on October 3, 1943. Considered one of his native country's greatest athletes, Ordenana made the most of his lone major league appearance with two hits in four at bats with three RBIs for the Bucs against Phillies, driving in all of the team's runs in an 11–3 loss.

What was his greatest day in the game turned out to be his last, as he spent the next ten years in the minors, in eleven leagues hitting .250 without a home run.

Joe Garagiola

As a ballplayer Joe Garagiola was very average, which he certainly was for the Pittsburgh Pirates, hitting .262 between 1951 and 1953. Like the great Bob Uecker, it was after his career was over that he became an American icon.

Garagiola was one of the great national broadcasters of all time with NBC, finding his way into the Hall of Fame by being given the Ford Frick Award in 1991. After he also appeared as a regular on the *Today Show* in the late 1960s and early 1970s, it would be accurate to say that he is the most famous number 2 in franchise history.

Hank Schenz

Hank Schenz had only 558 at bats in his major league career that included a .222 average in two seasons with the Bucs. Like Garagiola, it wasn't his play on the field that made Schenz a household name, but what he did off it . . . well, behind the scoreboard, that is. He admitted to using a telescope from the scoreboard at the Polo Grounds during the Giants' miraculous season in 1951 to steal the signs of the opposing catcher and signal to the New York hitters what was coming, which shrouded their pennant victory in controversy. It was a true maneuver that NFL New England Patriots coach Bill Belichick would be proud of.

Don Leppert

Leppert spent two seasons in Pittsburgh right after their 1960 world championship, hitting .266 before becoming a coach for the team between 1968 and 1973; Pirates fans of the era will always remember the sight of his cheek looking like a blowfish, full of chewing tobacco.

Bernie Carbo

Remembered as one of the stars of arguably the greatest World Series game of all time, (except for game seven of the 1960 World Series, of course) Bernie Carbo — who hit a home run to tie the sixth contest of the 1975 fall classic — became a Pittsburgh Pirate for a brief period of time in 1980, inking a free agent contract in September. While he hit .333 (less impressive considering it represented two hits for only six at bats) Carbo was unable to manufacture his Fenway magic in Three Rivers Stadium.

Fred Haney, Manager

After twelve years out of the majors as a manager following his unimpressive three-year run with the St. Louis Browns, Fred Haney continued his train wreck of a run as a major league skipper with the Bucs between 1953 and '55, producing a .353 winning percentage. For some reason unbeknownst to man, the Milwaukee Braves hired him to run their young club the following season.

A funny thing happens when a manger has a talented team: he looks like a genius. Haney not only won but won big, capturing the 1957 World Series, then winning the National League pennant again a year later.

#3: IT'S TPLUSH's WORLD, WE ARE JUST LIVING IN IT

ALL TIME NO. 3 ROSTER	YEAR
Sean Rodriguez	(2015)
Michael Martinez	(2014)
Travis Ishikawa	(2014)
Chase d'Arnaud	(2012)
Pedro Ciriaco	(2011)
Akinori Iwamura	(2010)
Nyjer Morgan	(2008–2009)
Nate McLouth	(2007)
Cesar Izturis	(2007)
Jeromy Burnitz	(2006)
Rob Mackowiak	(2005)
Chris Stynes	(2004)
Pokey Reese	(2002–2003)
Chad Hermansen	(1999–2001)
Shawon Dunston	(1997)
Jay Bell	(1989–1996)
Ruben Rodriguez	(1988)
Johnny Ray	(1981–1987)
Phil Garner	(1977–1981)
Richie Hebner	(1972–1976)
Frank Taveras	(1971–1972)
Ron Davis	(1969)
Bob Robertson	(1967)
Jim Pagliaroni	(1963–1964)
Orlando McFarlane	(1962)
RC Stevens	(1960)
Ted Kluszewski	(1958–1959)
Dee Fondy	(1957)
Dale Long	(1956–1957)
George Freese	(1955)
Bob Skinner	(1954)
Joe Garagiola	(1953)
Clyde McCullough	(1951–1952)
Bob Dillinger	(1950–1951)
Dale Coogan	(1950)
Eddie Bockman	(1949)
Johnny Riddle	(1948)
Al Gionfriddo	(1944–1946)
Bill Rodgers	(1944–1945)
Elbie Fletcher	(1939–1943, 1947)

NUMBER RETIRED: None

HALL OF FAMERS TO WEAR THE NUMBER: JOE GARAGIOLA (1991 Ford Frick Award winner)

FIRST PERFORMANCE WITH THE NUMBER

6/17/1939- In his first game after coming over from the Boston Braves, Elbie Fletcher, pinch-hitting for catcher Ray Berres, hit a double during an 11-2 loss to the Phillies.

FIRST HOME RUN WITH THE NUMBER

7/4/1939- In the second game of a double header at St. Louis, Elbie Fletcher was the offensive star with two hits that included his first home run in a Bucs uniform, and four RBIs, in a 6–3 win over the Cards.

FIRST VICTORY BY A PITCHER WITH THE NUMBER

No pitcher ever wore the number 3 for the Pirates.

MANAGER	
Harry Walker	(1965-1967)
COACHES	
Joe Lonnett	(1977)
Jay Bell	(2013)

BEST PIRATES TO WEAR THE NUMBER: (HR-RBI-AVE)

Jay Bell (78–423-.269)

It was one of the most one-sided trades in Pittsburgh Pirates history, taking the Cleveland Indians' disappointing shortstop prospect Jay Bell for Denny Gonzalez and the legendary Felix "The Cat" Fermin. It was also a stabilizing force for the infield that helped spur the Pirates to three straight eastern division crowns.

He became a solid force and important piece of the Pirates' championship puzzle and a sacrifice hit machine, accumulating a National League high 69 in 1990 and '91. Over the course of his eight seasons in the Steel City, Bell hit .269, was selected to play in an All-Star Game and won both a Gold Glove and Silver Slugger Award while finishing in the top 20 for the MVP race twice.

When he left the Bucs he developed power as he got older, hitting 38 homers for the Diamondbacks in 1999 at the age of thirty-three, before winning a world championship there two years later. The once disappointing prospect did eventually find his way and became the greatest number 3 on this list.

Elbie Fletcher (60–464-.279)

Elbie Fletcher, seen here being congratulated after a homer in 1943. (Photo courtesy of the Pittsburgh Pirates)

The first number 3 has remained one of the best throughout the years in Pittsburgh Pirates history. Elburt "Elbie" Fletcher won a newspaper contest and was given a chance to play with his hometown Boston Braves, appearing in his first major league game at the age of eighteen.

He was dealt to the Pirates in June of 1939 in another one-sided deal for Bill Schuster, and immediately found his batting swing, hitting .303 for the Bucs the rest of the season. The next year he knocked in 104 runs and began a string of three consecutive years when he led the league in on-base percentage. He remained a dangerous hitter until entering the Navy after the 1943 campaign, when he served his country proudly for two years in World War II.

Fletcher wasn't the same player after he returned from the service, but he still was successful enough to hang on to his lofty status here.

Johnny Ray (37–391-.286) and Richie Hebner (128–520-.277)

Johnny Ray, Richie Hebner. Richie Hebner, Johnny Ray. The decision couldn't be made as to who hung onto the last spot on this list, so they both share the honor.

While Ray was part of a rebuilding project in the early 1980s that went bad, he was the best piece of it. Acquired from the Astros with two other players in a trade for Phil Garner, Ray took the National League by storm hitting .281 while capturing *The Sporting News* Rookie of the Year Award in 1982.

An all-state football and basketball player in high school, Ray went on to win the Silver Slugger Award in 1983 and led the league in doubles two years.

A former grave digger in Boston, hence his nickname "the grave-digger," Richie Hebner was part of a group of dynamic young players who came through the Pirates system in the late 1960s, helping lead them to a World Series title in 1971.

Hebner became a great number 3 for one reason and one reason only: the team decided to retire Pie Traynor's number 20 in 1972, the same number Richie Hebner had been wearing, so he decided that 3 would be his number ... and history was made.

WORST THREE PIRATES TO WEAR THE NUMBER: (HR-RBI-AVE)

Chad Hermansen (12–29-.199)

The first-round pick in the 1995 amateur draft, Chad Hermansen was the rock upon which the new Pirates championship era was supposed to be built; instead, he was the poster child for the legendary streak of losing baseball.

His power in the minors was incredible: 60 homers in Nashville in 1998 and '99; in the majors it was on a par with Dal Maxvill's: 12 in his Bucco career, with a "stellar" .199 average in Pittsburgh.

Akinori Iwamura (2–9-.182)

A star in Japan and a fine player with the Tampa Bay Rays, much was expected from Iwamura when the Bucs acquired him as their highest paid player at $4.9 million. But he defied those expectations with two homers and a .192 average in 2010, causing the Bucs to designate him for assignment elsewhere even before his first season was completed in the 'Burgh.

Michael Martinez (0–2-.128) and Orlando McFarlane (0–2-.208)

It was only appropriate that there should be a tie for the third worst player, since there was one for the best, although this is a race that most would not want to win. Martinez was a .128 hitter for the club in his only season in 2014, while the great Orlando McFarlane, a former Cuban star, was a "scintillating" .087 in his only season wearing the number 3 in 1962.

OTHER INTERESTING PIRATES TO WEAR THE NUMBER

Dee Fondy

Dee Fondy was a fine major league hitter, with a .285 career average that included a .313 average in his only year in the Steel City during the 1957 campaign, performing well the majority of a campaign in which he was traded in May, but it was his off-the-field activities that caused his inclusion on this list.

A rare speedy player for a first baseman, Fondy was part of a regiment that landed on Utah Beach in Normandy during the D-Day invasion, and later was awarded the Purple Heart. He went to the Cubs along with a player named Chuck Connors, the same Chuck Connors who eventually became TV's famed Rifleman, and was also the last

player to bat at Ebbets Field before the Brooklyn Dodgers broke
the borough's hearts by moving
to California. That's enough off-
field activity to make Dee Fondy
a very interesting number 3.

Harry Walker

A good hitter with a .296 career
average and a NL batting title to
his credit, hitting .363 with the
Cardinals and Phillies in 1947,
Harry "The Hat" Walker brought
his famed hitting prowess to the

Richie Hebner (photo courtesy of the
Pittsburgh Pirates)

Pittsburgh Pirates in 1965 as their manager, where he was credited for
making Matty Alou, a light-hitting reserve, into a player who won a National League batting crown himself.

A World War II hero who won a Bronze Star and Purple Heart in the
European Theater, Walker's Pirates won more than ninety games his
first two seasons before he was replaced as manager by Danny Murtaugh following the team's 42–42 start in 1967.

Dale Long

For Dale Long the number 3 truly turned out to be his lucky number.
Hitting 27 home runs in 1956, Long went on a memorable eight-game
streak early in the season when he put his name among the greatest
ever to play the game, belting home runs in every contest. It was a
major league record so impressive that it has never been bettered in
the sixty seasons since.

Ted Kluszewski

Pictures of Ted Kluszewski in a sleeveless shirt for the Cincinnati Reds,
showing off his muscular biceps, are well known in baseball history.
The Cincinnati strongman hit over 40 home runs for three consecutive

seasons, including a league-leading 49 in 1954, when he also had a NL-high 141 RBIs.

By the time he came to Pittsburgh in 1958 he was not the same player; Forbes Field was not kind to the slugger, who hit only six home runs in a season and a half.

Bob Dillinger

Bob Dillinger started his major league career late, at the age of twenty-seven, after spending time in the service during World War II. When he finally arrived in 1947, for the St. Louis Browns it was worth the wait. He hit .309 in four seasons with them, leading the league three times in stolen bases and once in hits.

The thirty-two-year-old was purchased by the Bucs in May of 1950, and while he hit .288 his first of two seasons, he slumped to .233 a year later before being sold to the White Sox in mid-season.

Bill Rogers

The Harrisburg native who was a wartime player could brag he was a .400 hitter in his major league career between 1944 and '45; the problem is, he had only five major league at bats.

A former minor league pitcher who became an outfielder, Baseball-reference.com reminds us not to confuse him with "Rawmeat" Bill Rodgers, so we will not.

Phil Garner

Traded to the Pittsburgh Pirates in 1977 for pretty much every good prospect in their farm system, Garner became an integral part of the 1979 Fam-a-lee, helping the Bucs win a world championship. If there was a "top five" number 3s, Garner, who hit .500 with 12 hits in the '79 World Series, certainly would have been on that list. He will be remembered fondly in Bucco history. Garner eventually became a successful major league skipper, managing for fifteen seasons while winning the National League pennant with the Astros in 2005.

Travis Ishikawa

Ishikawa was so bad with the Pittsburgh Pirates in 2014 yet they took him back a year later, but he continued *not* to hit. In between, he was the 2014 NLCS MVP with the San Francisco Giants, hitting a three-run homer in the bottom of the ninth of game five that won the pennant. Maybe it's the air in Pittsburgh that doesn't agree with him.

Nyjer Morgan

A decent slap-hitter for the Bucs with a .286 average over three seasons, and a former hockey player who was with the Regina Pats of the Western Hockey League, Nyjer Morgan is more known for his alter ego, Tony Plush (or TPlush for short) who was at times funny and controversial. He'd take to Twitter, acted strange on the field at times, and generally made Tony Plush an icon . . . in his own mind. It was unfortunate that TPlush overshadowed the fact that Morgan was a pretty good player throughout his seven-year career.

Al Gionfriddo

A .266 hitter who batted only 580 times in his four-year career, the majority of them with the Bucs, Al Gionfriddo was known for exactly one thing, making a superb catch off the bat of the legendary Joe Di-Maggio in the sixth inning of game six in the 1947 World Series that apparently really irritated Joltin' Joe. It's a film clip that has become famous over the years, coupled with Red Barber's memorable call. The ironic thing about the historic performance is that it was Gionfriddo's last major league game.

Dale Coogan

Playing in exactly one major league season, when he hit .240 for the horrific Pittsburgh Pirates in 1950, Dale Coogan blasted one major league home run, against Ralph Branca on June 24⁻ before the game was called due to a curfew. When the contest was completed on August 1, Coogan was no longer with the team, having being sent to the minors from whence he would never return.

#4: WE CAN FINISH LAST WITHOUT YOU

ALL TIME NO. 4 ROSTER	YEAR
Mike LaValliere	(1987)
Mike Brown	(1985–1986)
Dale Berra	(1977–1984)
Jim Campanis	(1973)
Charlie Sands	(1971–1972)
George Brunet	(1970)
Rex Johnston	(1964)
Jerry May	(1964)
Bob Skinner	(1956–1963)
Sid Gordon	(1954–1955)
Ralph Kiner	(1947–1953)
Jack Saltzgaver	(1945)
Al Rubeling	(1943–1944)
Huck Geary	(1942–1943)
Stu Martin	(1941–1942)
Billy Cox	(1941)
Pep Young	(1940)
MANAGERS	
Larry Shepard	(1968–1969)
Chick Tanner	(1977)
COACHES	
Bob Skinner	(1974–1976)
Johnny Pesky	(1965–1967)

NUMBER RETIRED: RALPH KINER (1987)

HALL OF FAMERS TO WEAR THE NUMBER: RALPH KINER (1975)

FIRST PERFORMANCE WITH THE NUMBER

4/16/1940- After taking a 6–0 lead in the season opener, the Cardinals scored four runs in the bottom of the sixth to make it close, but Pittsburgh held on for a 6–4 victory. Pep Young was one-for-three with two strikeouts as he debuted the number 4 for the franchise.

FIRST HOME RUN WITH THE NUMBER

5/19/1940- Thirty-two-year old veteran Pep Young was two-for-four, with a two-run homer over the left-field wall at Shibe Park against Kirby Higbe in a 6–5 loss against the Phillies. Young had three RBIs on the day, pushing his batting average over .200 to .212.

FIRST VICTORY BY A PITCHER WITH THE NUMBER

10/1/1970- It was the last day of the 1970 season, and the newly crowned eastern division champions were playing the St. Louis Cardinals in a meaningless game. Starter Steve Blass allowed four runs in three innings before manager Danny Murtaugh, in the fourth, called on reliever George Brunet, whom they acquired for the September pennant run from Washington. Brunet was almost perfect in three innings, allowing two hits and striking out three in what would turn out to be a 9–5 victory, in which Brunet was given his one and only victory in a Pirates uniform.

BEST PIRATES TO WEAR THE NUMBER: (HR-RBI-AVE)

Ralph Kiner (301–801-.280)

It's tough to really appreciate what was more special about Ralph Kiner, his prodigious home run records or his legendary dating prowess. On the diamond Kiner had few peers. He had the most home runs in a player's first 1,000 games: 277 (broken by Ryan Howard; the player to reach 300 home runs the soonest; he won eight consecutive NL home run titles; hit the most home runs ever in a player's first three, four, five, six, seven, and eight seasons in major league history, and was elected to the Baseball Hall of Fame in 1975. He had his number retired by the Pirates in 1987, and had a statue placed inside PNC Park of his hands holding a bat while celebrating his home run titles (which was taken away to make room for a beer stand before the 2015 campaign). The only negative was that new general manager Branch Rickey traded him to the Cubs, pointing out that they finished last with him and they could do it without him! Other than the unceremonious way he left the Steel City, all his baseball marks were extremely impressive, until perhaps one compares them with the accomplishments of whom he dated. The list is a Hollywood Hall of Fame potpourri: Janet Leigh, Liz Taylor, Marilyn Monroe, Ava Gardner, and Jane Russell. The women he married included tennis star Nancy Chaffee and movie actress/swimming star Esther Williams. While it's a close call between the two as to which is more impressive, the whole ball of wax makes him the most fascinating number 4 of all time.

Ralph Kiner (left) and Johnny Mize (right). (Photo courtesy of the Pittsburgh Pirates)

Bob Skinner (90–462-.280)

There were other notable players on the Pittsburgh Pirates' 1960 world championship team — Vern Law, Dick Groat, Bill Mazeroski, and Roberto Clemente, to name a few — but make no mistake, Bob Skinner was just as important to their success as any of the others.

A Korean War vet, Skinner eclipsed the .300 plateau three times as a Pirate, including a career-high .321 in 1958. His resume included being selected as a two-time All-Star who also received votes in the MVP race on two occasions. Skinner was a natural hitter, which served him well after his major league career was over, as a long-time hitting coach for several teams, including the Pirates, where he helped the Fam-A-Lee at the plate in 1979.

Dale Berra (46–255-.238)

It hurts to list Dale Berra on a "best of" list; his incredible natural talent and penchant for not fulfilling that talent should realistically land him on a "worst of" list. What this rating basically says is, aside from Skinner and Kiner, there were basically no very good number 4s in Pittsburgh Pirates history.

A first-round pick by the Bucs in the 1975 amateur draft, the son of Hall of Fame Yankees catcher Yogi Berra made news during his career for all the wrong reasons. Implicated in the Pittsburgh cocaine trial, arrested for possession and public urination, his actions overshadowed the fact that he was a shortstop with some pop in his bat, twice hitting ten home runs and 25 doubles in a season. Like Chad Hermansen later on, he was the poster child for bad baseball, yet unlike Hermansen he is not at the top of the worst player list.

WORST PIRATES TO WEAR THE NUMBER: (HR-RBI-AVE)
Huck Geary- (1–15-.160)

There were some less-than-stellar players in Major League Baseball during World War II , and then there was Eugene "Huck" Geary. A .288 hitter in the minor leagues, Geary would not approach that mark in his two seasons with the Pirates in 1942 and '43. In 1943 he remarkably struck out only six times in 166 at bats. Unfortunately, when he made contact he wasn't much better, hitting a mere .151. Mercifully, he never played in the majors afterward, although he served his country proudly during the war.

Charlie Sands-(1–5-.192)

A Newport News native, catcher Charlie Sands had the honor of winning a ring for the 1971 world champion Pittsburgh Pirates, although, as the third catcher behind Manny Sanguillen and Milt May, he did so while sitting on the bench. It wasn't that Sands didn't have talent; he led the Dominican League in home runs following the Bucs' World Series campaign while showing power in the minors. Unfortunately, he was a prime example of the drawback to being selected a player in the Rule V draft and being kept on a major league roster instead of being allowed to develop in the minors, which is what happened when the Yankees took him in 1967. Regardless, had things turned out better he may have just been an afterthought instead of a notable bad player for the Bucs.

Rex Johnston-(0–0-.000)

Rex Johnston, who was a star at the University of Southern California, has the distinction of being the only professional athlete to play for both the Pittsburgh Pirates and Pittsburgh Steelers. He also has the distinction of being seriously considered as one of the worst players for both teams. Struggling with the Bucs farm system, he tried out and made the Steelers in 1960, running for twelve yards in four attempts in his only NFL season. When he finally made the majors in 1964, he "topped" his Steeler effort, going hitless in his only seven major league at bats, although he did walk three times.

OTHER NOTABLE PIRATES TO WEAR THE NUMBER

Jack Saltzgaver

A reserve with the New York Yankees between 1932 and 1937, Jack Saltzgaver thought his major league career was over at that point.

He languished in the minor leagues afterward until 1945, when most of the major league players were serving their country in World War II. It gave the forty-two-year-old an opportunity to revive his dream and he did not disappoint, with a career-high .325 average for the Bucs. He went on to manage in the minor leagues, where he won a league title in 1947 with Wilmington.

Billy Cox

More noted for his career with the Brooklyn Dodgers after being traded from the Pirates in 1948, Billy Cox was a fine player for Pittsburgh upon returning from World War II service, having fought in Guadalcanal. He lost thirty-five pounds while in the service, returning as only a 132-pound player. Despite his issues he hit well with the Bucs, finishing with a .280 average and smacking a career-high 15 home runs in 1947.

Sid Gordon

A slugger with the Giants and Braves, hitting 202 home runs while knocking in over 100 runs on three occasions, Sid Gordon came to the Bucs in 1954 at the age of thirty-six. He hit .306 in his first season with the Pirates, which was a career high. He also was the last starting right fielder for the franchise until 1973 who wasn't named Roberto Clemente, giving way to the Bucs legend at that position in 1955.

Jim Campanis

He was the son of famed Dodgers general manager Al Campanis, whose career ended unceremoniously on national TV when Ted Koppel wanted to know why there weren't black executives in major league baseball, and Campanis's embarrassing answer probably gave the true reason: ignorance. It would, unfortunately, be the main thing his son would be known for. Jim was quite simply a lousy hitter, with a .147 career average that included a one-for-six performance with the Pirates in 1973.

Johnny Pesky

Johnny Pesky was a Red Sox legend who hit .307 in ten seasons after returning from the service during World War II. He was, unfortunately, probably best known as the man the Red Sox Nation blamed for losing the 1946 World Series when he was accused of holding a relay throw a little too long, allowing Enos Slaughter of the Cardinals to score the winning run in the bottom of the eighth inning during the seventh game. Pesky came to Pittsburgh in 1965 as a coach, staying there for three seasons before managing their AAA team in Columbus in 1968. The Red Sox Nation forgave him, and now the right-field pole in Fenway is named Pesky's Pole.

#5: HE BROKE OUR HEARTS

ALL TIME NO. 5 ROSTER	YEAR
Josh Harrison	(2012–2015)
Ronny Cedeno	(2011)
Ramon Vazquez	(2009)
Chris Gomez	(2008)
Josh Phelps	(2007)
Joe Randa	(2006)
Tike Redman	(2000–2001,2003–2005)
Ed Sprague	(1999)
Tony Womack	(1997–1998)
Jacob Brumfield	(1995–1996)
Jerry Goff	(1994)
Lance Parrish	(1994)
Alex Cole	(1992)
Jose Gonzalez	(1991)
Sid Bream	(1985–1990)
Bill Madlock	(1979–1985)
Doe Boyland	(1979)
Duffy Dyer	(1975–1978)
Mike Ryan	(1974)
Dave Ricketts	(1970)
Orlando McFarlane	(1964)
Larry Elliot	(1963)
Howie Goss	(1962)
Hal Smith	(1960–1961)
Buddy Pritchard	(1957)
Preston Ward	(1953–1956)
Dick Hall	(1952–1953)
Tony Bartirome	(1952)
Jack Phillips	(1950–1952)
Ed Stevens	(1948)
Hank Greenberg	(1947)
Pete Coscarart	(1942–1946)
Arky Vaughan	(1940–1941)
COACHES	
Alex Grammas	(1965–1969)
Don Long	(2010)

NUMBER RETIRED: None

HALL OF FAMERS TO WEAR THE NUMBER: ARKY VAUGHAN (1985), HANK GREENBERG (1956)

FIRST PERFORMANCE WITH THE NUMBER

4/16/1940- In a 6–4 opening day victory against the St. Louis Cardinals, Arky Vaughan had a magnificent day with three hits in five at bats, scoring twice with two RBIs.

FIRST HOME RUN WITH THE NUMBER

5/25/1940- 1940 proved to be the beginning of a new era for Pirates Hall of Fame shortstop Arky Vaughan, as he shed his more traditional number 21 for the number 5,which seemingly caused his power outage at the beginning of the season. It would be almost two months before Vaughan smacked his first home run of the year. It came in the midst of a 12–7 Bucs victory, when Arky was two-for-four with four runs scored and three RBIs, finally ending the power shortage with his first home run of the season.

FIRST VICTORY BY A PITCHER WITH NUMBER

A Pirates pitcher has never won a game as a number 5.

BEST PIRATES TO WEAR THE NUMBER: (HR-RBI-AVE)

Bill Madlock (68–390-.297)

He was a cranky boy at times throughout his career, letting his fiery temper get in the way of his immense talent, but make no mistake: Bill Madlock was one of the premier hitters of his era. Winner of four batting titles, including two with the Pittsburgh Pirates in 1981 and '83, the man they dubbed "Mad Dog" was also a pivotal part of the franchise's last world championship team after coming over from the San Francisco Giants in mid-season. In 1980, his temper made the headlines once again when he hit an umpire with his glove during an argument, although he would later claim it was an accident.

Despite the fact he won the four titles, had over 2,000 hits, and hit .305 for his career, Madlock received little to no support in the Hall of Fame vote, garnering only 4.5 percent in 1993 in his one and only season on the ballot, perhaps due to his several run-ins with the baseball law. Even though the lords of baseball may not have liked him, his Pirates teammates did; he was selected captain of the team following Willie Stargell's retirement in 1982. Madlock is the last captain ever selected by the franchise.

Josh Harrison (24–126-.284)

He was a throw-in when the Pirates dealt John Grabow and Tom Gorzelanny to the Cubs in 2009, but sometimes the throw-in turns out to be the gem of the deal, and in this situation Josh Harrison was the gem.

After bouncing back and forth between the majors and minors, Harrison, a .306 hitter in the minor leagues, had his coming of age in 2014. First he was a super sub, then he was selected to play in his first All-Star Game. Finally he became the starting third baseman in a year when he hit .315 for the Bucs, which earned him a mega five-year $45 million contract. Even though he sat out some games n 2015 due to a torn UCL in his left thumb, the future certainly looks bright for the Cincinnati native, a gift from the Cubs who just keeps giving.

Sid Bream (57–293-.269)

Say it ain't so, Sid Bream. Having coming over from the Los Angeles Dodgers, you may not have lived up to the press clippings as one of the game's best prospects with Los Angeles after hitting 32 home runs with Albuquerque in 1983, but you solidified the situation at first base for Pittsburgh and proved to be one of the classiest athletes ever to grace the Steel City.

It wasn't your fault the Bucs didn't pursue you when you became a free agent in 1991, and we even gave you a standing ovation when you came back with the Braves and hit a home run at Three Rivers Stadium. So WHY, WHY did you have to break our hearts and score the winning run in game seven of the 1992 NLCS? We will try to forgive you.

WORST PIRATES TO WEAR THE NUMBER: (HR-RBI-AVE)
Buddy Pritchard- (0–0-.091)

Yet another USC star, Buddy Prtichard became a bonus baby with the Pittsburgh Pirates and proved to be not really worth the investment. His major league career consisted of 11 at bats and, after scoring a run in his first major league experience as a pinch-runner, he had only one hit, a single against Don Newcombe in the bottom of the fifth in a 3–2 victory against Brooklyn on May, 28, 1957. He was hitless in his final five at bats before being relegated to the minor leagues for the rest of his days in professional baseball.

Mike Ryan-(0–0-.100)

A light-hitting, great defensive backup catcher for most of his eleven-year major league career, Mike Ryan's last stop on the major league express was in Pittsburgh, cross state from the team he spent six years with, the Philadelphia Phillies. He was not exactly a gift, with three hits in 30 at bats in 1974, before bowing out gracefully from his big league career.

Doe Boyland-(0–1-.105)

Dorian "Doe" Boyland was a solid minor league player for the Pittsburgh Pirates, accumulating a .289 average in six seasons following

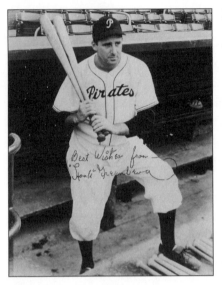

Hank Greenberg (photo courtesy of the Pittsburgh Pirates)

his selection in the second round of the 1976 amateur draft out of Wisconsin-Oshkosh. Boyland became a career major league pinch-hitter, and not much of one, with a two-for-nineteen performance in his major league career, which amounts to a .105 average. The only thing that keeps him below Pritchard and Ryan is the fact that he was the only one of the three to get an RBI.

OTHER NOTABLE PIRATES TO WEAR THE NUMBER

Hank Greenberg

It wasn't the best of partings when one of the greatest power hitters in the history of the game, Hank Greenberg, left the Detroit Tigers, but for the Pittsburgh Pirates and their young slugger Ralph Kiner, the move was very much a welcome sight. The new Pirates management crew, headed by the Galbreath family, made the disgruntled superstar the first $100,000 player in major league history. Although he was well past his prime, Greenberg hit 27 home runs in 1947, partially thanks to management's having moved in the left field fence by thirty feet, creating a bullpen section that was known as Greenberg Gardens. He was also a mentor to Kiner, helping him reach his potential that saw Kiner capture eight consecutive National League home run titles.

It was the only season Greenberg would play in Pittsburgh; he retired with 331 home runs, which included 58 in 1938, a number that would have been much higher had he not lost three full seasons and the better part of two more serving in the military during World War II. While in the service, the Hall of Famer proved to be a superstar there as well, being awarded a Presidential Unit Citation and four Battle Stars.

Tony Bartirome

As a player he was a light-hitting first baseman with no power on a bad team, with a .220 average and no homers in his only major league season in 1952. But Tony Bartirome still became a legend in Pittsburgh Pirates lore, albeit as a trainer instead of a player. He stayed with the Bucs from 1967–1985 when he left the team together with Chuck Tanner for the Atlanta Braves. Any true Pirates fan of the era will remember Bartirome rushing out to the field spraying his magic elixir (actually it was ethyl chloride) that would instantly soothe the bumps and bruises the players incurred.

Jack Phillips

Other than the fact that he was a decent hitting first baseman with a .283 career average over nine seasons, including .264 in four campaigns with the Bucs between 1949–1952, there really is no special reason to include Jack Phillips on this list—that is, unless we count the fact that he hit the first ultimate pinch-hit home run in major league history: a grand-slam walk-off homer that wins a game by one run. He hit his memorable shot for the Pirates on June 8, 1950 against the Phillies, a feat that went unmatched in major league lore for sixty years. After he retired, he eventually became the head coach at his alma mater, Clarkson College, where the baseball field is named in his honor. Ok, I guess there is a good reason to include him on this list.

Dick Hall

Dick Hall eventually became one of the best relievers in the game for the championship Baltimore Orioles teams in the 1960s and early 1970s, but when he was a young player in 1952 with the Pittsburgh Pirates donning the number 5, he was a poor hitting center fielder with a .215 batting average in his three seasons as an everyday player. Turns out he made a pretty shrewd move going to the mound, which extended his major league career to nineteen seasons.

Hal Smith

Hal Smith was a decent-hitting catcher in his major league career, but it was a single moment in the bottom of the eighth inning of the seventh game in the 1960 World Series that almost made him a Steel City icon. He smashed a three-run homer that gave the Bucs a 9–7 lead in the eighth inning of game seven that would have easily been remembered as the greatest long ball in franchise history . . . that is, had the Yankees not tied the score in the ninth and if a second baseman by the name of Bill Mazeroski had not gummed up Smith's place in history by hitting that walk-off homer in the bottom of the ninth. Oh well, hitting the second greatest home run in franchise history isn't a bad thing.

Howie Goss

Howie Goss certainly would have been at the top of the "worst to wear the number" list had this been a book about the Houston Astros. He recorded a strikeout in each of the first fourteen games in the 1963 campaign for the then Colt .45s, which was a major league record that stood for forty-nine years.

Dave Ricketts

The greatest Duquesne University athlete ever to play for the Pittsburgh Pirates was not Joe Beimel; no, it was a catcher by the name of Dave Ricketts, who hit .182 in his only season with the Bucs in 1970. It wasn't baseball that Ricketts was noted for, but as a star basketball player with the Dukes, who combined with his brother Dick to help lead the school to its only national championship in 1955, when they captured the NIT tournament.

Jerry Goff

While he "impressed" the Pirates faithful with his .080 batting average in 1994 and .210 mark in two seasons with the Bucs, it was his major league record six passed balls in one game that makes Jerry Goff important in baseball history.

Lance Parrish

Even though Clairton, PA's, own Lance Parrish played just one season in his hometown, hitting .270 in 126 at bats in 1994, he was an outstanding catcher with the Detroit Tigers for the majority of his nineteen-year career that saw him hit 324 home runs, including 33 in 1984 when the Tigers won the world championship.

Ed Sprague

Ed Sprague was a fine power-hitting third baseman with the Toronto Blue Jays to start his career, and he continued his success as a member of the Pittsburgh Pirates in 1999, hitting 22 home runs while being selected to play in his only All-Star game. Unfortunately, he signed only a one-year contract and left for greener pastures in San Diego following the '99 season

Ramon Vazquez

Playing his final season in Pittsburgh in 2009, Ramon Vazquez was a light-hitting utility infielder who had one day in the sun offensively in his major league career. He hit two of his 22 career home runs on August 8, 2007, with the Texas Rangers, while driving in seven. The importance of the day was that Texas scored 30 runs in the game, the first time an American League club ever achieved that lofty mark. Vazquez, who hit a homer in the ninth, scored the thirtieth run, the only major league player to do so in the twentieth century.

#6: CATCHERS RULE

ALL TIME NO. 6 ROSTER	YEAR
Starling Marte	(2012–2015)
Jeff Clement	(2010)
Robinzon Diaz	(2008)
Chris Duffy	(2006–2007)
Alfredo Amezaga	(2005)
Abraham Nunez	(2003)
Mike Benjamin	(1999–2002)
Lou Collier	(1997–1998)
Orlando Merced	(1991–1996)
Rafael Belliard	(1988–1990)
Tony Pena	(1980–1986)
Rennie Stennett	(1971–1979)
George Kopacz	(1970)
Bob Robertson	(1970)
Smoky Burgess	(1959–1964)
Dick Schofield	(1958)
Johnny O'Brien	(1955–1958)
Dick Smith	(1954–1955)
Mike Sandlock	(1953)
Lee Walls	(1952)
Dick Smith	(1951)
Rocky Nelson	(1951)
Stan Rojek	(1948–1951)
Billy Cox	(1947)
Lee Handley	(1940–1941, 1944–1946)
COACHES	
Clyde King	(1965–1967)
Don Leppert	(1968–1969)
Perry Hill	(2009)

NUMBER RETIRED: None

HALL OF FAMERS TO WEAR THE NUMBER: None

FIRST PERFORMANCE WITH THE NUMBER

4/16/1940- Pirate Lee Handley got the number 6 off to a good beginning with two singles in four at bats during a 6–4 victory against the St. Louis Cardinals at Sportsman's Park to begin the 1940 campaign.

FIRST HOME RUN WITH THE NUMBER

5/15/1940- The Polo Grounds was the place where a number 6 hit his first home run, as Lee Handley led the game off with a home run against the great Carl Hubbell. It would be just about all the offense the team mustered on the day as they lost to the Giants, 5–2.

FIRST VICTORY BY A PITCHER WITH THE NUMBER

No Pirate pitcher has ever worn the number 6.

BEST PIRATES TO WEAR THE NUMBER: (HR-RBI-AVE)

Tony Pena-(63–340-.286)

If someone were to be asked the trivia question, "Was there ever a catcher named to the Topps All-Star rookie team and also named as manager of the year?" they would need only look to Tony Pena as the answer to that absurd question. One of the most well-rounded catchers in Pittsburgh Pirate history, if not *the* most well-rounded, Pena had a strange style behind the plate: one leg stretched out with one underneath him. While looking unconventional, it worked for the Dominican-born backstop. His incredibly strong arm could nail runners even from that position, as he captured three straight National League Gold Glove Awards between 1983 and 1985. Pena also showed he knew how to wield a stick, batting .286 throughout his Pirates career. He was traded away in an April Fools deal in 1987 that brought Andy Van Slyke and Mike Lavalliere to the Steel City. While it was a great deal for the Pirates, it still took from them a memorable and beloved Pittsburgh legend.

Smoky Burgess-(51–265-.296)

It was said of Forrest "Smoky" Burgess that he could hit fastballs in his sleep, and when it came to his prowess as a pinch-hitter, no one was better. At one point in time he held the major league record for pinch-hits with 145, but when he came to the Bucs from the Reds with Don Hoak and Harvey Haddix in 1959 he became an everyday catcher.

Burgess didn't look like a prototypical baseball player. In fact, he didn't look like a prototypical athlete, looking more like a guy you'd sit down with at a bar for a beer . . . many beers.

He became an important cog in the Pirates' 1960 world championship machine and beyond, hitting over .300 in 1961 and '62. While many of his records are long gone, Burgess proves that catchers rule when it comes to the number 6.

Rennie Stennett-(38–388-.278)

He entered the major leagues with a vengeance in 1971, hitting .353 as a mid-season call-up who, unfortunately, was left off the post-season roster in favor of the veteran Jose Pagan. Rennie Stennett kept up his fine play with a .285 average between 1971 and 1977. As good as he was before his horrific leg injury in 1977, Stennett had a day for the ages on September 16, 1975, when he tied a major league record of seven hits in nine innings with a perfect seven-for-seven day during a 22–0 Pirates embarrassment of the Chicago Cubs. All in all, Stennett deservedly breaks up the catcher-dominated list for the best to wear the number 6.

WORST PIRATES TO WEAR THE NUMBER: (HR-RBI-AVE)

Dick Smith-(0–11-.134)

The Blandburg, Pennsylvania, native spewed PA blood, a product of both Penn State and Lock Haven, before being signed by the Pirates as an amateur free agent in 1949. He proved that maybe Pennsylvania blood didn't necessarily make good baseball players, however, batting only .134 in five abbreviated seasons with Pittsburgh.

George Kopacz-(0–0- .188)

When pinch-hitter is part of your lead bio as your position, generally you did not play long in the major leagues, a fact exemplified by George Kopacz. He was hitless in nine at bats with the Braves in 1966 and was relegated to the minor leagues for the next three seasons. Capturing the International League MVP in 1970, Kopacz got a second chance for big league glory with the Pirates. Glory was certainly fleeting with a three-for-sixteen performance in his Pirates career.

Jeff Clement-(7–13 .193)

A top 100 prospect for most of the latter part of the first decade in the twentieth century, the Pirates hoped they had made a steal by securing this one-time power-hitting minor leaguer from the Mariners. While his stats did resemble those of Bob Robertson, they were unfortunately Robertson's stats at the end of his career. When Clement returned to the team after a year away in 2012, he changed his number to 19; it did not help.

OTHER NOTABLE PIRATES TO WEAR THE NUMBER

Stan Rojek

Stan Rojek was a shortstop in the late 1940s for the Bucs who led the National League in at bats and plate appearances in 1948 while hitting .290. He was a decent hitter for the Pirates in an era of bad players who was nicknamed "reject" by his new Pirates teammates as a reference to the Dodgers' having given up on him and sending him to Pittsburgh. Rojek also served in the army, where he had a chance to refine his game playing for some of the best armed forces teams in the military.

Mike Sandlock

When Mike Sandlock went into the armed forces during World War II he brought with him the honor of a career 1.000 average, having singled in his only major league at bat for the Braves in 1942. When he returned, he played three seasons for the Dodgers before taking a seven-year minor league hiatus. The Pirates gave him one last major league opportunity when he was thirty-seven years old in 1953. He played one season in Pittsburgh, hitting .231, and his days in the big leagues ended at that point. Is it enough for him to be declared a notable Pirate? No, it's the fact that he is currently the oldest living former major league player, who just turned 100 years old on October 17, 2015.

Johnny O'Brien

One of the dynamic O'Brien twins who played for the Pirates in the 1950s, Johnny hit .260 in five seasons as a utility infielder. Serving a year in the military during the Korean conflict, O'Brien was much more renowned as a star basketball player for Seattle University before coming to Pittsburgh. At Seattle he became the first college player to eclipse 1,000 points in a season, scoring 2,733 in his career while being named an All-American in 1953. The greatest moment in his athletic career was when he scored 42 points as Seattle upset

Lee Handley (photo courtesy of the Pittsburgh Pirates)

the Harlem Globetrotters in 1952. He was drafted by the Milwaukee Hawks of the NBA in 1953, and chose the Pirates instead. Looking at his career baseball totals, perhaps he made a mistake: He had only four home runs and 59 RBIs in six major league seasons.

Lee Handley

Lee Handley was a Bradley University alum who became a fine hitting third baseman for the Pirates after Major League Baseball commissioner Landis declared him a free agent in 1936 when he was playing for the Reds. In Pittsburgh for eight of his ten major league seasons, where he hit .269 and led the NL in steals in 1939, Handley was handpicked by manager Pie Traynor to take over for himself, the Pirates Hall of Fame legend. He was good, but no Pie Traynor. Remembered by Jackie Robinson as the first opposing player to wish him well when Robinson broke the color barrier in 1947, Handley suffered two major setbacks in his career: a beaning in 1939, and an auto accident after the 1941 campaign that injured his arm so badly it caused him to temporarily quit baseball in 1942. He returned in 1944 and played four more seasons.

Orlando Merced

A friend of Roberto Clemente's son, Luis, Orlando Merced was a good hitter who eclipsed the .300 plateau twice in his seven-year Pirate career, and was an important component of the three-time eastern division champions in the early 1990s. When he left the Bucs after the 1996 campaign for Toronto, in return for a haul that included Craig Wilson, he never returned to the same level of play that he had achieved in

Pittsburgh, although he still has a Pirates connection, having marrying Bill Virdon's granddaughter.

Robinzon Diaz

Is there a player in Pirates history whose name induces more bitterness than Robinzon Diaz? Probably not. He was a decent prospect at catcher for Toronto who hit .281 in his brief major league career. The reason we should be bitter about Diaz is that the Bucs sent Jose Bautista and his mega home run power to the Blue Jays for a man who only had 135 career at bats for the Pirates, and 285 fewer home runs.

Chris Duffy

After hitting .341 in 126 at bats in his rookie year for the Pirates, Chris Duffy was firmly entrenched as the center fielder of the future for the team. He then donned the number 6 and became the center fielder of the past, hitting almost 100 points less in his two years with the digit.

Starling Marte

A minor league superstar who hit a home run on the first major league pitch that he faced, Starling Marte is quickly becoming a complete superstar for the Pittsburgh Pirates. A consistent .280 hitter with decent power, Marte is showing a rifle arm in left field and forming into what could be a Gold Glove outfielder for years to come as he won his first in 2015. It most likely won't be long before Marte can claim to be one of the greatest players of all time to wear number 6.

#7: YOUR SMILING FACE

ALL TIME NO. 7 ROSTER	YEAR
Alex Presley	(2012–2013)
Jose Bautista	(2005)
Abraham Nunez	(2004)
Kenny Lofton	(2003)
Armando Rios	(2002)
John Wehner	(1999, 2001)
Jeff King	(1989–1996)
Darnell Coles	(1987–1988)
Ruben Rodriguez	(1986)
Andy Van Slyke	(1987)
Barry Bonds	(1986)
Bob Robertson	(1970–1976)
Bill Virdon	(1968)
Andre Rodgers	(1967)
Bob Bailey	(1963–1966)
Dick Stuart	(1958–1962)
R C Stevens	(1958–1960)
Eddie O'Brien	(1955–1956)
Curt Roberts	(1954–1955)
Gene Hermanski	(1953)
Gus Bell	(1952)
Dick Hall	(1952)
Dick Smith	(1951–1953)
Danny Murtaugh	(1948–1951)
Whitey Wietelmann	(1947)
Maurice Van Robays	(1946)
Babe Dahlgren	(1944–1945)
Johnny Rizzo	(1940)
Eddie Yount	(1939)
MANAGER	
Chuck Tanner	(1978–1985)
John Russell	(2008–2010)
COACHES	
Jeff Cox	(2006–2007)

NUMBER RETIRED- None

HALL OF FAMERS TO WEAR THE NUMBER- None

FIRST PERFORMANCE WITH THE NUMBER

9/9/1939- Eddie Yount's career with the Pittsburgh Pirates was very abbreviated; nonetheless, he had the honor of debuting this number for the franchise in a 12–2 loss to St. Louis. He pinch-hit for pitcher Bill Swift in the ninth inning and promptly struck out. In fact, in his only other at bat in a Pirates uniform the next day he repeated his performance.

FIRST HOME RUN WITH THE NUMBER

5/29/1944- It took five years after the number 7 was first introduced before it would finally see its first home run. That day Babe Dahlgren smacked his first of the season in the fourth inning to tie the game against the Philadelphia Phillies at one. He would later win it with a sacrifice fly in the 11th inning, giving Pittsburgh a 3–2 victory. Dahlgren enjoyed breaking ground on the first homer so much he did it again a day later.

FIRST VICTORY BY A PITCHER WITH THE NUMBER

No pitcher ever wore the number 7.

BEST PIRATES TO WEAR THE NUMBER: (W-L-PCT-Tanner) (HR-RBI-AVE)

Chuck Tanner (711–685-.509)

It's fitting that Pittsburgh's own, actually New Castle's own, is the top number 7 in Pittsburgh Pirate history, the man who led the Fam-A-Lee so expertly to the team's last World Series title, Chuck Tanner.

He came to the Bucs in a trade with the Oakland A's for the 1977 campaign, and it was arguably the deal that was most important in achieving the glory that 1979 brought to the Pirate Nation. His enthusiastic spirit stayed with the city long after he left the club in 1985, as Tanner was a regular at both Three Rivers Stadium and PNC Park, always with a smile and a nice word for any fan with whom he came in contact. He was a truly class individual, and it was a sad day in the Steel City when he passed away in 2011.

Dick Stuart (117–290-.273)

For those who criticize Pedro Alvarez for his lack of defensive prowess at first base, they never met the man they called "Dr. Strangeglove," Dick Stuart, who made Alvarez look like a gold glover. While Stuart's glove seemed to be made of stone, his bat struck the ball with incredible power to the tune of 117 home runs in five seasons, 35 of them in 1961. After he was traded to the Red Sox in 1963, he continued his powerful way, smashing a career high 42 long balls that season while endearing himself to the Fenway faithful who dubbed him the Boston Strangler . . . you got it . . . for his defense.

Jeff King (99–493-.258)

They say patience is a virtue. With former first-round pick Jeff King it had to be that and more, as he struggled his first four seasons in a Pirates uniform until something clicked in 1993. He went on to crack the 100 RBI plateau twice in a Pirates uniform while hitting a career-high 30 homers during the 1996 campaign. King paid the Bucs back for their patience and then some, finally living up to his immense potential.

WORST PIRATES TO WEAR THE NUMBER: (HR-RBI-AVE)

Eddie Yount- (0–0-.000)

Eddie Yount's time in the majors was longer than Moonlight Graham's, but not by much. The first Pirate to wear the number 7 was a Wake Forest alum and who began his major league career with the A's in 1937, where he had two hits in seven at bats. Philadelphia traded him to Oakland of the Pacific Coast League after the season, and he reappeared in the majors two years later with the Bucs. If you read above in the first performance category, you'll notice Mr. Yount had two at bats in a Pirates uniform and struck out twice; it doesn't get much worse than that.

Rueben Rodriguez-(0–0-.125)

A one-for-eight major league career is certainly nothing to brag about, but at least Rueben Rodriguez made that hit count as he tripled in his next-to-last major league at bat against the Cubs in 1988.

Gene Hermanski-(1–4-.177)

Although a good-hitting outfielder with the great Brooklyn Dodger teams of the late 1940s and 1950s, when he hit .282 over seven seasons, Gene Hermanski unfortunately was not be able to maintain that level of play when he became a Pittsburgh Pirate in 1953. The Pirates were the polar opposite of the Dodgers in the 1950s as probably the worst franchise in the game; Hermanski hit accordingly in his final major league season. with a .177 average.

OTHER NOTABLE PIRATES TO WEAR THE NUMBER

Babe Dahlgren

Babe Dahlgren was a decent-hitting first baseman with adequate power who came to the Pirates late in his career, hitting .271 over his two seasons in Pittsburgh and knocking in 101 runs in 1944. Notable for sure, but the thing Dahlgren is most famous for in his major league career is the fact that he took over at first base for the New York Yankees

Danny Murtaugh sliding into home plate. (Photo courtesy of the Pittsburgh Pirates)

in 1939 after Lou Gehrig retired to battle ALS, more commonly known today as Lou Gehrig's disease.

Danny Murtaugh

Before Danny Murtaugh became the Bucs' manager, and one of the greatest managers in the game, he was a second baseman for the team between 1948 and 1951. Murtaugh as a player seemed to believe in the every-other-year system in which you succeed in alternate years while being awful in the others. He batted .290 and .294 in 1948 and '50, while battling the Mendoza Line in '49 and '51. Luckily, he was much more consistent as a manager.

Curt Roberts

While Puerto Rico–born Carlos Bernier may have been the first man of color to dot a Pirates roster the year before, in 1954 Curt Roberts was the franchise's first African American player. Signed by Branch Rickey in 1953, in the following season Roberts took over the starting nod at second, when he hit .232 his rookie season. It would be his last as a starter, as Johnny O'Brien took over in 1955 before they both gave way to the greatest defensive second baseman in the game's history, Bill Mazeroski, in 1956, which also proved to be Roberts's last season in the majors.

Eddie O'Brien

Eddie was the other half of the O'Brien brothers' combo for the Pirates in the 1950s. Like his brother, Johnny, Eddie was a phenomenal basketball player at the University of Seattle, averaging 13 points a game and helping lead the school to the NIT tournament in 1952 and the NCAA the following season. While he was only a .236 hitter with the Bucs, he would return to his alma mater in 1970, where he was the head baseball coach for fourteen years.

R.C. Stevens

If talk radio had been around in 1958, the city of Pittsburgh would have been buzzing about a budding superstar rookie by the name of R.C. Stevens. He had four hits in his first four major league at bats that included a walk-off hit in the fourteenth inning of his first game, and two consecutive pinch-hit home runs, the second of which won a game for the Pirates against the Cincinnati Reds.

Unfortunately, those fans who were gushing would soon realize that Stevens would not have the Hall of Fame career they had hoped for. After hitting .267 his rookie season, he had only eleven plate appearances for the Bucs over the next two years before moving to the Washington Senators, where his big league career ended in 1961.

Bob Robertson

Big Bob Robertson was being compared to Mickey Mantle when he came up to the majors in 1967. He did little to disappoint during his first two full seasons with the Bucs, smacking 53 home runs in 1970 and '71 before becoming a national hero with three homers against the Giants in game two of the 1971 NLCS. After missing a bunt single in the third contest of the World Series that season, Robertson launched another long ball, a three-run shot that helped win the game for Pittsburgh after they had fallen behind by two games early on.

With six homers in the post-season for a very Mantle-like performance, injuries then helped make him look more like Jeff Clement than the Mick, with a .224 average and only 59 more homers in eight seasons, relegating Robertson to this list of notables who wore the number 7, rather than the one at Cooperstown he looked to be headed for.

Bob Bailey

The Pittsburgh Pirates gave Bob Bailey the biggest signing bonus in baseball history at the time, $135,000. While he was a decent minor leaguer, capturing the International League's MVP award in 1962, he couldn't replicate that success in the majors, and the Bucs did not get their money's worth. He stayed with the Bucs for five seasons, hitting .257, and just as he was about to be labeled a bust after also failing with the Dodgers, he found a home with the Expos, hitting over 20 home runs on three occasions and ended up lasting in the big leagues for seventeen seasons.

Andre Rodgers

An average hitting infielder who started for three seasons in the early 1960s with the Chicago Cubs, Andre Rodgers came to the Steel City in 1965 and played his last three years here as a bench player. His claim to fame in the game: he was the first person from the Bahamas to play major league baseball, and was the son of a famous cricket player.

Darnell Coles

Darnell Coles burst on to the scene in his fourth major league season with the Tigers, hitting 20 home runs and driving in 86 in 1986. While he played fourteen seasons, he was never able to achieve that success again, especially in his two years in Pittsburgh, where he hit 11 home runs in 1987 and '88. As bad as he was with the Bucs, he did have one spectacular day in the second game of a doubleheader against the Cubs on September 30, 1987, when he tied a Pirates record, hitting three home runs in a single game.

Kenny Lofton

With almost 2,500 hits, a .296 average, and 622 stolen bases — leading the American League five times in the latter category — Kenny Lofton was a phenomenal player whose career was coming to an end when he became a Pirate in 2003 at the age of thirty-six. He still had something left, hitting .277 before becoming part of one of the worst deals in Pittsburgh history: the ill-fated Aramis Ramirez trade.

Bill Virdon, Jose Bautista, Barry Bonds, John Wehner, and Andy Van Slyke

It wasn't the main career number for these Pirates stars, but a temporary stop. Barry Bonds and Andy Van Slyke wore the number 7 when they first came aboard the Pirates express, before donning their more famous 24 and 18 respectively, and Bill Virdon put it on in 1968, three years after he retired, when he had a handful of at bats in July upon returning to the club as a player/coach. Announcer John Wehner wore his new digit for the final three years of his career after returning from the Florida Marlins, while Jose Bautista proudly wore it his second season with the team.

#8: POPS

ALL TIME NO. 8 ROSTER	YEAR
Willie Stargell	(1962–1982)
Coot Veal	(1962)
Dick Barone	(1960)
Harry Bright	(1958–1960)
Gene Freese	(1955–1958)
Gair Allie	(1954)
Bobby Del Greco	(1952)
Bill Howerton	(1951–1952)
Clyde McCullough	(1949–1950)
Monty Basgall	(1948)
Eddie Basinski	(1947)
Bob Elliott	(1939–1946)

NUMBER RETIRED: WILLIE STARGELL (1982)

HALL OF FAMERS TO WEAR THE NUMBER: WILLIE STARGELL (1988)

FIRST PERFORMANCE WITH THE NUMBER:

9/2/1939- In his first major league game, Bob Elliott announced his presence loudly after three consecutive outs with a seventh-inning single to right, knocking in one as he ended up on third after Enos Slaughter of the Cardinals misplayed the hit. Elliott then drove a two-run homer for his first long ball in the majors with Arky Vaughan on base in the ninth to power Pittsburgh to an 11–3 win against St. Louis.

First home run with the number

9/2/1939- See the above game.

First victory by a pitcher with the number

No Pirates pitcher ever wore the number 8.

BEST PIRATES TO WEAR THE NUMBER: (HR-RBI-AVE)
Willie Stargell (475–1540-.282)

One of the great things about baseball is that all stadiums have different dimensions; they are not limited by the rules of the game. While some players do find that to be a great thing, one who didn't was Willie Stargell. Forced to play in Forbes Field, he found that the massive park reduced his total of career home runs, certainly costing him a

Bob Elliott (photo courtesy of the Pittsburgh Pirates)

shot at 500, which would have made his induction into Cooperstown a certainty. One need look no further than his first four years at Three Rivers Stadium, when he smacked 156, averaging almost 40 a year. Luckily, Forbes Field would not cost him a shot at the Hall of Fame, as a miracle season in 1979, when the thirty-nine-year-old slugger captured the MVP awards in the National League, NLCS, and World Series, which made Willie Stargell a deserved selection in his first year of eligibility, and a Pittsburgh sports icon.

Bob Elliott (50–633-.292)

There really shouldn't be another player next to Willie Stargell on this list, but Bob Elliott was such a phenomenal player for the Pirates that it wouldn't be right for him to be anywhere else. Though he eclipsed the 100 RBIs plateau three times for the Bucs in his eight years in Pittsburgh, while hitting .292, the franchise inexplicably sent him to the Boston Braves for a group of soon-to-be-ineffective Pirates who included Billy Herman, Elmer Singleton, Stan Wentzel, and Whitey Wietelmann. Elliott made them pay, capturing the 1947 MVP award before helping lead the Braves to the NL title in 1948. Yes, it is safe to say it was a bad trade.

WORST PIRATES TO WEAR THE NUMBER: (HR-RBI-AVE)

Eddie Basinski (4–17-.199)

In his biography on the baseball-reference.com bullpen website, Eddie Basinski is quoted to have said, "Any man who can't hit .300 in this league ought to go get a lunch bucket." It was a quizzical statement, as the former wartime starter at short for the Brooklyn Dodgers in 1945 came to the Bucs in 1947 probably wondering how big a lunch box he should get for not being able to hit .200.

Gair Allie (3–30-.199)

You don't get to be the worst team in the league by having good players, and in the 1950s Gair Allie was the poster child for that point. Playing one season in the majors in 1954, Allie started at short for Dick Groat, who spent two years in the Armed Forces during the Korean conflict, and hit a resounding .199. He left for the military the next season himself, and luckily for the suffering Pirates faithful they would never see him on the field again.

OTHER NOTABLE PIRATES TO WEAR THE NUMBER

Clyde McCullough

A seven-year veteran catcher with the Cubs who missed two other seasons while he served in the Armed Forces during World War II, Clyde McCullough came to Pittsburgh in 1949, just as the franchise was falling deeply into its second-worst era. He performed admirably in his four years in a Pirates uniform, with a .258 average that includes a career-high .297 in 1951. Mc-Cullough returned to Chicago for the remaining four campaigns of his career and then became a successful minor league manager, capturing *The Sporting News*'s Minor League Manager of the Year Award with Tidewater in 1969, while winning four league championships in his managing career.

Willie Stargell (photo courtesy of the Pittsburgh Pirates)

Bobby Del Greco

Bobby Del Greco was a Pittsburgh kid through and through when he came to the Bucs in 1952. In a tryout with the team before that, there were thirty players trying to make the squad for GM Branch Rickey, and the Hall of Fame GM felt Del Greco was the best. Had he been as good as another Pittsburgh kid, Neil Walker, the story would have had a happy ending, but after Del Greco's two failed seasons with the Pirates, St. Louis thought enough of him to give up reigning Rookie of the Year Bill Virdon, which turned out to be a steal for Pittsburgh. Following his playing days, Del Greco returned to his hometown, where he became a driver for the *Pittsburgh Post-Gazette* and threw batting practice for the team into the 1990s.

Coot Veal

OK, he only batted once for the Bucs in 1962 and struck out; but, come on, his name was Coot, he belongs on this list.

#9: DOUBLE-PLAY MADNESS

NUMBER RETIRED: BILL MAZEROSKI (1987)

HALL OF FAMERS TO WEAR THE NUMBER: BILL MAZEROSKI (2001), PAUL WANER (1952)

FIRST PERFORMANCE WITH THE NUMBER

4/16/1940- On opening day, thirty-seven-year-old veteran Paul Waner pinch-hit for Pep Young in a 6–4 victory by the Bucs over St. Louis. He struck out in that appearance.

FIRST HOME RUN WITH THE NUMBER

5/18/1940- Although the Pirates lost to the Braves 15–5 on this day, Paul Waner launched his first home run of the year as he went three-for-five with two RBIs.

FIRST VICTORY BY A PITCHER WITH THE NUMBER

No pitcher ever won a game wearing the number nine.

BEST PIRATES TO WEAR THE NUMBER: (HR-RBI-AVE)

Bill Mazeroski (138–853-.260)

He was the Pirates' starting second baseman by the time he turned twenty years old, and never let go of the position until injuries had gotten the best of him fourteen years later. In between, Bill Mazeroski had a memorable career, one that may have been best known for the major league's only seventh game walk-off home run in a World Series, but it should have been remembered for the fact that he was arguably the greatest defensive second baseman in the history of the game. When

Bill Mazeroski (photo courtesy of the Pittsburgh Pirates)

it came to double plays he was a machine, turning 1,706 of them, more than any other second baseman in the game's history. "Maz" is widely criticized as not deserving the Hall of Fame honor he was given by the veteran's committee in 2001, but as important as defense is in the course of the game there can be no one more deserving. The number 9 ended with Maz in Pirates history, and that is also an honor of which he is richly worthy.

WORST PIRATES TO WEAR THE NUMBER: (HR-RBI-AVE)

Nick Koback (0–0-.121)

Nick Koback looked to be a young phenom playing his first major league game, when he was eighteen. It was certainly his high point: three years later, he no longer was a young phenom, ending his major league career with an *un*phenom-like .121 average.

OTHER NOTABLE PIRATES TO WEAR THE NUMBER

Vince DiMaggio

The Pirates jumped on the DiMaggio bandwagon during the war years, bringing Vince to the majors in 1940 following a spectacular 46-home run performance with Kansas City of the American Association. Would he be a power-hitting DiMaggio, on a par with Mantle and Ruth? The answer was, unfortunately, no; he was probably the worst of the DiMaggio brothers. It didn't mean he was a bad player; he certainly was not. It's just that Joe and Domenic were that damn good.

During the war years Vince was one of the team's top sluggers, with 79 homers in five seasons, driving in 100 in 1941. He just didn't do what his brother Joe did, nor have the ability to put World Series rings on his teammate's fingers.

Ed Fitz Gerald

A catcher so bold he had to split his name in half, Ed Fitz Gerald had more than his share of suffering as a backup catcher on some of the worst Pirates teams ever to grace the field. While not quite one of the best hitting catchers of his day, registering a .247 career average with the Bucs, he was decent defensively, tossing out 40 percent of the runners who dared to try and steal against him, including 59 percent of them in 1949. Perhaps the most notable achievement for the backstop was his service to his country during World War II, when he was stationed in both the Aleutian Islands and Germany.

Paul Waner, Ray Mueller, and Curt Roberts

Even though 9 was not their regular number, Paul Waner wore the digit in his last season in the Steel City, as did the team's first African American player, Curt Roberts, and its pre-war catcher, Ray Mueller, who set a National League record for backstops by playing in 233 consecutive games with Cincinnati and donned the number 9 in 1950, ten years after he initially left the team.

#10: THE FIRST

ALL TIME NO. 10 ROSTER	YEAR
Jordy Mercer	(2013–2015)
Eric Fryer	(2012)
Josh Rodriguez	(2011)
Tony Beasley	(2010)
Brian Bixler	(2008–2009)
Rajai Davis	(2006–2007)
Alvaro Espinoza	(2003–2005)
Abraham Nunez	(1998–2002)
Kevin Elster	(1997)
Johnnie LeMaster	(1985)
Tim Foli	(1979–1981, 1985)
Benny Distefano	(1984)
Richie Hebner	(1982–1983)
Ken Reitz	(1982)
Frank Taveras	(1972–1979)
Richie Zisk	(1971)
Dave Cash	(1970)
Richie Hebner	(1970)
George Kopacz	(1970)
Gary Kolb	(1968–1969)
Jim Pagliaroni	(1965–1967)
Danny Kravitz	(1959–1960)
Dick Rand	(1957)
Jack Shepard	(1953–1956)
Danny O'Connell	(1953)
Jack Merson	(1951–1952)
Johnny Berardino	(1950, 1952)
Monty Basgall	(1949–1951)
Earl Turner	(1948, 1950)
Clyde Kluttz	(1947–1948)
Hank Camelli	(1944–1946)
Babe Phelps	(1942)
Ed Leip	(1940–1942)
Lloyd Waner	(1932–1941)
MANAGER	
Jim Leyland	(1987–1996)
COACHES	
Tony Beasley	(2010)
Virgil Trucks	(1961–1963)

NUMBER RETIRED: None

HALL OF FAMERS TO WEAR THE NUMBER: LLOYD WANER (1967)

FIRST PERFORMANCE WITH THE NUMBER

6/30/1932- As the first player to come to bat with a number on his back in Pittsburgh Pirates history, Lloyd Waner had a decent performance in the Bucs' 9–6 win against the Cardinals; he had two hits in six at bats, including a triple and an RBI.

FIRST HOME RUN WITH THE NUMBER

6/21/1934- On June 24, 1932, six days before the Pirates donned uniform numbers, Lloyd Waner hit his second home run of the year. It would be almost two years later to the day when he hit his next, the first while wearing a number. It was a solo shot in the second game of a double header that saw Pittsburgh lose to Brooklyn 8–7.

FIRST VICTORY BY A PITCHER WITH THE NUMBER

No Pirates pitcher ever won a game wearing the number 10.

BEST PIRATES TO WEAR THE NUMBER: (HR-RBI-AVE) (W-L-PCT. For Leyland)

Lloyd Waner (27–598-.316)

Waner started off with a bang, hitting .355 with a league high 133 runs in his rookie campaign of 1927. He never stopped until he had accumulated 2,459 hits, setting major league records for runs by a rookie in a season, and singles by a rookie in a season. While he earned baseball's highest honor, being elected to the Hall of Fame in 1967, and was a tremendous defensive center fielder, he was nevertheless the game's ultimate slap hitter with the dubious rating as having the worst secondary average of any of the top 100 outfielders, as rated by Bill James in his "Historical Baseball Abstract."

One of the famous Waner brothers, Lloyd will go down in Pittsburgh Pirates history as a pioneer of sorts, a main player in this book as the first Bucco to come to bat with a number on his back, which he did on June 30, 1932, beginning an era in the most unassuming of ways with a fly-out.

Jim Leyland (851–863-.496)

His hiring was met with a collective yawn in 1986 by a Pirates Nation that was getting tired of losing, and that figured this career minor league manager would lead them to more of the same. After he won 64 games in his first year, and the team stood at 53–71 a year later, it appeared that they were right. A true players' manager who turned out to be a magnificent acquisition by general manager Syd Thrift, Leyland turned the team around to end the 1987 campaign with a 27–11 mark before leading them to three consecutive eastern division titles between 1990 and '92. While his career in the Steel City ended in a less-than-stellar manner — the team aggressively cut costs, replacing championship-caliber players with twenty-five guys named Moe — he would eventually win a world championship with Florida in 1997, and went on to two World Series while at the helm of the Tigers.

Tim Foli (4–125-.269)

Frank Taveras was an exciting force at shortstop for the Pittsburgh Pirates; he could be magnificent and lousy at the same time. Tim Foli was a stable, good-fielding, decent hitter who made very few highlight films in his career. When the Mets took the Bucs' thrill-a-minute player in exchange for Mr. Stability, the results were staggering. Foli stabilized the Pirates' infield defensively, while also hitting .291 as a pivotal part of the team's last world championship season in 1979. While he's rated higher than Taveras in this book, Bill James has him as the 125th best shortstop in the history of the game, ten spots behind the man for whom he was traded. Perhaps Bill James doesn't consider helping lead a team to a World Series title as important.

WORST PIRATES TO WEAR THE NUMBER: (HR-RBI-AVE)

Ken Reitz (0–0-.000)

Kenny Reitz was a fan favorite in St. Louis in the 1970s as their decent-hitting third baseman who hit .263 over eight years, seven as a starter. In Pittsburgh he was not as much revered, going hitless in eleven at bats and landing himself as the worst number 10 in team history.

Josh Rodriguez (0–1-.083)

Josh Rodriguez's major league career lasted a brief span between April 5⁻ and 21, 2011, when he mustered only a hit and a walk in fourteen plate appearances, both of which came in an extra-inning win against Colorado on April 8.

Gary Kolb (2–9-.186)

Gary Kolb wasn't much of a player when he came to Pittsburgh in 1968 and he left that way in '69, with a .186 average based on an an unimpressive three hits for 37 at bats. A football player at Illinois, Kolb had questionable luck in his career, leaving St. Louis the year before the Cardinals won the Series in 1964, and then exiting Pittsburgh two seasons before they captured their fourth world championship.

OTHER NOTABLE PIRATES TO WEAR THE NUMBER

Babe Phelps

Nicknames like Babe are supposed to be reserved for the great hitters in baseball history . . . or maybe just for people who act like children. Nonetheless, in the case of Babe Phelps, good hitter certainly was an appropriate description of him. He was a lifetime .310 hitter in eleven major league seasons that included a .294 mark with nine homers in 257 at bats with the Bucs in 1941, his final year in the majors.

Jack Shepard

It seemed as though the Pittsburgh Pirates boasted quite a few .250 hitting catchers in their forgettable losing era in the 1950s, and Jack Shepard proved to be one of them. Well, perhaps that's a bit of an understatement: Shepard was actually a .260 hitter between 1953 and '56. At his alma mater, Stanford University, they give the player with the highest batting average the Jack Shepard Award; perhaps they don't quite understand that .260 is not a revered batting average.

Jack Merson

Jack Merson had all the makings of a superstar when he arrived in the major leagues with the Bucs in 1951. In only his second major league game after a September call-up, he had four hits and six RBIs in an 11–4 victory over the Brooklyn Dodgers. By his seventh game he was hitting .538, knocking in 10 runs. It was a small sample for sure, but was he to be the slugger who could lift the Pirates out of the cellar? The answer was no. He slumped to .246 in 1952, and was out of the major leagues the following season. Perhaps Stanford is crafting an award in his honor, too.

Danny O'Connell

A talented infielder with the Bucs, Braves, Cardinals, Giants, and Senators, Danny O'Connell played his first two major league seasons for the Pittsburgh Pirates. Hitting .292 his rookie season in 1950,

Johnny Berardino (photo courtesy of the Pittsburgh Pirates)

O'Connell spent the next two years serving in the army during the Korean conflict. He returned in 1953 and picked up where he left off, with a .294 average before heading off to the Braves.

Jim Pagliaroni

Keeping the seat warm for Manny Sanguillen as starting catcher for the Pirates in the mid-1960s, Jim Pagliaroni was much more powerful than Sangy, hitting 49 homers in four seasons following his acquisition from the Red Sox. After leaving the Bucs, Pags experienced the two biggest highlights of his major league career: being on the receiving end of Catfish Hunter's perfect game in 1968, and being part of the team that Jim Bouton made legendary in his book, *Ball Four*, the Seattle Pilots.

Johnny Berardino

Johnny Berardino was a decent infielder for the St. Louis Browns before becoming a forgettable one in Pittsburgh. He was a better actor than ball player though, playing Dr. Steve Hardy on the ABC-TV soap, *General Hospital,* for thirty-three years until he passed away in 1996.

Frank Taveras

He was exciting to watch as a Pirates shortstop, fast as hell, swiping 300 bases over his career, including a league-leading 70 in 1977.But as exciting as Frankie Taveras was, his ability on the field was not exactly his strongest point. Neither was his legendary lack of power: He, hit one homer over the course of his eight-year Pirates career. Taveras made a huge contribution to the 1979 world champion Pirates, though, as the trading chip that GM Pete Peterson used to get Tim Foli from the Mets.

Jordy Mercer

Jordy Mercer is the shortstop for the Bucs who has started in each of their winning seasons following a disastrous twenty-year stretch of losing baseball. While his potential hasn't quite been fulfilled yet, Mercer hopes to continue to man the starting spot at short and help lead them to their first World Series since 1979.

Paul Waner (left) and Lloyd Waner (right). (Photo courtesy of the Pittsburgh Pirates)

Kevin Elster

A member of the great New York Mets teams of the mid-to-late 1980s, Kevin Elster came to the Steel City late in his career as part of the 1997 "Freak Show," where he backed up another Kevin, Polcovich, hitting only .225.

Rajai Davis

A decent prospect with the team, no one would have imagined the success Rajai Davis would have in the majors as he became another example of bad decisions in Pittsburgh during the mind-numbing twenty-year streak without a winning baseball team. He has gone on to enjoy a ten-year major league career, and is currently with the Detroit Tigers.

Dave Cash, Richie Zisk, and Richie Hebner

Dave Cash and Richie Zisk wore number 10 toward the beginning of their careers in 1970 and '71, respectively, while Hebner put it on at the end of his, returning to the Pirates in 1982 and '83.

Virgil Trucks

A coach for the Bucs following their world championship in 1960, Virgil Trucks was a hell of a pitcher in his seventeen-year career, winning 177 games, primarily for the Detroit Tigers. He had one of the strangest seasons in 1952, with a very poor 5–19 mark; but, remarkably, two of his five wins were no-hitters.

#11: A LONG TIME COMING

ALL TIME NO. 11 ROSTER	YEAR
Humberto Cota	(2001–2007)
Dale Sveum	(1999)
Jose Guillen	(1997–1999)
Mike Kingery	(1996)
Don Slaught	(1990–1995)
Glenn Wilson	(1988–1989)
Mike Diaz	(1986)
Joe Orsulak	(1984–1986)
Lee Mazzilli	(1983)
Jim Smith	(1982)
Kurt Bevacqua	(1980–1981)
Alberto Lois	(1979)
Mario Mendoza	(1973, 1975–1978)
Dal Maxvill	(1973–1974)
Jerry McNertney	(1973)
Jose Pagan	(1965–1972)
Dick Schofield	(1958–1965)
Paul Smith	(1957–1958)
Toby Atwell	(1953–1956)
Howie Pollet	(1952–1953, 1956)
George Metkovich	(1951)
Danny O'Connell	(1950)
Nanny Fernandez	(1950)
Dixie Walker	(1948–1949)
Billy Herman	(1947)
Al Tate	(1946)
Tommy O'Brien	(1943–1945)
Jimmy Wasdell	(1942–1943)
Spud Davis	(1940–1941)
Paul Waner	(1932–1939)

NUMBER RETIRED:
PAUL WANER (2007)

HALL OF FAMERS TO WEAR THE NUMBER: PAUL WANER (1952), BILLY HERMAN (1975)

FIRST PERFORMANCE WITH THE NUMBER

6/30/1932- In the first game in which the Pittsburgh Pirates ever wore numbers, Paul Waner debuted number 11 in a positive way with two singles in four at bats, as well as an RBI and a walk in a 9–6 victory over the Cardinals.

FIRST HOME RUN WITH THE NUMBER

8/2/1932- The Pirates would lose to the Phillies this day, 11–6, but in the process Paul Waner hit his sixth homer of the season, his only hit in five at bats.

FIRST VICTORY BY A PITCHER WITH THE NUMBER

5/7/1952- Pitching in one of the worst eras of Pirates baseball, Howie Pollet came into this contest against the Phillies with an 0–3 mark. He tossed a complete-game gem, allowing five hits while striking out five in a 5–1 victory. It was a highlight, as Pollet finished the season 7–16.

Paul Waner (photo courtesy of the
Pittsburgh Pirates)

BEST PIRATES TO WEAR THE NUMBER: (HR-RBI-AVE)

Paul Waner (109–1177-.340)

Why did it take so long for the Pirates front office to honor Paul Waner by retiring his number, which they finally did in 2007 after being visited by members of his family? He was a .340 lifetime hitter, won three batting titles, was named the 1927 National League MVP, and was elected to the Hall of Fame in 1952. He had some of the greatest statistics in franchise history, and arguably was their third greatest player. Better late than never, as the honor was a long time coming and richly deserved.

Don Slaught (21–184-.305)

A backup catcher with the three-time eastern division champions in the early 1990s, Don Slaught proved to be a hitting machine, finishing his Pirates career with a .305 average that included a phenomenal season in 1992, when he hit .345.

Jose Pagan (33–189-.263)

Jose Pagan was an important utility player with the Pittsburgh Pirates in the late 1960s and early 70s. While his .263 average over an eight-year Pirates career may have been nothing spectacular, his clutch double in the eighth inning of game seven during the 1971 World Series would prove to be one of the greatest hits in franchise history; it was the game-winning RBI in a 2–1 world championship-clinching win.

WORST PIRATES TO WEAR THE NUMBER: (HR-RBI-AVE)
Mario Mendoza (1–36-.204)

Mario Mendoza may not have technically been the worst player to wear this number, but since he has a category named after him that doesn't exactly celebrate his hitting prowess, there was no choice but to insert him here. The Mendoza Line has come to refer to a .200 average and is used to describe poor hitters, depending on whether they are above or below that vaunted line. For the record, Mendoza was slightly above his own line with a .215 career average, .204 in a Pirates uniform.

Dal Maxvill (0–17-.188)

Odds that the all-field, no-hit Dal Maxvill would be worse in a Pirates uniform than he had actually been in his career at the plate were long indeed, yet Maxvill did just that, hitting a mere .188 . . . 12 points below the Mendoza line.

Billy Herman (0–6-.213)

Billy Herman had a wonderful Hall of Fame career with the Cubs and Dodgers before coming to the Steel City, where management hoped he would lead not only on the field, but also on the bench as their manager in 1947; he did neither. He hit only .213, and was not effective as a manger either, with a team record of 61–92 before he was replaced as manager by Bill Burwell.

OTHER NOTABLE PIRATES TO WEAR THE NUMBER
Spud Davis

Spud Davis came to the Pirates late in his sixteen-year career when he was thirty-five years old in 1940, but, like Smoky Burgess after him, man, could he hit! Even as his career was coming to an end, Davis hit over .300 twice for the Bucs in four seasons, finishing his major league career with a .305 average. He later would manage the team for only three games in 1946, going 1–2.

Jimmy Wasdell

The main purpose of including Jimmy Wasdell in Pittsburgh Pirate history is to prove just how bad the Arky Vaughan trade was. He was part of a four-player haul that, when all were put together, equalled half the player Vaughan was. Wasdell actually had a decent eleven-year major league career, but a .260 hitter did not compare to a Hall of Fame shortstop.

Lee Howard

Serving three years in the military during World War II is enough to have a person be referred to as a hero. Doing that time in the horror that was the Pacific Theater takes it to the next level. The fact that he pitched only five games in his major league career for the Pirates is inconsequential.

Dixie Walker

The brother of Pirates manager Harry Walker, Dixie had a wonderful eighteen-year career, mostly with Brooklyn and the Yankees. He hit .306 and led the NL in RBIs in 1945 with 124.. He was thirty-seven years of age in 1948 when he became a Pittsburgh Pirate, and while it was his last two seasons in the show, he still proved he could hit, as he matched his career average at .306 with the Bucs.

Nanny Fernandez

A World War II vet who was the American Association MVP in 1949, Nanny Fernandez's major league career was a brief one, four seasons to be exact, including his last with the Bucs in 1949. He achieved the rank of corporal in the military, and had one of the game's great nicknames, enough to include him in this list.

Lee Mazzilli

A native New Yorker, Lee Mazzilli had a fine start to his career with his hometown New York Mets. A former speed skater in his youth, Mazzilli's career was on a downward slope when the Yankees dealt him to Pittsburgh in 1982. The mid-80s were not the best of times for the Bucs, and Mazzilli's time here mirrored that as he hit.244 in four seasons before being released in 1986.

Joe Orsulak

When he began his major league career in Pittsburgh, not many would have guessed he could last fourteen seasons. Although he had no power, the former sixth-round draft pick proved to be a decent hitter, especially in his official rookie season in 1985 when he hit .300 and finished sixth in the Rookie of the Year vote. Unfortunately, he would enjoy most of that major league career away from Pittsburgh, since the Bucs dealt him to Baltimore in 1987 for a guy named Rico Rossy.

Jose Guillen

He was supposed to be the next Roberto Clemente for the Pittsburgh Pirates, having being brought up to the team after being named the Carolina League MVP in 1996, an A ball affiliate. By his second season his arm was ripe with Clemente talent, and he was showing some power that led fans to believe he was the real McCoy. The Bucs, probably scared of having winning baseball, surprisingly dealt him to Tampa Bay the next season. While he eventually showed more power, hitting 31 home runs in 2003, he decided to embrace the steroid era, which ended his major league career in 2010 after it was learned that he was having human growth hormones shipped to him.

Humberto Cota

He played seven seasons behind the plate for the Bucs and never really established himself in Pirates lore, hitting .233, except for the fact that he has been the last Pirate to wear the number 11.

Toby Atwell

Toby Atwell spent three years in the US Army Air Corps during World War II, and got a late start in his major league career as a rookie in

1952 with the Cubs at the age of twenty-eight. He made the All-Star Game that season and promptly became another in a long line of average Pirates catchers in the 1950s. Even though he hit only .250 in his career with the Bucs, he did have a fine season in 1954 with a .289 average.

Dick Schofield

A hero in 1960 when he took over for Dick Groat at short after the MVP broke his wrist late in the year, Dick Schofield hit .333 for the season, including a .397 mark as a starter in September. It was the highlight of a nineteen-year career in which he averaged a meager .227.

Tony Pena and Catfish Metkovich

Pena wore the number 10 for one season, his first with the Bucs in 1980, while the man they called Catfish also had it for one season, in 1951.

#12: NOT JUST FOR QUARTERBACKS ANYMORE

ALL TIME NO. 12 ROSTER	YEAR
Corey Hart	(2015)
Clint Barmes	(2012–2014)
Chase d'Arnaud	(2011)
Freddy Sanchez	(2004–2009)
Matt Stairs	(2003)
Jack Wilson	(2001–2002)
Wil Cordero	(2000)
John Wehner	(1994–1996, 2000)
Turner Ward	(1997–1999)
Glenn Wilson	(1993)
Mike LaValliere	(1987–1993)
Bill Almon	(1986–1987)
Trench Davis	(1985)
Brian Harper	(1982–1984)
Doe Boyland	(1981)
Bob Beall	(1980)
Dock Ellis	(1979)
Matt Alexander	(1978)
Mike Edwards	(1977)
Fernando Gonzalez	(1977)
Craig Reynolds	(1976)
John Morlan	(1973–1974)
Chuck Goggin	(1972–1973)
Gene Garber	(1972)
Carl Taylor	(1971)
Jerry May	(1964–1970)
Gene Freese	(1964–1965)
Don Hoak	(1959–1962)
Jim Pendleton	(1957–1958)
Dick Cole	(1953–1956)
Jack Maguire	(1951)
Monty Basgall	(1951)
Johnny Hopp	(1948–1950)
Culley Rikard	(1947)
Al Lopez	(1940–1946)
Ray Berres	(1940)
Johnny Rizzo	(1938–1939)
Bud Hafey	(1936)
Claude Passeau	(1935)
Freddie Lindstrom	(1933–1934)
Adam Comorosky	(1932)
COACHES	
Carlos Garcia	(2010)

NUMBER RETIRED: None

HALL OF FAMERS TO WEAR THE NUMBER: AL LOPEZ (1977), FREDDIE LINDSTROM (1976)

FIRST PERFORMANCE WITH THE NUMBER

7/1/1932- Adam Comorosky was hitless in a pinch-hitting performance for pitcher Larry French in a 5–3 loss to Dizzy Dean and the St. Louis Cardinals.

FIRST HOME RUN WITH THE NUMBER

7/26/1932- Leading off in a 7–3 loss to the New York Giants at the Polo Grounds, Adam Comorosky was three-for-four on the day with his first home run of the year, a solo shot off Hall of Famer Carl Hubbell.

FIRST VICTORY BY A PITCHER WITH THE NUMBER

8/3/1973- Rookie John Morlan pitched seven effective innings, allowing only four hits and an earned run while striking out five in the Bucs' 3–1 victory over Philadelphia for his first major league victory.

BEST PIRATES TO WEAR THE NUMBER: (HR-RBI-AVE)

Don Hoak (41–253–.281)

He had a football player mentality and even wore a quarterback's number; it's not just for quarterbacks anymore. The Tiger came to the Steel City in 1959 in a mega-deal with Cincinnati, along with Harvey Haddix and Smoky Burgess. While Burgess and Haddix were important in the 1960 title run, Hoak was much more, hitting .294 and finishing second to teammate Dick Groat in the NL's MVP race. His fiery personality and great leadership made him one of the greatest players ever to wear a Pirates uniform. Hoak tragically died in a car accident in 1969, suffering a heart attack while performing the heroic act of chasing after his brother-in-law's car, which had been stolen.

Freddie Sanchez (37–289-.301)

One of the few great trades the Pittsburgh Pirates made in their twenty-year steak of losing baseball was grabbing Freddie Sanchez from the Boston Red Sox. Hitting .301 in his five-plus seasons with the team, Sanchez put his name alongside such franchise greats as Dave Parker, Roberto Clemente, and Honus Wagner (and, yes, even Debs Garms) by capturing the National League batting title in 2006 with a .344 average.

Adam Comorosky (28–417-.285)

While he actually only wore the number one season, the first year the Bucs actually wore numbers, in 1932, Adam Comorosky had a fine career with the Pirates, hitting .285 while a member of the 1927 National League champions. He led the league in triples in 1930, when he had a career year with 12 homers and 119 RBIs, the only time he would have double digits in home runs and more than 100 RBIs in the same year.

WORST PIRATES TO WEAR THE NUMBER: (HR-RBI-AVE) (W-L-ERA)

Claude Passeau (0–1-12.00)

Claude Passeau did have an excellent career with the Phillies and Cubs, winning 162 games. Unfortunately, he did not have an excellent career in Pittsburgh, where he pitched in only one game, his first major league game in 1935, allowing seven hits and two walks in three innings, giving up four runs.

Jack Maguire (0–0-.000)

In 1951 Jack Maguire had a perfect record for the Pirates — in a bad way — going hitless in six plate appearances with a walk and a run, before being put on waivers by the team.

Wil Cordero (16–51-.282),

He may not have hit poorly for the team, with a .282 average and 16 homers in 89 games, but Wil Cordero turned out to be a very bad signing for the Pirates, at least from a character standpoint, which made him one of the worst to wear the number. Despite a history of issues including domestic violence, the losing Bucs gave him a three-year, $9 million contract. After Cordero gave a half-hearted effort and took a week off when the Bucs needed his bat claiming a stomach flu, Pittsburgh realized what a mistake they made and sent him and his $9 million contract to Cleveland.

OTHER NOTABLE PIRATES TO WEAR THE NUMBER

Freddie Lindstrom

A Hall of Famer who remains the youngest player ever to appear in a World Series, at the age of eighteen in 1924, Freddie Lindstrom hit .311 over a thirteen-year career that included a two-year stop in the Steel City late in his career, where he had a .302 average.

Johnny Rizzo

There are few home run hitters who belong in the same class as Ralph Kiner, but for one year Johnny Rizzo was exactly that. He hit a team rookie record 23 homers in 1938 with 111 RBIs. Ralph Kiner was only able to tie the mark in his first season as it was a record the two held jointly until 2004, when Jason Bay broke it by a single long ball.

Johnny Hopp

A star outfielder and first baseman with the St. Louis Cardinals during the war years, when he once hit .336, Johnny Hopp was acquired by the Bucs in 1948 along with second baseman and future manager Danny Murtaugh. He did well for the Bucs, especially in 1949 and '50, when he hit .335 and .340, respectively.

Dick Cole

A .253 hitter with Pittsburgh, Dick Cole was more important in Pirates history later in his life as a scouting supervisor for the team between 1971 and '74.

Jim Pendleton

While being a.306 hitter over his Pirate career is impressive, that record is tempered a bit by the fact that he had only 62 at bats. What was interesting about Jim Pendleton was the fact that he played in the Negro Leagues, for the Chicago American Giants in 1948, where he had only a .154 average in 13 at bats for Chicago. His other claim to fame is that he hit three home runs in one game his rookie year with the Braves, in a 19–4 trouncing of these same Pirates in 1953. No other rookie has ever hit more in a game.

Ray Berres

Ray Berres was a poor-hitting, excellent-fielding catcher for the Bucs with a .225 average over four seasons. He went on to do two things of note in his life: He became an excellent pitching coach for the White Sox under Al Lopez, and fell eight months short of living to the age of 100.

Jerry May

He was the Pirates' main catcher before Manny Sanguillen, and had a career that was very nondescript. The most memorable thing about it was the fact that he was the catcher for the famous Dock Ellis "LSD no-hitter" in 1970, when he wore reflective tape on his fingers so the drug-induced hurler could see the target.

Chuck Goggin

Chuck Goggin came to the plate only nine times in two seasons with the Pirates in 1972 and '73 and batted .375, but he was a hero nonetheless serving in Vietnam, a time when most players stayed home using the Army Reserves in an attempt to keep their playing careers alive. Although he was injured stepping on a landmine, it luckily was not severe enough to derail his major league aspirations.

Mike LaValliere (photo courtesy of the Pittsburgh Pirates)

Matt Alexander

In 1978 Matt Alexander had the distinction of playing seven games while never coming to bat; he was used only as a pinch-running specialist, all while wearing the number 12. He changed numbers afterwards and continued to be primarily a pinch-runner, although he would hit .444 in 27 at bats as a Pirate.

Bill Almon

Bill Almon was the first player picked in the entire 1974 amateur draft by San Diego. Even though he had a disappointing career for a first pick, he played fifteen seasons, including three decent ones with the Bucs, hitting .246.

Mike LaValliere

"Spanky" was a throw-in when the Pirates traded Tony Pena for Andy Van Slyke, but he turned out to be one of the best catchers in Pittsburgh

Pirates history, capturing a Gold Glove in 1987, and he hit .278 over seven seasons. There was a part of the field between where the outfielders and infielders stood called "Spankyland," where his hits often fell, as he didn't possess much power.

John Wehner

A hometown man from the Steel City, John Wehner,has had a great career as an announcer for the Pirates, but during his career as a utility player he had two areas of distinction: hitting the last home run at Three Rivers Stadium, and he shares the major league record for most games without committing an error at third base with 99 (a streak he shares with Jeff Cirillo) that strangely took him nine years to accomplish. It ironically also ended during the final contest at Three Rivers, a game in which he also made the final out in the stadium. Make that *three* things he's known for.

Al Lopez

One of the game's great defensive catchers, Al Lopez played for the Bucs between 1940 and 1946, part of a nineteen-year major league career. He,was elected to the baseball Hall of Fame in 1977. His election was not due to his .261 average, but for his tremendously successful stint as a manager, achieving a .584 winning percentage, winning 1,410 games over seventeen seasons with the Indians and White Sox,and capturing two American League pennants in the process.

Gene Garber and Dock Ellis

Gene Garber was a great reliever with other teams throughout his major league career, but certainly not with the Bucs, where he had a 7.11 ERA in 1972, the only year he wore number 12 as a young prospect. Dock Ellis wore it when he returned to the Bucs in 1979, pitching in his last three major league contests for the soon-to-be world champions.

#13: UNLUCKY 13

ALL TIME NO. 13 ROSTER	YEAR
Ronny Cedeno	(2009–2010)
Nate McLouth	(2008–2009)
Cesar Izturis	(2007)
Adrian Brown	(1998–2002)
Carlos Garcia	(1994–1996)
Jose Lind	(1987–1992)
Rich Reteria	(1986)
Trench Davis	(1986)
Steve Kemp	(1985)
Fernando Gonzalez	(1977–1978)
Roberto Clemente	(1955)
Eddie Pellagrini	(1953–1954)
Bill Pierro	(1950)
Marv Rickert	(1950)
Kirby Higbe	(1947–1949)
Luke Hamlin	(1942)
MANAGER	
Clint Hurdle	(2011–2014)
COACHES	
John Russell	(2003–2005)

NUMBER RETIRED: None

HALL OF FAMERS TO WEAR THE NUMBER: ROBERTO CLEMENTE (1973)

FIRST PERFORMANCE WITH THE NUMBER

4/16/1942- Luke Hamlin got the start in the third game of the season for the Pittsburgh Pirates and he was bad, very bad. Allowing six hits and five runs in two innings, Hamlin could not take advantage of the 3–0 lead the Bucs gave him in the top of the second, and the team eventually lost 8–7 in 12 innings.

FIRST HOME RUN WITH THE NUMBER

5/26/1953- In the first at bat of his Pittsburgh Pirates career, Eddie Pellagrini smacked a ninth-inning, pinch-hit two-run homer against the Phillies. Unfortunately, the team was down 7–3 at the time, so it was an exciting, albeit meaningless, shot to begin his Pirates career.

FIRST VICTORY BY A PITCHER WITH THE NUMBER

4/22/1942- After being thrashed in his first start of the season, former Dodger Luke Hamlin was much better in his second, allowing a run and seven hits in a complete-game 9–1 victory over the Cubs.

BEST PIRATES TO WEAR THE NUMBER: (HR-RBI-AVE) (W-L-PCT For Hurdle)

Clint Hurdle (431–379-.532)

As a player, Clint Hurdle was a disappointment for a first-round pick, never fully living up to his potential despite the fact he graced the cover of *Sports Illustrated*. As a manager he more than lived up to it, first leading the Colorado Rockies to their lone World Series appearance, then performing a Moses-like feat as he brought the Pittsburgh Pirates out of their losing ways to three consecutive playoff appearances. Pirates Nation continues to appreciate him for having made the unlucky 13 a very lucky one for the Steel City.

Jose Lind (8–249-.255)

He was pulled over for a traffic violation and was found to have no pants . . . or underpants, on for that matter, with many beers on the floor of his car, as well as cocaine in his possession; which apparently explains the lack of pants. He also made an egregious error in game seven of the 1992 NLCS that helped lead to such a heartbreaking defeat. Despite those facts, Jose Lind was not only a phenomenal defensive second baseman for the three-time eastern division champions, capturing a Gold Glove in 1992, but he wasn't an embarrassment at the plate, like he was in the driver's seat.

WORST PIRATES TO WEAR THE NUMBER: (HR-RBI-AVE) (W-L-ERA)

Trench Davis (0–1-.133)

Trench Davis may have had a great name, but it did not translate on to the field. He spent time with the Bucs in the mid-1980s; his claim to fame was that he was the man they sent back to the minors when they decided to bring up Barry Bonds, who didn't have as great a name but was decidedly better on the field.

Marv Rickert (0–4-.150)

After playing only three games for the Boston Braves in 1948, Marv Rickert was thrust upon the national scene in the World Series, taking over in left field for Jeff Heath, who had broken his ankle right before the Series began. Predictably, he was not at Heath's level, hitting only .211. When he came to Pittsburgh in 1950, he was not at a major leaguer's level, with a .150 average in 20 at bats.

Bill Piero (0–2-10.55)

One of the Pirates' best young pitchers in 1950, Bill Piero lost both his decisions that year with a 10.55 ERA. A year later he developed encephalitis and struggled to survive, much less continue his career. Luckily, he did survive, living until almost the age of eighty when he passed away in 2006. Unfortunately, his baseball career did not survive: he would never play another major league game.

OTHER NOTABLE PIRATES TO WEAR THE NUMBER

Roberto Clemente

Clemente's little-known rookie number was 13, until he donned another more famous one a year later: 21.

Luke Hamlin

A former 20-game winner with the Brooklyn Dodgers, Luke Hamlin came to Pittsburgh as part of the Arky Vaughan trade in 1942. If Pittsburgh thought they were getting the talent of a 20-game winner they were sadly mistaken, as Hamlin fell 16 victories short of the mark. He would play one more major league season with the A's before being relegated back to the minors, where he would eventually be elected to the International League Hall of Fame in 1955.

Kirby Higbe

In the film on Jackie Robinson's life, *42,* pitcher Kirby Higbe— a vocal dissenter on Robinson becoming a Dodger, who even signed a petition to keep him off the team — screamed in disgust when he learned that he had been traded to Pittsburgh by Brooklyn GM Branch Rickey. Before his embarrassing display, Higbe had actually been a fine pitcher for the Dodgers, winning a league-high 22 games in 1941. He also was involved in combat in Germany during World War II, where he fought bravely despite the fact that the horrors of war he witnessed had affected him emotionally.

Getting back to the situation at hand, it was in Pittsburgh where he was 19–26 over two seasons before ending his career with the Giants.

Eddie Pellagrini

Pellagrini's major league career got off to a late start as he spent time in the Navy during World War II. By the time he got to Pittsburgh, his career was pretty much over. The Pirates proved to be the last stop for the utility infielder; he hit .237 in two seasons with the Bucs. His main success would come as the head coach for Boston College, where his teams went to three College World Series in his thirty-one years at the helm.

Red Swanson

The Pittsburgh Pirates invested heavily in pitcher Red Swanson, giving him a $20,000 bonus to sign out of LSU, which made him--you got it, a bonus baby. Bonus Babies had to stay with the major league team two seasons, and Red proved quickly that he was not ready to do that, wining only three games in his three-season career. He did receive some press for wearing an eye protector in an effort to protect himself from being hit by a line drive; not sure if rubber and wire would defeat a line drive coming at you, but there is a complete certainty that he was a bad investment for the Bucs.

Steve Kemp

Steve Kemp had a great career for the Detroit Tigers, eclipsing the 100 RBI mark twice. The New York Yankees signed him to a free agent contract, realized that it was a bad signing, and dumped him off on Pittsburgh for, among others, a young Jay Buhner. Pittsburgh realized that they had been duped and, unfortunately, released him after a little more than a season with the team

Carlos Garcia

A decent-hitting second baseman, who hit .278 for the Bucs in seven seasons and was named to play in the 1994 All-Star game at Three Rivers Stadium, Carlos Garcia still is a big presence in the Pirates organization, managing both Bradenton and Altoona over the past five years.

Nate McLouth

Not much was made of the promotion of Nate McLouth when he came
to the Bucs in 2005, but three years
later he was the face of the franchise
with 26 homers, a league-high 46
doubles, an All-Star Game selection
and a Gold Glove in centerfield. The
next season Neal Huntington inexplicably sent him to the Braves. In

Nate McLouth (photo courtesy of
author)

retrospect, Huntington first showed us his brilliance with that trade as
McLouth would never be the same, and he got 40 percent of his starting rotation with Charlie Morton and Jeff Locke in return.

#14: OPERATION SHUTDOWN

ALL TIME NO. 14 ROSTER	YEAR
Jaff Decker	(2014–2015)
John Buck	(2013)
Gaby Sanchez	(2012–2013)
Casey McGehee	(2012)
John Bowker	(2011)
Jose Castillo	(2004–2007)
Derek Bell	(2001)
Emil Brown	(2000)
Luis Sojo	(2000)
Freddy Garcia	(1998–1999)
Mark Parent	(1995)
Brian Hunter	(1994)
Tom Prince	(1990–1993)
Ken Oberkfell	(1988–1989)
Mike Diaz	(1987–1988)
Dave Tomlin	(1985)
Milt May	(1983–1984)
John Milner	(1982–1983)
Willie Montanez	(1981–1982)
Ed Ott	(1977–1980)
Art Howe	(1974–1975)
Kurt Bevacqua	(1974)
Johnny Jeter	(1969)
Jim Bunning	(1968–1969)
Gene Alley	(1964–1967, 1970–1973)
Ted Savage	(1963)
Larry Elliot	(1962–1963)
Jim Marshall	(1962)
Rocky Nelson	(1959–1961)
John Powers	(1955–1958)
Jerry Lynch	(1954, 1956)
Felipe Montemayor	(1953–1955)
Pete Naton	(1953)
Sonny Senerchia	(1952)
George Strickland	(1950–1952)
Dino Restelli	(1949, 1951)
Max West	(1948)
Gene Woodling	(1947)
Billy Sullivan	(1947)
Frankie Zak	(1944, 1946)
Johnny Wyrostek	(1942–1943)
Bud Stewart	(1941–1942)

NUMBER RETIRED: None

HALL OF FAMERS TO WEAR THE NUMBER: HEINIE MANUSH (1964), CHUCK KLIEN (1980), JIM BUNNING (1996)

FIRST PERFORMANCE WITH THE NUMBER

6/30/1932- Oglethorpe University's Dave Barbee was in left field when the Pirates first wore numbers on their uniforms; he was the first to wear 14. He had a single, a walk, and an RBI in three at bats in the 9–6 win against the Cardinals.

FIRST HOME RUN WITH THE NUMBER

6/24/1933- After Dave Barbee hit five home runs before he wore 14, he hit none afterwards, which left it up to Adam Comorosky to do the honors of hitting one for the first time with number 14 on his back. He only hit one during the season, but it was enough to include him here as it came during a 15–3 rout of the Dodgers at Ebbets Field.

FIRST VICTORY BY A PITCHER WITH THE NUMBER

4/14/1968- It took until 1968 for a number 14 to win a major league game, but

Ray Mueller	(1940)
Chuck Klein	(1939)
Heinie Manush	(1939)
Fred Schulte	(1936–1937)
Babe Herman	(1935)
Wally Roettger	(1934)
Adam Comorosky	(1933)
Dave Barbee	(1932)
MANAGER	
Jim Leyland	(1986)
COACHES	
Gary Varsho	(2008–2010)

he did so in a big way as Hall of Famer Jim Bunning turned the trick. On this day, he shut out the Dodgers on five hits while striking out eight in a 3–0 victory.

BEST PIRATES TO WEAR THE NUMBER: (HR-RBI-AVE)

Gene Alley (55–342-.254)

Gene Alley was the other end of the legendary double-play combination with the Pittsburgh Pirates in the 1960s. While injuries would curtail his effectiveness, he won two Gold Gloves in his career and was also selected to the All-Star Game twice.

Ed Ott (31–173-.269)

Ed Ott formed a superb catching duo with Steve Nicosia that was an important part of the Pirates' last world championship season in 1979. He was also noted for his wrestling skills, as his most memorable major league moment occurred in 1977 when the Mets' Felix Millan took a swipe at him after an aggressive slide at second. Ott picked him up and slammed him to the ground severely, hurting Millan's shoulder and ending his season in the process.

Gene Alley (photo courtesy of the Pittsburgh Pirates)

Jose Castillo (33–181-.256)

Jose Castillo made the jump from AA in 2004, and became a good second baseman with decent power in his four years with

Pittsburgh. Actually, having Castillo on this list truly shows that there is not much star power with the number 14.

WORST PIRATES TO WEAR THE NUMBER: (HR-RBI-AVE)

Derek Bell (5–13-.173)

He came to the Pirates as a celebrated free agent, showing that the team was willing to spend money as they opened PNC Park. Actually, while the team thought he was celebrated, many scratched their heads since he was coming off two subpar seasons. Before the season was too old it became apparent that Bell was perhaps the worst free agent signing ever. Operation Shutdown cemented him as one of the most hated players in Pittsburgh sports history.

Felipe Montemayor (2–10-.173)

The native Mexican did not set the world on fire in his two major league seasons, finishing with a .173 average.

Johnny Wyrostek (0–4-.140)

An outfielder who was selected to play in two All-Star Games in 1950 and '51 with Cincinnati, Johnny Wyrostek spent his first two seasons in Pittsburgh, where he didn't play to that level, hitting only .140.

OTHER NOTABLE PIRATES TO WEAR THE NUMBER

Jim Leyland and Milt May

Manager Jim Leyland wore uniform number 14 in his first season, while May wore it in his final two after returning to the Pirates.

Heinie Manush

Manush was a Hall of Famer with a long career in the American League before the .330 hitter came to the Steel City. He was a shell of his former self at that point, with a .160 average over his final two major league seasons.

Wally Roettger

While he played only one season in Pittsburgh, his last in the majors in 1934, hitting .245, Wally Roettger went on to become a successful college baseball and basketball coach. He led the baseball program at Illinois for sixteen years and was head basketball coach at Illinois Wesleyan for ten seasons. He played in the majors between 1925 and 1934.

Babe Herman

Babe Herman was a fabulous player with the Brooklyn Dodgers, twice having over 100 RBIs, including 130 in 1930 when he hit a career-high 35 home runs. The .324 lifetime hitter was still playing at a high level in 1935 when he came to the Bucs. But injuries caused a slow start with the Pirates, and he and his high salary were quickly shipped off to the Reds, where he resumed his fine play, hitting .335 the rest of the way in Cincinnati.

Chuck Klein

Chuck Klein played one season with the Pirates, in 1939. Unlike fellow Hall of Famer Heinie Manush, he played well, hitting .300 before heading back to the Phillies, where he ended his career five years later.

Bud Stewart

Bud Stewart played his first two major league seasons with the Pirates, where he hit .242. He became the first player to lead both leagues in pinch-hits and was also an extra in the movie, *The Monte Stratton Story.*

Frankie Zak

A reserve shortstop in his three major league seasons, Frankie Zak had the honor of being the strangest All-Star selection in major league history. It was 1944, the game was at Forbes Field, and Eddie Miller was selected as a back-up for Marty Marion. Miller was injured and, when looking for a replacement, Pirates starter Frankie Gustine was not in

Frankie Zak (photo courtesy of the Pittsburgh Pirates)

town, so they called upon rookie Zak, who was selected because the game was in Pittsburgh and, quite simply, so was he.

Gene Woodling

Before Gene Woodling went on to success with the New York Yankees in the first half of the 1950s, he spent a season in Pittsburgh with Hank Greenberg and Ralph Kiner in 1947, when he hit .266 in 87 at bats.

Dino Restelli

His was the epitome of a fast start, hitting seven home runs in his first twelve major league games in 1949 that included a two-home run performance in only his second contest. Instead of being the next Babe Ruth, Dino Restelli crashed to earth quickly, hitting only six more major league homers over the rest of his two-year career.

Wally Judnich

An outstanding hitter early in his major league career with the St. Louis Browns, Wally Judnich lost three prime seasons while serving in the military during World War II. When he returned, he did not perform at his previous level and ended his career with the Bucs in 1949, hitting only .229.

Sonny Senerchia

Sonny Senerchia doubled as a jazz musician who appeared at Carnegie Hall at the age of ten, and was a race car driver, as well as a baseball player. His career was brief: he played one major league season, in 1952, hitting .220.

Jerry Lynch

Jerry "The Hat" Lynch played for thirteen major league seasons, beginning his career with the Bucs and then ending it there, too. The left fielder went on to be more noted as an owner of the famed Western Pennsylvania golf course Champion Lakes with fellow Buc Dick Groat.

Rocky Nelson

A minor league legend, Rocky Nelson finally found success later in his major league career with Pittsburgh, where he was a pivotal part of the 1960 world championship team and hit a clutch two-run homer in game seven of the World Series.

Jim Bunning

Hoping to add some pitching depth to their potent offense, Pittsburgh dealt for future Hall of Fame pitcher Jim Bunning in 1968. Unfortunately, it proved to be the beginning of the descent of his career, as the man who went on to become a United States Senator was only 17–23 with the team over two seasons.

Art Howe

Hitting only .195 in his first two seasons in the majors with Pittsburgh, Howe went on to enjoy a fine career with the Astros. He later became noted as a manager, first with Houston and then with the Oakland Athletics, where he did not look very impressive in the movie, *Moneyball*, about his general manager.

Ken Oberkfell

A great third baseman with the St. Louis Cardinals in the late 1970s and early 1980s, hitting .292 for the Cards, Ken Oberkfell was a Pirate late in his sixteen-year career, falling below the Mendoza Line with a .181 average.

#15: THE ORIGINAL

ALL TIME NO. 15 ROSTER	YEAR
Andrew Lambo	(2015)
Ike Davis	(2014)
Andy LaRoche	(2008–2010)
Keith Osik	(1997–2002)
Denny Neagle	(1993–1996)
Doug Drabek	(1987–1992)
Pat Clements	(1985–1986)
George Hendrick	(1985)
Ron Wotus	(1983–1984)
Enrique Romo	(1979–1982)
Mike Easler	(1977)
Tommy Helms	(1976–1977)
Miguel Dilone	(1975)
Gene Clines	(1970–1974)
Jose Martinez	(1969–1970)
Manny Mota	(1963–1968)
Tom Sturdivant	(1961–1963)
Roman Mejias	(1959–1961)
Frank Thomas	(1951–1958)
Erv Dusak	(1951–1952)
Wally Westlake	(1947–1951)
Elbie Fletcher	(1946)
Lloyd Waner	(1944–1945)
Alf Anderson	(1941–1942)
Johnny Dickshot	(1936–1937)
Bill Brubaker	(1933, 1940)
Gus Dugas	(1932)
COACHES	
Rusty Kuntz	(2003–2005)
Jim Lett	(2006–2007)
Luis Silverio	(2011–2012)

NUMBER RETIRED: None

HALL OF FAMERS TO WEAR THE NUMBER: LLOYD WANER (1967)

FIRST PERFORMANCE WITH THE NUMBER

7/1/1932- Gus Dugas, a little-used out-fielder, pinch-hit for pitcher Steve Swetonic in a 5–3 loss against Dizzy Dean and the Cardinals. Dean was gone when Dugas came up, and even though he didn't face a Hall of Famer he came up empty against reliever Jim Lindsey.

FIRST HOME RUN WITH THE NUMBER

7/30/1932- In the first game of the month, Gus Dugas premiered the number 15 with an unsuccessful pinch-hitting appearance. Even though he was only one-for-four starting in right field during a 13–3 loss to the Phillies, the one hit proved to be the first home run by a number 15.

FIRST VICTORY BY A PITCHER WITH THE NUMBER

8/8/1961- After coming over from Washington in his second start in a Pirates uniform, Tom Sturdivant defeated the Cubs 3–2 in a complete game victory in which he allowed seven hits, struck out five and walked five.

BEST PIRATES TO WEAR THE NUMBER: (HR-RBI-AVE) (W-L-ERA)

Frank Thomas (163–562-.275)

In the post-Ralph Kiner era, the man who was the face of the franchise was Frank Thomas. In six full seasons, he never hit fewer than 23 homers and twice hit more than 30 while knocking in over 100 runs on some very bad teams; he was selected to play in three All-Star Games. After a phenomenal 1958 campaign, when he finished fourth in the MVP race as the team celebrated its first winning campaign in ten years, he was traded to the Reds. He still remains in the area and refers to himself as the "Original" Frank Thomas, as compared to the Hall of Fame slugger who has the same name.

Doug Drabek (photo courtesy of the Pittsburgh Pirates)

Doug Drabek (92–62-3.02)

It was one of the great trades in Pittsburgh Pirates history. In Doug Drabek the Bucs got a prospect who had struggled with the Yankees and then blossomed with the Pirates. Leading the league in wins and winning percentage in 1990, Drabek became the second Pirate ever to capture the Cy Young Award. In his last game in a Bucs uniform, he pitched magnificently during the ill-fated 1992 NLCS game seven, but was exhausted in the ninth and couldn't complete the job; Stan Belinda, unfortunately, finished the game and the team suffered perhaps the worst loss in its history, with Drabek going down as the official loser of the game.

Wally Westlake (97–378-.281)

Combining with Ralph Kiner to form a powerful one-two punch on some lousy Pirate teams, Wally Westlake hit almost 100 home runs over five seasons, the best being 1949 with 23 long balls and 104 RBIs. The highlight of his time in the Steel City was hitting for the cycle both in 1948 and '49, when he would be the last to do it in Pittsburgh until Jason Kendall equaled that achievement in 2000. Westlake was having a fine 1951 campaign, when he would eventually be selected to play in his only All-Star Game, but the Bucs traded him to St. Louis for a bunch of guys including Joe Garagiola, who collectively helped them maintain their last-place finishes.

WORST PIRATES TO WEAR THE NUMBER: (HR-RBI-AVE) (W-L-ERA)

George Hendrick (2–25-.230)

If Derek Bell is the number one Pirates enemy in recent history, then George Hendrick comes in a close second. Much was expected from the slugger when he came over from the Cards in 1985; instead, what was given was an extremely lackadaisical effort that still ruffles the feathers of Pirates fans who had the misfortune to witness it.

Roy Wise (0–0-9.00)

During World War II there were many who appeared in major league games, due to lack of available personnel, who weren't really of major league caliber; Roy Wise was part of that crew. Appearing in two games in 1944, Wise confounded the experts on May 12 with two hitless innings against the Braves, when he walked two. A day later, all things were right with the world again as he gave up four hits and three runs in an inning. He never pitched again.

Andy LaRoche (19–92-.226)

A top prospect in the Dodgers' farm system, where he reached as high as being ranked fourteenth by "Baseball Prospectus" in 2007, Andy LaRoche proved in Pittsburgh that rating prospects is a very inexact science; he played like a top ten bust here with a .226 average.

OTHER NOTABLE PIRATES TO WEAR THE NUMBER

Johnny Dickshot

Hitting .250 in three seasons with the Pirates, Johnny Dickshot had the unique moniker of "Ugly," often claiming that there was no uglier player in the game. In looking at his picture it's a point well taken.

Lloyd Waner and Elbie Fletcher

After being dealt away in 1941, Lloyd Waner returned to the Pirates in 1944 for his last two seasons, when he wore number 15. Elbie Fletcher donned quite a few numbers for the team, wearing 15 in 1946.

Tom Sturdivant

A converted infielder, Tom Sturdivant turned himself into an effective pitcher who won 16 games twice with the New York Yankees in the 1950s, including a league-leading .727 winning percentage in 1957. A year later he injured his arm and was never the same, although he pitched well for the Bucs in his three seasons with the team, winning a total of 14 games with a 3.49 ERA, splitting time between the starting rotation and the bullpen.

Manny Mota

Pinch-hitter extraordinaire Manny Mota was a near .300 hitter in his six seasons in the Burgh, hitting .297. In 1979, while playing for the Dodgers, his 146th stolen base would break the all-time pinch-hit record set by another former Pirate, Smoky Burgess.

Jose Martinez

Cuban-born Jose Martinez never amounted to much as a major league ball player, hitting .286 over two years in a Pirates uniform, his only two seasons in the majors, but he had a long career as a coach that included a world championship with the Royals in 1985.

Gene Clines

With any other team Gene Clines could have been a star outfielder, hitting .300 twice with the team including .334 in 1972, but in Pittsburgh's crowded star outfield in the early 1970s he was reduced to nothing more than a reserve. Struggling against right-handed pitching also hurt his playing time; Clines was only a .262 hitter against them in his career, 30 points lower than he hit against southpaws.

Tommy Helms

Tommy Helms was a great second baseman with the Big Red Machines of the late 1960s and early 1970s, when he won the Rookie of the Year Award, two Gold Gloves, and was named to two All-Star teams. By the time the Bucs got him he was at the end of his career and was only a utility infielder hitting .242 in a black-and-gold uniform.

Enrique Romo

An important part of the Pirates bullpen during their last world championship in 1979, Enrique Romo won ten games for the team with five saves and a 2.99 ERA. Four years later in 1983, he refused to report to spring training and refused to contact the team. His wife would say only that he was unhappy with the Bucs and the fact that they were fining him $500 a day, which led him to play in Mexico. He has pretty much never been heard from again.

Ron Wotus

Ron Wotus had a very brief major league career that consisted of 58 at bats over two seasons in Pittsburgh, where he hit .207. He went on to become a successful minor league manager and a long-time coach with the San Francisco Giants.

Denny Neagle

Denny Neagle was a fine pitcher in Pittsburgh, winning 27 games over two seasons before being dealt to Atlanta, where he became a 20-game winner.

#16: NO RESPECT

ALL TIME NO. 16 ROSTER	YEAR
Pedro Ciriaco	(2010)
Eric Hinske	(2009)
Doug Mientkiewicz	(2008)
Salomon Torres	(2004–2007)
Jose Hernandez	(2003)
Aramis Ramirez	(1998–2003)
Joe Randa	(1997)
Nelson Liriano	(1995–1996)
Tom Foley	(1993–1994)
Bob Kipper	(1987–1991)
Hipolito Pena	(1986)
Lee Mazzilli	(1984–1986)
Steve Nicosia	(1979–1983)
Will McEnaney	(1978)
John Milner	(1978)
Al Oliver	(1969–1977)
Chris Cannizzaro	(1968)
Andre Rodgers	(1966)
Del Crandall	(1965)
Ron Brand	(1963)
Tom Parsons	(1963)
Johnny Logan	(1961–1962)
Gene Baker	(1960–1961)
Bob Porterfield	(1958–1959)
Eddie O'Brien	(1957–1958)
Lee Walls	(1956–1957)
Tom Saffell	(1955)
Pete Castiglione	(1947–1953)
Frankie Gustine	(1939–1948)
Woody Jensen	(1932–1939)
COACHES	
Nick Leyva	(2011–2015)

NUMBER RETIRED: None

HALL OF FAMERS TO WEAR THE NUMBER: None

FIRST PERFORMANCE WITH THE NUMBER

4/21/1933- Woody Jensen singled and scored while pinch-hitting for Bill Swift in a 5–1 victory against the Cincinnati Reds.

FIRST HOME RUN WITH THE NUMBER

5/15/1935- It took more than three seasons while wearing the number 16 before Woody Jensen finally hit a home run in it. After the Bucs fell behind the Phillies 5–4 in the first inning, they would score 16 more runs to crush Philadelphia 20–5. Jensen was three-for-six with his first home run since 1931, and three runs scored, in the win.

FIRST VICTORY BY A PITCHER WITH THE NUMBER

5/11/1958- In his first game for the Bucs after coming over from the Red Sox, Bob Porterfield was magnificent in tossing an eleven-inning shutout over Philadelphia 1–0.

BEST PIRATES TO WEAR THE NUMBER: (HR-RBI-AVE)

Al Oliver (135–717-.296)

He is the Rodney Dangerfield of baseball when it comes to the Hall of Fame candidate; he gets no respect. Whether it was his brash attitude

Al Oliver sliding into second. (Photo courtesy of the Pittsburgh Pirates)

with management or the same with reporters, Oliver has gotten little or no support when it comes to baseball's highest honor, despite the fact he had 2,746 hits and 1,326 RBIs plus winning a batting title with eight All-Star Game selections. Despite all that, he received just 4.3 per cent of the vote in his only appearance on the ballot in 1991. Hopefully, the Veteran's Committee will overlook his attitude someday and give his candidacy the respect it deserves.

Woody Jensen (26–235-.285)

Spending his entire nine-year career with the Pittsburgh Pirates, Woody Jensen was a slap-hitting left fielder who walked only 69 times in his entire Pirates career. Jensen hit .324 in 1935, and because he walked so few times it allowed him to set a major league record with 696 at bats, batting leadoff with Lloyd Waner dropping to second. It was a record that lasted until another Pirate, Matty Alou, broke it by two thirty-three years later.

Frankie Gustine (34–451-.268)

In ten seasons as a Pirate, the popular Frankie Gustine started at second, third, and shortstop at various times for the Bucs. The three-time

All-Star was a great friend and pallbearer at the funerals of two Pirates icons, Pie Traynor and Honus Wagner. He also coached baseball at Point Park for seven seasons after his retirement, and was part owner of the Sheraton Inn located on the Southside of Pittsburgh.

WORST PIRATES TO WEAR THE NUMBER: (HR-RBI-AVE) (W-L-ERA)

Tom Parsons (0–1-8.31)

If not for a chance to pitch with the horrific Mets in 1964, Tom Parsons's poor performance in his first and only start for the Pirates would have been the end of his major league career. Thank God for expansion.

Hipolito Pena (0–6-5.56)

Losing all six decisions in his two-year career in 1986 and '87, Hipolito Pena at least would win one major league game after he was dealt to the Yankees in 1988.

Del Crandall (2–10-.214)

A heavy-hitting catcher with the great Milwaukee Braves teams in the 1950s, when he hit 170 homers over thirteen seasons while being named to eight All-Star games and receiving four Gold Gloves, Del Crandall came to the Pirates in his next-to-last major league season in 1965 and hit .214.

OTHER NOTABLE PIRATES TO WEAR THE NUMBER

Lee Walls

Lee Walls looked more like a college professor than a baseball player, but after three nondescript seasons with the Pirates he was a one-year wonder in 1958 in Chicago where he hit 24 of his career 66 home runs, including what still remains a Cubs record eight in April, and was named to the All-Star team.

Bob Porterfield

Like Lee Walls above him on this list, Bob Porterfield was a one-year wonder with Washington, leading the American League in wins in 1953 with 22, and being named *The Sporting News* Pitcher of the Year. He was 5–8 with the Bucs over his final two major league seasons in 1958 and '59.

Eddie O'Brien

Former college basketball superstar Eddie O'Brien wore 16 his final two seasons in a Pirates uniform.

Gene Baker

While he hit only .259 over his four seasons with the Pirates, the former Negro League player with the Kansas City Monarchs was a pioneer in the game. He became the first African American minor league manager with an affiliated team in 1958, leading Batavia. Then in 1962, after Danny Murtaugh was thrown out of a contest, Baker, who was a Pirates coach at the time, took over the team for the rest of the game, becoming the first African American to manage a major league team. He finished his time in baseball as the head Midwestern scout for the Bucs, holding the position for twenty-three seasons.

Johnny Logan

A fine-hitting shortstop with Milwaukee for most of his thirteen-year major league career, Johnny Logan ended his days in the majors averaging .249 for the Bucs in a backup roll. He played in Japan after he left the Pirates, and became the first player to participate both in an American World Series and a Japanese one.

Steve Nicosia

Steve Nicosia combined with Ed Ott to form a dynamic catching duo for the world champion Pirates in 1979. Although only a .242 hitter in his six seasons in a Pittsburgh uniform, he hit .288 in 1979.

Bob Kipper

Bob Kipper was a struggling starter with potential his first two seasons in a Pirates uniform before becoming a decent reliever. He was nicknamed "Round Tripper" Kipper for his penchant for giving up homers, which he did 72 times in 520 innings during his Bucs career.

Joe Randa

In the midst of the amazing "Freak Show" in 1997, Joe Randa was a key component as the team's third baseman, hitting .302. In true Pirates form during the era, the fear that keeping him would lead to winning apparently led management to deal him to the Royals. He returned in 2006, which was a freak show in the sense that the Bucs lost in a freakishly high manner.

Aramis Ramirez

Ramirez was a budding superstar with the Pirates in the early twenty-first century, hitting 34 homers with 112 RBIs in 2001 at the age of twenty-one. Two years later, he was dealt for financial reasons in one of the worst trades the Pirates Nation would ever see. He became a star with the Cubs and Brewers, before eventually returning to the city where it all started for his final major league season in 2015. It's a different atmosphere in Pittsburgh now: Ramirez enjoyed a playoff game at PNC Park with the team, a contest unimaginable when he was a rookie.

Salomon Torres

After not playing major or minor league baseball in this country for four seasons, Salomon Torres had an impressive six-year career out of the Pirates bullpen between 2002 and 2007, tying the franchise record with Kent Tekulve for most games pitced in a season with 94 in 2006.

Doug Mientkiewicz

Doug Mientkiewicz had a memorable long name, and was a decent first baseman for the Minnesota Twins at the beginning of his career.

He signed with Boston in 2004 and while he hit only .215, he had the honor of catching the final out of the 2004 World Series, giving the Red Sox their first world championship in 86 years. He decided to keep the ball, which apparently made him public enemy number one in Boston until he agreed to donate it to the Hall of Fame in 2006. He played for the Pirates two years later, in 2008, hitting .277 in his next-to-last major league season. Luckily for Mientkiewicz, the Bucs gave him no chance to catch the final ball of a World Series.

#17: AN IMPERFECT NO-HITTER

ALL TIME NO. 17 ROSTER	YEAR
Aramis Ramirez	(2015)
Pedro Florimon	(2015)
Gaby Sanchez	(2013–2014)
John McDonald	(2013)
Drew Sutton	(2012)
Pedro Alvarez	(2010)
Eric Hacker	(2009)
Sean Burnett	(2009)
Bobby Hill	(2003–2005)
Mendy Lopez	(2002)
Armando Rios	(2001)
Emil Brown	(2001)
Joe Oliver	(1999)
Doug Strange	(1998)
Dale Sveum	(1996–1997)
Charlie Hayes	(1996)
Mackey Sasser	(1995)
Bob Walk	(1986–1993)
Trench Davis	(1985)
Jerry Dybzinski	(1985)
Scott Loucks	(1985)
Mike Brown	(1985)
Lee Lacy	(1979–1984)
Ellie Rodriguez	(1978)
Phil Garner	(1977)
Doug Bair	(1976)
Odell Jones	(1976)
Dock Ellis	(1970–1975)
Ed Acosta	(1970)
Donn Clendenon	(1961–1968)
George Perez	(1958)
Danny Kravitz	(1956–1957)
Red Swanson	(1955–1956)
Hardy Peterson	(1955, 1957–1958)
Dick Hall	(1954)
Carlos Bernier	(1953)
Brandy Davis	(1952–1953)
Tom Saffell	(1951)
Ted Beard	(1948–1952)
Bobby Rhawn	(1949)
Phil Masi	(1949)
Marv Rackley	(1949)
Grady Wilson	(1948)
Jim Russell	(1947)

NUMBER RETIRED: None

HALL OF FAMERS TO WEAR THE NUMBER: None

FIRST PERFORMANCE WITH THE NUMBER

4/19/1938- The self-proclaimed ugliest man in baseball, Johnny Dickshot, wore the number 17 in 1938. He pinch-hit for Lloyd Waner in the opener, getting out in the process. The Pirates would rally for two runs in the ninth to defeat St. Louis 4–3.

FIRST HOME RUN WITH THE NUMBER

5/27/1939- Fern Bell was a rookie who would enjoy a fine season, hitting .286 as an outfielder with the Bucs in 1939. On this date he was a star, with a home run and five RBIs, knocking in one on a sacrifice fly, two on a single, and the other two RBIs on the first home run by a 17. He'd be out of the majors a year later, then fought in the Pacific Theater with the Navy in 1944 and '45.

FIRST VICTORY BY A PITCHER WITH THE NUMBER

4/9/1970- It wasn't until the second game of the 1970 season that a number 17 won a ball game, fittingly the greatest to wear the number who had the honor. That day

Vic Barnhart	(1944–1946)
Len Gilmore	(1944)
Maurice Van Robays	(1939–1943)
Fern Bell	(1939)
Johnny Dickshot	(1938)
COACHES	
Bobby Cuellar	(2006–2007)
Lou Frazier	(2008)
Jeff Banister	(2011)

Dock Ellis would toss a five-hit complete game, striking out 13 in a 2–1 victory against the Mets. Also fittingly, he walked five in the contest, a preview of what the Padres would experience in the famed LSD no-hitter later in the season.

BEST PIRATES TO WEAR THE NUMBER: (HR-RBI-AVE)

Dock Ellis (96–80-3.16)

From wearing curlers to hitting the first three Cincinnati Reds in one game, saying Dock Ellis was colorful could be one of the great understatements. What gets lost in the story was that he was a hell of a pitcher, winning 19 games in 1971, including 13 in a row, and

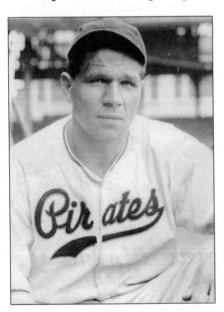

Johnny Dickshot (photo courtesy of the Pittsburgh Pirates)

being named the starting pitcher in the 1971 All-Star Game against another African American, Vida Blue. As great as his career was, Ellis was most famous for his admission that he was high on LSD when he pitched a no-hitter against the San Diego Padres in 1970. It was that game that was the inspiration for a great documentary about his life titled, *No-No: A Dockumentary,* in which he walked eight Padres in that famous contest; perhaps the most imperfect no-hitter in the history of the game.

Donn Clendenon (108–488-.280)

A power-hitting first baseman for the Bucs who hit 28 homers in 1966 while knocking in 98, Donn Clendenon was a great all-around athlete; he chose the Pirates over pro football's Cleveland Browns and basketball's New York Knicks and Harlem Globetrotters. He was given up in the expansion draft to the Montreal Expos, and eventually found his way to the Mets in 1969, where he had a World Series for the ages, hitting three home runs and being named World Series MVP. After retiring, he received his law degree from Duquesne University.

Donn Clendenon (photo courtesy of the Pittsburgh Pirates)

Lee Lacy (35–172-.304)

Coming to the Bucs from the Dodgers in 1979, just in time to win a World Series ring, Lee Lacy formed a great left-field platoon with Bill Robinson and hit .304 over his six-year Pirates career that included .335 in 1980 and a National League second-best .321 in 1984. In between, he showed his great speed by swiping 40 bases in 1982.

WORST PIRATES TO WEAR THE NUMBER: (HR-RBI-AVE) (W-L-ERA)

Grady Wilson (0–0-.100)

Grady Wilson is as well-known as the character who was Fred Sanford's best friend in the famed TV series, *Sanford and Son*; this would be a different and much less famous Grady Wilson. A four-year army vet during World War II, this Grady Wilson had a less-than-stellar career in a major league uniform, racking up one hit in ten at bats, and two errors, in twelve major league games for the Bucs in 1948. By the way, the more famous Grady had a spin off-series that was as brief as baseball Grady's major league career; it lasted just ten episodes. Your Grady Wilson fact of the day!

John McDonald (0–1-.065)

A decent-fielding utility infielder, John McDonald proved so much of a hazard at the plate for the Pirates in 2013 with only two hits in 31 at bats, that he was sent to the Indians as part of a conditional deal before the season ended; the condition probably was that he never step to the plate for the Bucs again.

Brandy Davis (0–3-.187)

He was the butt of many of Joe Garagiola's jokes on the *Tonight Show,* and was also talked about in a book on scouting, "Dollar Sign on the Muscle," where presumably it was claimed that scouts can be wrong. Brandy Davis could have been the poster child for bad Pirates baseball in the 1950s, since he batted only .187 over two seasons. Remarkably he led the 1952 Pirates in stolen bases with nine.

Len Gilmore (0–1-7.88)

Here, my friends, is the only pitcher from the great Indiana University of Pennsylvania who threw a meaningful pitch in a major league game. After a fine 21–5 campaign in Albany in 1944, Gilmore got a chance to live his dream, pitching in the major leagues on the final day of the season. It would prove to be his only day in the majors, after he allowed seven runs and 13 hits in the complete-game loss.

POTENTIALLY THE WORST PIRATE TO WEAR THE NUMBER: (HR-RBI-AVE)

Pedro Florimon (0–1-.087)

Potentially one of the worst Pirate of all time to wear the number 17, "potentially" only because he could return and either get off this list or entrench himself in it. Pedro Florimon showed just how cruel baseball can be; he was DFA'd (designated for assignment) the day after he hit a game-winning triple in the bottom of the 15th inning against Arizona.

OTHER NOTABLE PIRATES TO WEAR THE NUMBER

Maurice Van Robays

Maurice Van Robays had one of the most magnificent rookie seasons in Pittsburgh Pirates history in 1940, knocking in 116 runs and hitting 11 home runs. A veteran of World War II, missing the 1944 and 1945 campaigns, Van Robays also had the honor of naming Rip Sewell's famous "eephus" pitch. claiming simply that "an eephus wasn't anything," just like Sewell's famed pitch. Unfortunately, the rest of his career proved to be an eephus. While he hit over .280 on two occasions in his six years with the Pirates, he would never again come close to reaching the lofty milestone of 100 RBIs.

Vic Barnhart

Vic Barnhart had good bloodlines, the son of Pirate Clyde Barnhart. Unfortunately, his talent never reached his father's level. Vic hit .270 between 1944 and '46 in only 204 at bats. His claim to fame is the fact that he and his father both played with Hall of Famer Lloyd Waner.

Phil Masi

A great defensive catcher who was a four-time All-Star in his fourteen-year major league career, Phil Masi had the honor of being the opposing catcher in Jackie Robinson's debut. Masi was dealt to the Bucs midway in the 1949 campaign after eleven years with the Boston Braves. He hit .274 in 48 games before being sold to the White Sox the next season.

Marv Rackley

Marv Rackley was a fine-hitting backup catcher with a .317 lifetime average who was traded to the Pirates in 1949 by Brooklyn for Johnny Hopp and $25,000. When he came to the Steel City he hit .314 in 35 at bats, but was found to have a sore arm, prompting claims that the great Dodger GM Branch Rickey had sent the Bucs damaged goods. Eventually, the trade was voided and the Pirates got Hopp and their money back.

Ted Beard

A minor league star who was a poor-hitting outfielder in the majors for seven seasons, falling two points below the Mendoza Line, Ted Beard might have been a bust on the diamond, but he was a genuine American hero in the military for three years during World War II. He was a medic in the Pacific Theater, a very dangerous job in a very deadly war zone.

Tom Saffell

Another forgettable Pirates outfielder in the late 1940s and early 1950s, who hit .238 in four seasons with the Bucs, Tom Saffell was also an American hero, flying sixty-one bombing missions in the European Theater during World War II.

Carlos Bernier

While Curt Roberts is given credit as the first African American to appear with the franchise, Carlos Bernier was the first man of color. The fiery Puerto Rican was a star in his native country, but it didn't translate on the field with the Pirates; he hit .213 in 1953, his lone season in the majors. He had a troubled life afterwards, eventually committing suicide in 1989.

Harding Peterson

A little-used catcher with the Pirates in the late 1950s, Harding Peterson would become the farm director for the team and helped build the world champions as a general manager in 1979; ironically, in the process he emptied the farm system he had built up so proudly.

Pedro Alvarez, Phil Garner, and Aramis Ramirez

Phil Garner and Pedro Alvarez each wore the number 17 in his first season in a Pirates uniform, while Ramirez did so in his last, coming back to the Pirates during the 2015 pennant chase.

Mike Brown

Mike Brown was thought to be the face of the future for the franchise when he came to the Bucs from the Angels in 1985; it didn't hurt that he hit .332 the rest of the season. What did hurt was his .220 average the next year, which ended his brief stay in the Steel City.

Bob Walk

He was a reliable, tough pitcher who captured 82 games in his ten-year Pirates career while playing a pivotal role on their three eastern division championship squads. After his career ended he became, and still remains, one of the great color men in baseball; he has been with the club since 1994 in that capacity.

Charlie Hayes

Playing with the Bucs for one season in 1996, the fourteen-year veteran was dealt to the Yankees at the trading deadline and went on to win a World Series with the Bronx Bombers. Since then he has contributed to the Pirates as the father of their second first-round draft pick in 2015, Ke'Bryan Hayes.

Armando Rios and Bobby Hill

As we talk about a "poster child" at various times in this book, these two would be prime candidates for the Pirates regime's failed attempts to build a winner in the 'Burgh during their twenty-year streak of losing baseball. Rios played two games for Pittsburgh after coming over for Jason Schmidt, then blew out his knee. (The Bucs got Ryan Vogelsong also, but, of course, gave up on him before he became a star with the Giants.) Bobby Hill was a key piece of the ill-fated Aramis Ramirez trade, hitting only .263 with two homers in parts of three seasons with Pittsburgh.

#18: WHERE BALLS GO TO DIE

ALL TIME NO. 18 ROSTER	YEAR
Neil Walker	(2010–2015)
Jeff Salazar	(2009)
Craig Monroe	(2009)
Jason Michaels	(2008)
Masumi Kuwata	(2007)
Steve Pearce	(2007)
Jose Hernandez	(2006)
Sean Burnett	(2005)
Jason Kendall	(1996–2004)
Andy Van Slyke	(1987–1994)
Bob Walk	(1984–1985)
Gene Tenace	(1983–1984)
Omar Moreno	(1977–1982)
Willie Randolph	(1975)
Craig Reynolds	(1975)
Mario Mendoza	(1974)
Vic Davalillo	(1971–1973)
Matty Alou	(1966–1970)
Bill Virdon	(1956–1965)
Bobby Del Greco	(1956)
Jerry Lynch	(1955)
Laurin Pepper	(1954)
Cal Abrams	(1953–1954)
Gus Bell	(1950–1951)
Tom Saffell	(1949–1950)
Murry Dickson	(1949)
Eddie Bockman	(1948)
Al Gionfriddo	(1947)
Hank Behrman	(1947)
Johnny Barrett	(1942–1946)
Debs Garms	(1940–1941)

NUMBER RETIRED: None

HALL OF FAMERS TO WEAR THE NUMBER: None

FIRST PERFORMANCE WITH THE NUMBER

4/16/1940- Debs Garms began his greatest season in a major league uniform on opening day, with two hits and a run in five at bats against the Cardinals in a 6–4 win.

FIRST HOME RUN WITH THE NUMBER

4/26/1940- Ten days later, Garms hit his first homer of the season, a three-run shot in the bottom of the eighth off Bob Weiland, helping Pittsburgh to a 10–4 victory against St. Louis.

FIRST VICTORY BY A PITCHER WITH THE NUMBER

4/27/1949- After being acquired from the St. Louis Cardinals, Murry Dickson won his second start against the Cards in a complete-game 7–1 victory in which he allowed seven hits and no earned runs while striking out five and walking four in the process. Dickson would wear the number 18 only until mid-season, when he switched to the uniform he wore the rest of his time with the Bucs, 22.

BEST PIRATES TO WEAR THE NUMBER: (HR-RBI-AVE)

Andy Van Slyke (117–564-.283)

The best of a great group of center fielders to wear number 18, Andy Van Slyke shared something with Bill Virdon: He was a young castoff sent to the Pittsburgh Pirates, where he became a superstar. Van Slyke would win five Gold Gloves in the Steel City, while capturing two Silver Slugger awards and the 1988 *Sporting News* National League Player of the Year.

Andy Van Slyke (photo courtesy of the Pittsburgh Pirates)

Jason Kendall (67–471-.306)

Catcher Jason Kendall donned 18 after Van Slyke and kept the success going, breaking up the block of center fielders as the greatest to wear the number. One of the great catchers in Pirate history, Kendall hit .306 with the team. The three-time All-Star had a tremendous career, finishing fifth in games played behind the plate; only Ivan Rodriguez had more assists as a catcher than Kendall's 13,019.

Matty Alou (6–202-.327)

A slap hitter when he was with the Giants, Pirates manager Harry Walker turned this little-respected reserve outfielder into a National League batting titlist in 1966 with a .342 average. The man who took over for Bill Virdon in center learned to choke up on the bat and hit it to left instead of pulling the ball. It made all the difference in the world, turning him into a superstar.

Jason Kendall (left) and Manny Sanguillen (right). (Photo courtesy of the Pittsburgh Pirates)

Bill Virdon (72–425-.266)

A St. Louis Cardinals disappointment turned out to be a Pittsburgh Pirates fortune. After Virdon won the 1955 Rookie of the Year Award in St. Louis, the Cards quickly gave up on him and sent him to the Pirates. For ten years he manned the vast centerfield in Forbes Field and turned the area into a place where balls went to die. An important member of the 1960 world champions, Virdon won the Gold Glove in 1962. He later managed the Bucs to the eastern division title in 1972.

WORST PIRATES TO WEAR THE NUMBER: (HR-RBI-AVE) (W-L-ERA)

Jeff Salazar (0–1-.043)

Following a fine minor league career, Jeff Salazar was a decent defensive center fielder for Colorado and Arizona, where he hit a combined .247 over three seasons. Unlike the many outfielders who can proudly say they wore the number 18 with the Bucs, Salazar was not one of them, going one-for-23 in his Pirates career in 2009, his last season in the majors.

Hank Behrman (0–2-9.12)

Sandwiched in between two tours of duty in Brooklyn, where he was acquired in 1947 as part of the Kirby Higbe trade, Hank Behrman was horrific in his stop in Pittsburgh, eclipsing the dreaded 2.000 mark in WHIP at 2.027 in 24 2/3 innings, during the 1947 campaign before the World War II vet was cut loose.

Masumi Kuwata (0–1-9.43)

Many pitchers from Japan came to the United States and had success; Masumi Kuwata was not one of them. The thirty-nine-year-old former star in Japanese baseball was awful in his lone major league season in 2007, losing his only decision with a 9.43 ERA, allowing six home runs in only 21 innings pitched.

Willie Randolph (0–3-.164)

As many great moves as the Pirates did make in the 1970s, Willie Randolph was an exception. The young prospect hit only .164 for the team in 1975, and was dealt to the Yankees for Doc Medich. Medich was a bust for the Pirates, while Randolph went on to an eighteen-year career as a six-time All-Star with the Bronx Bombers.

OTHER NOTABLE PIRATES TO WEAR THE NUMBER

Deb Garms

You'd think Debs was a nickname, but, alas, it was the first name of one of the most obscure batting champions in major league history, Debs Garms. Although he hit .355 in 1940, his first season with the Pirates, in only 385 at bats, there was controversy surrounding the title since it was believed that a batter needed 400 at bats to qualify. When questioned, Commissioner Ford Frick stated that the 400 at bats rule was only an American League rule and that Garms did, in fact, win the batting title.

This man, who broke up Johnny Vander Meer's record-setting no-hit streak in 1938 — and who also temporarily held the record of seven consecutive pinch-hits in 1941, a record that was forgotten by some record keepers at that time — was never given the full respect of his accomplishment, which also set the stage for batting title requirements that would come later on. By the way, he also had a nickname, Tex.

Johnny Barrett

An outfielder with the Pittsburgh Pirates, Johnny Barrett saw most of his success and playing time with the team during World War II. He led the National League in triples and stolen bases in 1944, but hurt his knee in 1946 before being dealt to the Braves. It was the .251 hitter's final major league campaign.

Gus Bell

Only scratching the surface of his potential, Gus Bell hit 16 home runs in 1950 and '51 for the Pirates, with a league-leading 12 triples in 1950.

Teams go through bad losing eras due to dumb transactions, and with Bell the Pirates proved that adage correct by sending him to the Reds for three players that included Cal Abrams, Gail Henley, and Joe Rossi, none of whom would be the slugging superstar that Bell became in Cincinnati. Later in his career, in 1962, he had the honor of getting the first hit in New York Mets history.

Cal Abrams

Part of one of the worst trades in Pirates history, Cal Abrams was a non-factor as a player, but a hero fighting for his country in World War II. Abrams fought in the Pacific and was awarded a Philippines Liberation Ribbon with one bronze star and two battle stars.

Vic Davalillo

A good-hitting reserve outfielder during his sixteen-year major league career, Vic Davalillo spend three years in Pittsburgh during their championship run in the early 1970s, hitting .290 for his Bucco career; that included a fine .318 average in 1972.

Omar Moreno

Yet another center fielder to wear the number 18, the speedy Omar Moreno twice led the National League in stolen bases; he swiped 96 in 1980. Stealing a total of 487 in his career, Moreno had the honor of securing the final out in the 1979 World Series.

Gene Tenace

The 1972 World Series MVP who had an .817 career OPS, Gene Tenace ended his career in Pittsburgh in 1983 as a shell of himself, hitting only .177.

Neil Walker

The home-grown Neil Walker was a first-round draft pick in 2004 out of Pine-Richland High School in nearby Gibsonia, PA, where he was both a football and baseball star. Starting out as a catcher in the minors before moving to third, Walker eventually found his niche in the majors at second and became one of the best power-hitting second basemen in franchise history. He belted 93 homers in his seven-year career, including a team record 23 for a second baseman in 2014. It was a sad day in the 'Burgh when he was dealt to the New York Mets after the 2015 campaign.

#19: THE LOSING RECORD

ALL TIME NO. 19 ROSTER	YEAR
Chris Stewart	(2014–2015)
Michael McKenry	(2013)
Jeff Clement	(2012)
Chris Snyder	(2010–2011)
Ryan Church	(2010)
Neil Walker	(2009)
Jose Bautista	(2006–2008)
Ty Wigginton	(2004–2005)
Reggie Sanders	(2003)
Alex Hernandez	(2000)
Luis Sojo	(2000)
Emil Brown	(1997, 1999)
Dan Plesac	(1995–1996)
Curt Wilkerson	(1991)
Wally Backman	(1990)
Albert Hall	(1989)
Gary Redus	(1988–89)
Terry Harper	(1987)
Rod Scurry	(1981–1985)
Jim Rooker	(1973–1980)
Joe Gibbon	(1969–1970)
Jim Shellenback	(1969)
Pedro Ramos	(1969)
Pete Mikkelsen	(1966–1967)
Bob Friend	(1953–1965)
Red Munger	(1952)
Bill Werle	(1949–1952)
Jack Cassini	(1949)
Gene Mauch	(1947)
Jimmy Bloodworth	(1947)
Hugh Mulcahy	(1947)
Maurice Van Robays	(1946)
Max Butcher	(1939–1945)
COACHES	
Goldie Holt	(1948)
Mick Kelleher	(1986)
Bill Virdon	(1993–1994, 2001–2002)

NUMBER RETIRED: None

HALL OF FAMERS TO WEAR THE NUMBER: None

FIRST PERFORMANCE WITH THE NUMBER

7/30/1939- In his first game in a Pirates uniform, Max Butcher entered the game in relief of Bill Swift in the seventh inning, allowing three hits and a run in 1 2/3 innings during a 7–5 loss to the Dodgers.

FIRST HOME RUN WITH THE NUMBER

8/2/1946- Returning from the war in 1946, Maurice Van Robays donned the number 19 and hit his first and only home run of the season, the final one of his career. He plated Ralph Kiner and Jim Russell in front of him in the second inning, giving the Bucs a 3–0 advantage en route to a 6–0 win against the New York Giants. It was his lone hit in three at bats that day.

FIRST VICTORY BY A PITCHER WITH THE NUMBER

8/20/1939- Coming over from the Phillies with a 2–13 record, Max Butcher pitched well for the Bucs, although he lost his first two decisions. Finally, against the Cubs he tossed six shutout innings in the second game of a double header, which was shortened to six innings, for a 5–0 victory.

BEST PIRATES TO WEAR THE NUMBER: (W-L-ERA)

Bob Friend (191–218-3.55)

Proof positive that a won-loss record is more indicative of the team a player pitches for than of his own talent, Bob Friend is the only pitcher in major league history with 200 losses who did not win 200 games. Despite the fact that he pitched on some poor Pirates teams, he had some wonderful seasons in the process: In 1955 he became the first hurler with a last-place team to capture the ERA title; in 1958 he led the NL in wins with 22, finishing third in the Cy Young race; and in the world championship season of 1960 Friend was 18–12, although a miserable 0–2 in the World Series with a 13.50 ERA was probably not his finest moment. A losing record maybe, but he was one of the greatest pitchers ever to take the mound in a Pirates uniform.

Maurice Van Robays (photo courtesy of the Pittsburgh Pirates)

Jim Rooker (82–65-3.29)

Announcer, political candidate, author, bar owner, Jim Rooker made his initial mark in Pittsburgh as a pitcher for the Pirates. While he had a fine career following his trade from the Kansas City Royals in 1973, perhaps his greatest moment in a Pirates uniform came towards the end

Jim Rooker (photo courtesy of the Pittsburgh Pirates)

of his career in 1979 when Chuck Tanner surprisingly called on him to start game five of the World Series with the Bucs facing elimination. He allowed only one run and three hits in five innings, spurring the Pirates to a win that was the catalyst to their memorable comeback and world championship.

Rod Scurry (17–28-3.15)

Despite his less than stellar record, Rod Scurry was a tremendous reliever for the club in the early 1980s, a period that included his memorable 1982 campaign when he had 14 saves, a 1.74 ERA, and in which he allowed only 79 hits in 103–2/3 innings. Unfortunately, drugs ruined his career and life; he died tragically of an apparent overdose in 1992.

WORST PIRATES TO WEAR THE NUMBER: (HR-RBI-AVE) (W-L-ERA)

Jack Cassini (0–0-.000)

Jack Cassini had a better career than did Moonlight Graham, barely. While he did at least get into a major league game (eight to be exact, he never had a major league at bat, being inserted as a pinch-runner each time during the 1949 campaign when he scored three runs.

Ryan Church (3–18-.182)

Much was expected from Ryan Church when he came to the Bucs in 2010, and not much was delivered as he hit only .182 before the team gave up and sent him to Arizona in July.

OTHER NOTABLE PIRATES TO WEAR THE NUMBER

Max Butcher

The West Virginia native was 28–47 when he came to the Bucs in 1939 in exchange for Pirates great Gus Suhr; it was yet another instance where a pitcher's record is a very misleading stat. With some good Pirates teams during the World War II years, he reversed the trend, going 67–60 over his seven seasons in Pittsburgh.

Jimmy Bloodworth

A defensive specialist at second with limited offensive skills, Jimmy Bloodworth had an eleven-year major league career separated by two years in the military during World War II, and found himself for one season with the Pirates, hitting .250 in 1947.

Gene Mauch

Becoming one of the great managers in the history of the game, winning 1,902 games in twenty-six seasons without ever having the honor of managing in a World Series, Gene Mauch spent a brief amount of time with the Bucs in 1947, hitting .300 in 30 at bats.

Hugh Mulcahy

Nicknamed "LP" due to the fact he had the letter LP next to his name in the box score for some very bad Phillies teams in the 1940s (that's right, LP means losing pitcher), Hugh Mulcahy was probably the greatest example of a won-loss record being insignificant compared to other pitching stats. He was 45–89 during his career, twice losing more than 20 games, yet he was named to an All-Star team and received votes for MVP twice. Finishing his career with the Pirates in 1947 with an 0–0 record and 4.05 ERA, Mulcahy's real mark in major league history was his service during World War II. Losing four years of his career while in the military, Mulcahy was stationed in the Philippines entertaining the troops as part of a baseball team when he lost thirty-five pounds after a severe case of dysentery. He was awarded a Bronze Star and, remarkably, was able to recover and resume his career.

Bill Werle

Bill Werle pitched for some bad Pirates teams in the 1950s but looked as if he could be something special when he went 12–13 in his rookie season in 1949. But he eventually succumbed to the level of his teammates and was never as effective with the Bucs again.

Pete Mikkelsen

A non-descript reliever who spent two of his nine major league seasons in Pittsburgh during the 1966 and 1967 campaigns with a 10–10 record, Pete Mikkelsen is better known for a dispute he had with the Topps Card company in 1968, which caused him not to have a card produced during his final five major league seasons. At least he was famous for something.

Jim Shellenback

Spending the first three years of his major league career with the Pirates, when the reliever was 1–1 with a 3.35 ERA between 1966 and 1969, Jim Shellenback went on to a long career as a pitching coach in the Minnesota Twins farm system, thirty-seven seasons to be exact, the last twenty-one with their Elizabethton affiliate.

Wally Backman

A star second baseman with the New York Mets during their championship seasons in the 1980s, a stint that included his hitting .320 in 1986, Wally Backman signed with the Pirates, who were looking for a veteran to complement their strong young club. He was exactly what they needed as they began their run of three straight eastern division championships. Playing mostly as a backup at third, Backman hit .292 in his one year in the Steel City.

Dan Plesac

A fine reliever over his eighteen-year major league career, Dan Plesac spent two of them with the Pirates in 1995 and 1996, winning 10 games with 14 saves and a 3.86 ERA. After his career he became a fine analyst on the MLB network.

Luis Sojo

Mostly a utility infielder during his thirteen-year major league career, Luis Sojo hit .286 in his time with the Pirates in 2000. A five-time batting champ in the Venezuelan Winter League, Sojo turned out to be a good luck charm in the majors as he was part of five World Series championship teams.

Reggie Sanders

A slugging outfielder who slammed 305 home runs in his seventeen-year major league career, Reggie Sanders was thirty-five years of age when he had a wonderful season with the Bucs in 2003, hitting 31 home runs and 85 RBIs.

Jose Bautista

"Joey Bats." It still hurts to see him so successful with the Toronto Blue Jays, knowing he could have done the same in the Steel City. The Pirates gave up on him way too quickly, and the proof is the 238 home runs he has hit since one of the worst trades in franchise history that included 54 of the round-trippers for Toronto in 2010.

Gary Redus and Neil Walker

Gary Redus wore the number 19 in his first two seasons with the Bucs, while Neil Walker donned it in his brief first major league experience in 2009.

#20: PIE A LA MODE

ALL TIME NO. 20 ROSTER	YEAR
Richie Hebner	(1968–1971)
Al Luplow	(1967)
Jesse Gonder	(1966–1967)
Frank Carpin	(1965)
John Gelnar	(1964, 1967)
Walt Moryn	(1961)
Gino Cimoli	(1960–1961)
Hardy Peterson	(1959)
Hank Foiles	(1957–1959)
Red Munger	(1956)
Red Swanson	(1955)
Sam Jethroe	(1954)
Jim Mangan	(1952, 1954)
Ron Kline	(1952)
Paul Pettit	(1951, 1953)
Vern Law	(1950–1951)
Tiny Bonham	(1949)
Ken Heintzelman	(1946–1947)
Boom-Boom Beck	(1945)
Ray Starr	(1944–1945)
Bob Klinger	(1940–1943)
Lee Handley	(1938–1939)
Pie Traynor	(1932–1936)

NUMBER RETIRED: PIE TRAYNOR (1972)

HALL OF FAMERS TO WEAR THE NUMBER: PIE TRAYNOR (1948)

FIRST PERFORMANCE WITH THE NUMBER

6/30/1932- In what could have been the greatest first performance while wearing a number, Pie Traynor had four singles in five at bats while scoring twice and knocking in one in the Pirates' 9–6 victory over the Cardinals, which just happened to be the first game the team played while wearing numbers. On the negative side, the Hall of Famer had both of the Bucs' errors in the game.

FIRST HOME RUN WITH THE NUMBER

8/31/1932- Pie Traynor didn't hit many home runs in the 1932 campaign, knocking out only two, but on the last day in August he hit an important one, a two-run shot in the fourth, scoring Adam Comorosky in front of him to give the Bucs a 2–0 lead. They would hold on to defeat Brooklyn, 2–1.

FIRST VICTORY BY A PITCHER WITH THE NUMBER

4/16/1940- Wearing the number 20 for the first time in his third major league season, Bob Klinger was the starting pitcher on opening day and tossed 5 2/3 innings, allowing four runs, all in the sixth inning, on five hits and four walks. As poorly as he pitched that day, the Bucs were ahead 6–4 when they pulled him. Johnny Lanning and Dick Lanahan shut out St. Louis the rest of the way and they held on to beat the Cards.

BEST PIRATES TO WEAR THE NUMBER: (HR-RBI-AVE)

Pie Traynor (58–1,273-.320)

There's not too much to the story. As a kid he liked pie; hence, the name Harold Traynor was a thing of the past. To those who saw him play, Pie Traynor was one of, if not the greatest, third baseman in the history of the game (in the pre Schmidt-Brett era, of course). He hit .320 in the course of his seventeen-year major league career, all with the Bucs, and

Pie Traynor (photo courtesy of the Pittsburgh Pirates)

eventually would go on to manage the team for six seasons, ending his tenure with a .530 winning percentage. The first Pirate to wear 20 was the best: He received the two greatest honors a player can get— election to the Hall of Fame, and having his number retired by the team he played for. Certainly, if there was a pie lover's hall of fame he would have been included there, too..

WORST PIRATES TO WEAR THE NUMBER: (HR-RBI-AVE) (W-L-ERA)

Jim Mangan (0–4-.179)

A star catcher in college at Santa Clara, Jim Mangan was far from a star in the majors with the Bucs, playing sparingly in two seasons during the 1952 and '54 campaigns when he hit .179 in 39 at bats.

Paul Pettit (1–2-7.34)

A bonus baby in the early 1950s, Paul Pettit never lived up to his lofty scouting report with a career 1.826 WHIP in parts of two seasons with the Bucs. While he never made it back to the majors, Pettit became quite a hitter in the minors when he switched to the outfield and first base. He hit 86 homers and hit .272, including 20 homers for both Salinas and Hollywood in 1954 and 1957.

Al Luplow (1–8–.184)

Al Luplow was a fine football player as well as baseball player at Michigan State. The outfielder had a decent season in 1962 with the Indians, slamming 14 home runs with a .277 average, but when it came to his days in the Steel City in 1967 he didn't exactly challenge Roberto Clemente for his spot in right; his .184 average proved to be the death blow to his major league career.

OTHER NOTABLE PIRATES TO WEAR THE NUMBER

Red Munger

A fine pitcher with the St. Louis Cardinals, where he was 74–49 as a member of two world championship teams (he missed out on a third while serving in the Army in 1945), Red Munger would spend the final two seasons of his career in 1952 and 1956 pitching ineffectively for the Pirates.

Bob Klinger

A long-time minor leaguer who spent eight seasons in the majors, six of them with the Pirates, Bob Klinger had a decent run, winning 62 games, including a fine 12–5 rookie campaign in 1938. He left the Bucs in 1944 when he went into the Navy during the war, and when he returned in 1946 he signed with the Red Sox.

Ray Starr

Starr was All-Star with the Reds in 1942, when he finished twenty-third in the MVP race. The Pirates were hoping for the same type of performance when they acquired him in 1944. Instead, they got two seasons of ineffective pitching that included a poor 1.723 WHIP with the Bucs.

Boom Boom Beck

He was forty years old in the last season of baseball during the war years in 1945 when the Pirates picked him up. Walter "Boom Boom" Beck did not disappoint, having a fine season, primarily out of the bullpen, with a 6–1 mark and 2.14 ERA. He went on to manage in the Pirates' system for three seasons.

Vern Law and Tiny Bonham

Vern Law wore the number 20 for his first two seasons in 1950 and '51, while Tiny Bonham wore it in his last season in a Pirate uniform, 1949. That was the year Bonham was operated on for appendicitis in September, and passed away days later with complications from the surgery.

Sam Jethroe

A star with the Cleveland Buckeyes of the Negro American League, Sam Jethroe didn't get to the major leagues until he was thirty-three, leading the senior circuit in steals twice with the Braves, in 1950 and '51. He was at the end of his career when he came to the Pirates in 1954, going hitless in one at bat.

Bill Bell

Bill Bell wasn't much of a major leaguer, with an 0–1 mark and 4.32 ERA in parts of two major league seasons, but the Duke alum was a minor league legend as he tossed back-to-back no-hitters for the Bucs' Bristol affiliate in 1952, striking out 37 batters in the process, including 20 in the second gem.

Hank Foiles

An All-Star selection for the Bucs in 1957 when he hit .270, catcher Hank Foiles never came close to that success again. His next biggest contribution to the team was the fact that he was traded to the Kansas City A's for World Series hero Hal Smith.

Gino Cimoli

An important reserve outfielder on the 1960 world champion Pirates, who was outstanding defensively, Gino Cimoli got his spot in the sun during the World Series after Bob Skinner was injured in the first game. He took over in left field until Skinner returned in the final contest, and hit .250 in 20 at bats.

Richie Hebner

His bio is included under the number 3, but Richie Hebner was the last Pirate to wear number 20. Pie Traynor had taken a liking to Hebner, and while Richie would have liked to have seen Traynor's number retired while Pie was alive, unfortunately that never happened. The Bucs officially honored the Hall of Famer during a ceremony before the home opener in 1972, which was a little more than a month after Traynor had passed away.

#21: THE TRAGIC NUMBER

ALL TIME NO. 21 ROSTER	YEAR
Roberto Clemente	(1956–1972)
Paul Smith	(1953, 1955)
Ron Necciai	(1952)
Murry Dickson	(1951)
Gus Bell	(1950)
Tom Saffell	(1950–1951)
Elmer Riddle	(1949)
Fritz Ostermueller	(1944–1948)
Wally Hebert	(1943)
Joe Bowman	(1940–1941)
Gus Suhr	(1936)
Arky Vaughan	(1932–1935, 1936–1939)

NUMBER RETIRED: ROBERTO CLEMENTE (1973)

HALL OF FAMERS TO WEAR THE NUMBER: ROBERTO CLEMENTE (1973), ARKY VAUGHAN (1985)

FIRST PERFORMANCE WITH THE NUMBER

6/30/1932- Rookie Arky Vaughan had a fine day in the first game in which the Pirates wore numbers on their uniforms, going three-for-five with a double, two runs scored, and a run batted in during the Bucs' 9–6 win over the Cardinals.

FIRST HOME RUN WITH THE NUMBER

7/26/1932- Arky Vaughan cracked his first major league home run on this day, a solo shot, as the Pirates beat the Giants 7–5 in ten innings during the second game of a double header. He would not wait too long for his second, hitting it the next day.

FIRST VICTORY BY A PITCHER WITH THE NUMBER

4/22/1940- In the second game of the 1940 campaign, the Pirates sent Joe Bowman to the mound to face Claude Passeau and the Chicago Cubs. Bowman, who was 33–38 in his five-year Pirates career, was not effective, allowing seven

Roberto Clemente (photo courtesy of the Pittsburgh Pirates)

Arky Vaughan (photo courtesy of the Pittsburgh Pirates)

hits and five runs, three earned, in six innings that day. His defense didn't help, committing four errors. Luckily, the Pirates' offense was sharp in a 9–5 victory.

BEST PIRATES TO WEAR THE NUMBER: (HR-RBI-AVE)

Roberto Clemente (240–1,305-.317)

A four-time National League batting champion; a hero not only in his native Puerto Rico but in all Latin American nations; a pioneer who battled not only racial discrimination but discrimination against his nationality as well; a man who has forty schools and more than 200 parks named in his honor, and a player who is considered the biggest icon in the history of the city he played in for seventeen seasons: all of these describe the man who was Roberto Clemente.

He helped lead the franchise to two World Series championships, the second in 1971 in front of a baseball nation that didn't quite appreciate his greatness. In his last at bat of the 1972 campaign he had his 3,000[th] hit; it would be his last. On New Year's Eve the Pirate great would be killed in a plane crash while trying to deliver relief supplies to earthquake ravaged Nicaragua. He became only the second man to have the five-year waiting time period waived for his immediate induction into the Hall of Fame. Clemente also had his number 21 retired at the Pirates' home opener in 1973. Forty-four years later, Pirates fans still mourn the death of one of the greatest human beings ever to grace the Steel City, and without a doubt he remains the most beloved person in the city's history.

Arky Vaughan (84–764-.324)

Next to Honus Wagner, the greatest Pirates shortstop in the history of the franchise was Floyd "Arky" Vaughan. As consistent as one could ask a player to be, Vaughan never hit below .300 in his ten years in a Pirates uniform that included a modern team record .385 single season average, in 1935. He also has the honor of being one of only four players in major league history to have hit two home runs in a single All-Star Game, achieving the feat in 1941. Like Clemente after him, Vaughan died a premature death, trying to save a friend in a lake after the boat capsized during a fishing trip, with both men tragically drowning.

For years, time forgot Arky Vaughan's excellence, until the Veterans Committee made things right in 1985 and he was elected to his rightful spot in the Baseball Hall of Fame.

WORST PIRATES TO WEAR THE NUMBER: (W-L-ERA)
Ron Necciai (1–6-7.48)

Like Clemente and Vaughan, Ron Necciai is a baseball legend; the problem was that his legend was in the minors and not with the Bucs. A local son from nearby Gallatin, he had a contest on May 13, 1952 when he performed a feat never equalled in the annals of professional baseball; it occurred during a game with the Pirates affiliate in Bristol. Necciai struck out 27 batters that day in the process of tossing a no-hitter. He actually would have fallen one short of the amazing feat if his catcher hadn't let the final out get past him with the batter reaching first on a third-strike passed ball. He then struck out the final batter for his record 27th. In his next start, the hurler punched out 24 more and hoped to resume his glory at the major league level. With a 1–6 mark and 7.48 ERA in his only major league experience, it's obvious he did not.

OTHER NOTABLE PIRATES TO WEAR THE NUMBER

Gus Suhr and Gus Bell

The great Pirates first baseman wore the number 21 for a brief period of time in 1936. The slugger Gus Bell wore it in his rookie campaign in 1950.

Wally Hebert

Awful in his first three seasons with the St. Louis Browns between 1931 and 1933, when he was 11–25 due partially to a sore arm, Wally Hebert returned to the minors and thought he would never get another chance to pitch in the majors; that is, until the Pirates took a chance on him ten years later, in 1943. At the age of thirty-five, Hebert pitched well, going 10–11 with a 2.98 ERA. It should have been the beginning of a new career, but he retired following the season citing the difficulty of traveling with his family while playing the game.

Fritz Ostermueller

A fine pitcher for the Bucs in the mid- to late 1940's, Fritz Ostermueller was 49–42 with a 3.48 ERA. While forgotten for the most part over the years since, Ostermueller was brought to the national forefront in 2013 during the movie *42*, in which there was a scene of him beaning Jackie Robinson, injuring the Hall of Famer and casting the Pirates pitcher as a racist. The problem was that, according to his family and some historians, Ostermueller was not a racist. The other fallacy was that Robinson was hit in the arm by the pitch, and not the head as suggested by the film. It's certainly not the way his family wanted him to be remembered.

Paul Smith

An MVP in the Southern League with the Pirates affiliate in New Orleans in 1952, Paul Smith hit .283 in his rookie season with the Bucs a year later. Conflicting reports of either a concussion keeping him out of the lineup in 1954, or the fact that the Pirates thought he would be drafted resulted in Smith being stuck in the minors until 1957; he played sparingly with the team for two seasons before ending his major league career with the Cubs in 1958. The important thing about Paul Smith is that he is the answer to the trivia question, "Who was the last Pirate before Clemente to wear the number 21?"

#22: CUTCH

ALL TIME NO. 22 ROSTER	YEAR
Andrew McCutchen	(2009–2015)
Xavier Nady	(2006–2008)
Ryan Vogelsong	(2003–2006)
Gary Matthews Jr.	(2001)
Jason Schmidt	(1998–2001)
Freddy Garcia	(1995, 1997)
Gary Varsho	(1994)
John Wehner	(1992–1994)
Steve Buechele	(1991–1992)
Jeff Richardson	(1991)
Dann Bilardello	(1990)
Logan Easley	(1989)
Al Pedrique	(1987–1988)
John Cangelosi	(1987)
Lee Tunnell	(1983–1985)
Bob Owchinko	(1983)
Odell Jones	(1981)
Bert Blyleven	(1978–1980)
Jerry Hairston	(1977)
Terry Forester	(1977)
Richie Zisk	(1971–1976)
Mudcat Grant	(1970–1971)
Chuck Hartenstein	(1970)
George Brunet	(1970)
Gene Alley	(1968–1969)
Woodie Fryman	(1966–1967)
Joe Gibbon	(1960–1965)
Ron Kline	(1955–1959)
Gene Hermanski	(1953)
Murry Dickson	(1949–1950, 1952–1953)
Nick Strincevich	(1944–1948)
Hank Camelli	(1943)
Dutch Dietz	(1941–1943)
Danny MacFayden	(1940)
Red Juelich	(1939)
Tommy Thevenow	(1938)
Lee Handley	(1937)
Cookie Lavagetto	(1934–1936)
Tony Piet	(1932–1933)

NUMBER RETIRED: None

HALL OF FAMERS TO WEAR THE NUMBER: BERT BLYLEVEN (2011)

FIRST PERFORMANCE WITH THE NUMBER

6/30/1932- In the 9–6 victory over the Cardinals when the Pirates first wore numbers on their uniforms, Tony Piet was the starting second baseman and had a single in four at bats. He scored two runs and was hit by a pitch in the contest.

FIRST HOME RUN WITH THE NUMBER

7/26/1932- Tony Piet clubbed his second home run of the season in a 9–8 ten-inning victory over the Braves. He had two hits in the game, scoring three times with an RBI.

FIRST VICTORY BY A PITCHER WITH THE NUMBER:

6/23/1940- Newcomer Danny Mac-Fayden captured his first victory in a Pirates uniform, defeating Brooklyn 8–5. He pitched 8 1/3 innings allowing five runs, four earned on nine hits, and three walks. Mace Brown came on in the ninth to save the game for MacFayden.

Andrew McCutchen (photo courtesy of Christina Bortak)

BEST PIRATES TO WEAR THE NUMBER: (HR-RBI-AVE) (W-L-ERA)

Andrew McCutchen (151–558-.298)

Many Pirates fans were distraught with the consistent losing when management decided once again to rebuild in 2008, despite the fact the team looked as though it had pieced together a successful offensive team. Fear not, Pirate fans, your savior was on his way. Andrew McCutchen was a much-heralded first-round pick in 2005, and has more than lived up to his lofty hype. Earning three consecutive top three finishes in the MVP race, including the award itself in 2013, Cutch has done wonderful things in the 'Burgh, most notably helping end the franchise's embarrassing twenty-year stretch of losing seasons and leading them to the post-season for three consecutive years. The great part is that the McCutchen story is still unfolding for the Bucs and, hopefully, it will take the Pirate nation to the next step: its first World Series venture in five decades.

Richie Zisk (69–324-.299)

One of a long line of great hitting outfielders for the Pittsburgh Pirates in the 1970s, Richie Zisk eclipsed 100 RBIs once and hit 20 or more home runs on two occasions. Rather than try to re-sign him with one year left on his contract, the Pirates sent Zisk to the White Sox for Goose Gossage and Terry Forster. Zisk had his finest season for Chicago with 30 home runs and an All-Star Game appearance.

Murry Dickson (66–85-3.83)

Playing for the Bucs in only five of his eighteen major league seasons, Murry Dickson was a great pitcher with some bad teams. A 20-game winner with a poor Pirates club in 1951, Dickson pitched well in his

Bucco career, even though his won-loss record may say otherwise. Being able to keep his ERA respectable in such a bad era of baseball was impressive enough, but his war record was even more so. Serving in the Army during World War II, Dickson landed on Omaha Beach on D-Day and not only survived, but then fought his way through Europe as part of a squad that helped liberate the continent. He also fought in the Battle of the Bulge. For his efforts he was awarded four battle stars.

WORST PIRATES TO WEAR THE NUMBER: (HR-RBI-AVE) (W-L-ERA)

Dann Bilardello (2–11-.171)

A former first-round pick of the Dodgers in 1978, Dann Bilardello spent the first four seasons of his career as a backup catcher with the Reds and Expos. After a less-than-stellar season as a reserve with the Pirates in 1989, he was downright pathetic in 1990, going two for 37. He spent two more years with the Padres before ending his major league career, and currently is part of the St. Louis Cardinal system as a minor league manager.

Ryan Vogelsong (10–19-6.00)

Acquired by the Pirates from the Giants in the Jason Schmidt trade, Ryan Vogelsong was a top prospect who never lived up to his potential with the Pirates. He was left unsigned and ended up in Japan for three seasons but didn't seem to improve. Vogelsong eventually found himself back with San Francisco and, after five seasons out of the majors, at long last finally reached his potential. He was 13–7 in 2011 and was named to the All-Star Game, finishing ninth in the Cy Young vote. He remained with the Giants since, as a pivotal member of two world championship teams, until he signed a one year deal with the Bucs for the 2016 campaign, giving him an opportunity to exercise him from this list with a good performance.

Jerry Hairston (2–6-.192)

Jerry Hairston enjoyed fourteen major league seasons with the White Sox in two tenures there. Sandwiched in between was half of a bad season in Pittsburgh during the 1977 campaign, when he hit only .192. So bad was he that Hairston was relegated to the Mexican Leagues before returning to Chicago in 1981.

OTHER NOTABLE PIRATES TO WEAR THE NUMBER

Tony Piet

A feisty, speedy second baseman who hit .294 over his three seasons with the Bucs, second baseman Tony Piet went on to play eight seasons in the major leagues with the Pirates, Reds, White Sox, and Tigers. His best season would be his last in Pittsburgh during the 1933 campaign, when he had a .323 average.

Cookie Lavagetto

A good player for the Pirates in his first three major league seasons, Cookie Lavagetto made a national name for himself with the Dodgers in the 1947 World Series when he broke up Bill Bevens's no-hitter attempt with two outs in the ninth, lacing a double that knocked in two runs and won the contest for Brooklyn 3–2. It would be the last major league hit for the man who missed four seasons while serving in the navy during World War II and was hitless in the remainder of the Series, never returning to the majors afterward.

Danny MacFayden

Looking more like an accountant than a baseball player, Danny Mac-Fayden had a fine seventeen-year major league career, winning more than ten games in each of six seasons while garnering 132 major league victories. He spent one season in a Pirates uniform towards the end of his career, in 1940, when his record was 5–4 with two saves and a fine 3.55 ERA.

Dutch Dietz

Dutch Dietz was a fine reliever for the team during the war years in the 1940s; he went 13–15 for the Bucs in his career with an ERA of 3.55.

His best season was 1941 with a 7–2 mark and a career-low 2.33 ERA. Dietz entered the army in 1944, which signaled the end of his major league career.

Nick Strincevich

Signing first with the Bronx Bombers during the Babe Ruth era, Nick Strincevich pitched seven seasons with the Pirates in the 1940s, the strongest of which were at the end of World War II between 1944 and '46, when he won 40 of his 42 victories in a Pittsburgh uniform. His Pirates career in 1941 had not gotten off to a good start after he fractured his skull, the result of being hit by a line drive during spring training batting practice.

Ron Kline

Beginning his career with his hometown Pittsburgh Pirates (Kline was from Callery, PA, in nearby Butler County) Ron Kline was a good starter in the 1950s on some bad teams, twice leading the league in losses. When he returned in 1968 he was a successful full-time reliever, going 12–5 for the Bucs with a miniscule 1.68 ERA.

Joe Gibbon

Beginning his career with the 1960 world champion Pirates, Joe Gibbon was effective going back and forth between the starting rotation and the bullpen, accumulating 39 wins in six seasons. He was sent to the Giants in 1966, then returned three years later, in 1969, to record a 5–1 mark and a spectacular ERA of 1.93. He pitched one more season for the eastern division champs in 1970, then left the Bucs for Cincinnati, never to return for a third stint with the Bucs.

Woody Fryman

Woody Fryman played in Pittsburgh during the first two of his eighteen major league seasons. He had a fabulous rookie campaign in 1966, going 12–9 before falling to 3–8 a year later. He was sent to the Phillies after that, along with Don Money and two other players in exchange for Hall of Famer Jim Bunning.

Gene Alley

Gene Alley wore the number 22 toward the end of his time in Pittsburgh, in 1968 and '69.

George Brunet

Brunet is the all-time minor league strikeout record holder, with 3,155. He spent one of his fifteen major league seasons with the Bucs in 1970, going 1–1 with a 2.70 ERA.

Mudcat Grant

One of the early great African American pitchers in the major leagues, Mudcat Grant became the first to win 20 games in the American League. A star in the 1967 World Series, when he won two games, Grant captured 145 wins over the course of his fourteen-year major league career. He was thirty-four when he came to the Bucs in 1970, pitching effectively down the stretch from the bullpen. Grant was a member of the 1971 world champions, although he didn't end the season here, having been purchased by the A's before the year was over.

Bert Blyleven

He could be difficult over his twenty-two-year major league career, when he won 287 games and in Pittsburgh, often criticized manager Chuck Tanner for pulling him out of the game too early. A curveball specialist, Blyleven overcame his sulky ways to go 12–5 in 1979. He was on the mound when the Bucs defeated the Reds in game three of the NLCS to capture their seventh National League pennant. After many years of being passed over, he was finally elected to the Hall of Fame in 2011.

Al Pedrique

A member of the Topps All-Rookie team with the 1987 Bucs, when he hit .301, Al Pedrique quickly faltered, hitting only .180 a year later before ending up with the Tigers. He was out of the majors after a brief try with Detroit in 1989. Pedrique has since become a successful minor league manager, and is currently with Trenton in the Yankees system.

Steve Buechele

Steve Buechele was a slugging third baseman with the Texas Rangers whom the Pirates acquired at the trading deadline in 1991 as they were vying for their second consecutive eastern division championship. While he hit .304 in the NLCS that season, he never quite reached the level the Bucs had hoped for, and was shipped off to the Cubs in 1992 in a trade for for Danny Jackson.

Xavier Nady

Xavier Nady was another top prospect who had difficulties living up to his potential. After coming over from the Mets, he was able to figure things out and hit 20 home runs in 2007. Nady was off to a magnificent start a year later, with 13 long balls and a .330 average by mid- season, when the Pirates decided they would rebuild again and sent him to the Yankees. It was just as well; injuries all but ended his success in the majors.

#23: A MANAGER'S NIGHTMARE

ALL TIME NO. 23 ROSTER	YEAR
Pedro Florimon	(2015)
Steve Lombardozzi	(2015)
Travis Snider	(2012–2015)
Matt Diaz	(2011)
John Bowker	(2010)
Robinzon Diaz	(2009)
Lloyd McClendon	(1990–1994)
R.J. Reynolds	(1986–1990)
Steve Kemp	(1986)
Randy Niemann	(1983)
Tom Griffin	(1982)
Grant Jackson	(1978–1982)
Ed Kirkpatrick	(1974–1977)
Luke Walker	(1968–1973)
George Spriggs	(1965–1967)
Don Bosch	(1966)
Steve Blass	(1964–1965)
Julio Gotay	(1963–1964)
Johnny Logan	(1963)
Cal Neeman	(1962)
Joe Christopher	(1959–1961)
Gene Baker	(1957–1958)
Laurin Pepper	(1955–1957)
George O'Donnell	(1954)
Walker Cooper	(1954)
Jim Waugh	(1952–1953)
Lenny Yochim	(1951)
Cliff Chambers	(1949–1951)
Mel Queen	(1947–1948)
Lou Tost	(1947)
Frank Colman	(1942–1946)
Cookie Cuccurullo	(1943)
Frank Kalin	(1940)
Pep Rambert	(1939–1940)
Bill Brubaker	(1934)
Val Picinich	(1933)
MANAGERS	
Lloyd McClendon	(1997–2005)
Jim Tracy	(2006–2007)
COACHES	
Grant Jackson	(1984–1985)
Gene Lamont	(1996)
Jeff Andrews	(2008)

NUMBER RETIRED: None

HALL OF FAMERS TO WEAR THE NUMBER: None

FIRST PERFORMANCE WITH THE NUMBER

6/25/1933- After being released by Brooklyn earlier in the season, catcher Val Picinich was picked up by the Bucs and was hitless in three at bats with a walk in his first game in a Pirates uniform during a 5–2 victory over his old team.

FIRST HOME RUN WITH THE NUMBER

6/30/1933- Val Picinich hit his lone home run in his final season in the majors, against the Phillies. It was a solo shot, his only hit of the day in a 5–4 loss.

FIRST VICTORY BY A PITCHER WITH THE NUMBER

6/17/1947- In his first start in a Pirates uniform after coming over from the Yankees, Mel Queen had a complete-game victory allowing only one run, but giving up eight hits and five walks in the process, as Pittsburgh beat Brooklyn 7–1.

BEST PIRATES TO WEAR THE NUMBER: (HR-RBI-AVE) (W-L-ERA)

Grant Jackson (29–19-3.23)

A starter early in his eighteen-year career, Grant "Buc" Jackson became a hell of a reliever with the Orioles. When he came from the Yankees to Pittsburgh in 1977 he continued his dominance in the pen, winning 29 games in six seasons with 36 saves. He was at his best when the team needed it most—in 1979, when he was 8–5 with a career-high 14 saves and 2.96 ERA, helping Pittsburgh to the world championship.

R.J. Reynolds (31–234-.269)

He was part of the Pirates' rebuilding effort in the 1980s, after they acquired him from the Dodgers in 1985. While he was a very good player for them over the course of six seasons, his major league career ended in 1990 and he wouldn't get to enjoy the full success that rebuilding the team had brought to the franchise by that point.

Luke Walker (40–42-3.47)

A key member of the Pirates rotation in 1970, when he was 15–6 and took a no-hitter into the ninth against the Dodgers a year later, Luke Walker won 40 games for the Bucs in his eight seasons in a Pirates uniform.

WORST PIRATES TO WEAR THE NUMBER: (W-L-ERA) (HR-RBI-AVE)
Pep Rambert (0–1-8.25)

A fine hitting outfielder, as well as a pitcher. in his long minor league career, Pep Rambert was put on the mound in his brief major league tenure between 1939 and 1940. Perhaps the outfield would have been a better choice.

Laurin Pepper (2–8-7.06)

An All-American halfback out of Southern Mississippi, Laurin Pepper became a bonus baby for the Pittsburgh Pirates, outbidding his Forbes Field neighbors, the Steelers, for his services. Because he received a

$35,000 bonus with the team he had to stay in the majors for two seasons. As it turned out, the Steelers probably sent a thank-you note for saving them money, for Pepper was not a good major league pitcher. He went on to become a head high school football coach for twenty-nine seasons in Mississippi, where the football field is named after him.

George Spriggs (0–5–.182)

A great minor leaguer who won the American Association's MVP Award in 1970, George Spriggs was anything but an MVP with the Bucs between 1965 and '67, when he hit .182. Becoming a member of the expansion Kansas City Royals in 1969 did nothing for Spriggs's major league efforts; he hit only .195 in two seasons there.

WORST PIRATES MANAGERS TO WEAR THE NUMBER

Lloyd McClendon and Jim Tracy

The number 23 was a popular one for managers during the Pirates' mind-numbing twenty-year streak of losing seasons. These two wore 23 on the Pirates' bench for seven years, more than one-third of those forgettable seasons.

OTHER NOTABLE PIRATES TO WEAR THE NUMBER

Val Picinich

A good defensive catcher, Val Picinich quietly lasted eighteen years behind the plate without playing in 100 games. His main purpose at the beginning of his career was to be Walter Johnson's personal catcher. He ended his long stay in 1933 with the Bucs hitting .250. He unfortunately passed away at the age of forty-six, suffering from pneumonia.

Frank Colman

A Canadian who played with the Bucs during the war years after he was rejected from serving his country because of a leg injury, Frank

Colman was a serviceable utility player for the team, hitting .233 over five seasons.

Cliff Chambers

After two good seasons in a Pirates uniform, winning 25 games in 1949 and '50, Cliff Chambers fell off a bit in '51. He won only three games, but one happened to be the team's first no-hitter in forty-four years, against the Braves. While he walked eight in the contest, it was a day when Chambers had been felled by the flu, yet pitched the second game of a doubleheader after spending the first sleeping in the locker room. Despite the gem, he was traded to the Cardinals the following month.

Cliff Chambers (photo courtesy of the Pittsburgh Pirates)

Jim Waugh

On August 9, 1952, pitcher Jim Waugh won his first major league game, defeating the Cubs 4–3 in a complete-game effort. He was only eighteen at the time, the youngest pitcher to win a game with the franchise. His bright future clouded quickly, however, as he lasted only one more season with the Bucs and was out of the majors before his twentieth birthday, managing a career 6.43 ERA.

Walker Cooper

An eight-time All-Star Game selection and runner-up for the National League MVP in 1943, catcher Walker Cooper enjoyed a fabulous eighteen-year career, and was a pivotal part of the St. Louis Cardinals championship teams during the World War II years. The .285 career hitter came to Pittsburgh late in his career, when Cooper was thirty-nine years old, in 1954. He hit .200 before being put on waivers, and was picked up by the Cubs.

Joe Christopher

A back-up outfielder for the Pirates in his first three major league seasons, Joe Christopher debuted in 1959 on the night Harvey Haddix pitched 12 perfect innings in Milwaukee. He was the first major league player from the Virgin Islands and had the honor of being a member of the 1962 original New York Mets.

Steve Blass

Steve Blass spent his rookie season in 1964 wearing the number 23.

Ed Kirkpatrick

Ed Kirkpatrick was a catcher whose major league career began at the age of seventeen, in 1962, with the Angels; he was mostly a reserve catcher with the Pirates for four seasons in the mid-1970s, when he hit .236. After he retired he was involved in an auto accident that put him in a wheelchair for the rest of his life, until he passed away in 2010.

Steve Kemp

A slugger with the Detroit Tigers, where he knocked in over 100 runs twice, the Pirates were hoping Steve Kemp could come back and give them the same production, even though he had been hit in the face by a line drive off the bat of Omar Moreno while with the Yankees in 1983 during batting practice; his statistics had suffered since. But Kemp could not return to his former level and hit only .246 in his two seasons with the Pirates.

Travis Snider

Travis Snider was a top prospect with Toronto who had never reached his potential, so the Pirates took a gamble on him in 2012. He seemed to come into his own late in the 2014 campaign, hitting .292 with nine homers the second half of the season, playing in place of struggling rookie Gregory Polanco. Inexplicably, Pittsburgh dealt him to Baltimore in 2015 for two minor league pitchers. The trade turned out to be gold, as Stephen Tarpley and Steven Brault have become two of the Pirates' top prospects, while Snider was later released from the Orioles and then picked up again by the Bucs for the stretch run that season.

#24: MVP HAVEN

ALL TIME NO. 24 ROSTER	YEAR
Pedro Alvarez	(2011–2015)
Delwyn Young	(2010)
Tom Gorzelanny	(2007–2009)
Ruben Mateo	(2004)
Brian Giles	(1999–2003)
Zane Smith	(1996)
Dennis Moeller	(1993)
Barry Bonds	(1986–1992)
Denny Gonzalez	(1985)
John Tudor	(1984)
Mike Easler	(1979–1983)
Will McEnaney	(1978)
Tommy Helms	(1977)
Bobby Tolan	(1977)
Tony Armas	(1977)
Omar Moreno	(1975–1976)
Dave Augustine	(1974)
Paul Popovich	(1974–1975)
John Lamb	(1970–1971)
Jim Nelson	(1970)
Manny Jimenez	(1967–1968)
Jerry Lynch	(1963–1966)
Dick Groat	(1952, 1955–1962)
Paul LaPalme	(1951, 1954)
Don Carlsen	(1951)
Hank Borowy	(1950)
Bob Chesnes	(1948–1950)
Ed Bahr	(1947)
Ed Albosta	(1946)
Bill Brandt	(1941–1943)
Ken Jungels	(1942)
Johnny Gee	(1939, 1941)
Arky Vaughan	(1936)
Gus Suhr	(1932–1935, 1937–1939)

NUMBER RETIRED: None

HALL OF FAMERS TO WEAR THE NUMBER: ARKY VAUGHAN (1985)

FIRST PERFORMANCE WITH THE NUMBER

6/30/1932- While the Pirates' offense was great in the 9–6 victory over St. Louis, Gus Suhr did not have one of his best days: a single and a walk in five plate appearances.

FIRST HOME RUN WITH THE NUMBER

7/24/1932- In the second game of a doubleheader against the Cubs, the Pirates defeated Chicago 7–5. The star of the contest was Gus Suhr, who belted his fourth home run of the year, a three-run shot, and scored twice in the victory.

FIRST VICTORY BY A PITCHER WITH THE NUMBER

9/21/1939- In the second start of his major league career, pitcher Johnny Gee struck out 11 in a 6–4 complete-game victory against the Boston Braves. While he won, it wasn't exactly a great performance; he gave up 12 hits and two walks in the win.

BEST PIRATES TO WEAR THE NUMBER: (HR-RBI-AVE)

Barry Bonds (176–556-.275)

Coming from baseball royalty — son of Giants great Bobby Bonds and godson of one of the game's greats, Willie Mays — Barry Bonds donned uniform number 24 in honor of his godfather. He was irascible off the field, but on it he was a thing of beauty, winning three Gold Glove awards and becoming the only Pirate to win two MVP awards, capturing the league's highest honor in 1990 and '92. While he went on to post some of the most incredible numbers in

Barry Bonds (photo courtesy of the Pittsburgh Pirates)

the history of the game, including the records for both home runs in a season with 73 and career homers at 762, he did it all under the dark cloud of the accusations of steroid use. Despite that fact, he is one of the greatest Pirates to wear the uniform, accusations or not.

Dick Groat (30–454-.290)

One of the great two-sports stars of all time, Dick Groat was a legendary basketball player at Duke who not only was the national player of the year, but the first basketball player at that prestigious institution to have his number retired. He went on to play in the NBA right after his senior season and had a wonderful year with the Fort Wayne Pistons, averaging 11.9 points per game. Even

Dick Groat (photo courtesy of the Pittsburgh Pirates)

though his future at basketball seemed bright, the Wilkinsburg native chose to sign with his hometown baseball team, the Pirates. It would turn out to be a wise decision, as he was one of the greatest players in franchise history, who led the National League in hitting in 1960 with a .325 average, earning the circuit's highest honor that year: the MVP Award. As successful as he was in baseball, the man who was inducted into both the college basketball and Baseball Hall of Fame chose to stay close to basketball after he retired. He remains today the long-time color man on the University of Pittsburgh basketball radio broadcasts.

Brian Giles (165–506-.308)

The Pirates were hoping for Brian Giles to live up to his potential after the Indians seemingly gave up on him, trading the power hitter to Pittsburgh for lefty reliever Ricardo Rincon, but what they got was far more than the Bucs could ever have imagined. He topped 30 home runs in four straight seasons, while knocking in more than 100 in three of them. Unfortunately, he was dealt to San Diego in another of a long line of salary dumps in 2003; fortunately, it brought Jason Bay to the 'Burgh.

Gus Suhr (84–818-.279)

He was the National League's version of Lou Gehrig . . . well, at least in a minor way. While Gehrig was setting his memorable iron man streak of 2,130 consecutive games played, Gus Suhr was setting a mark that no other National League player had achieved, playing in 822 consecutive contests on his own. The record ended not due to injury, but so that he could attend his mother's funeral in San Francisco. In between, he was not only an incredibly durable player but a hell of a hitter, three times topping the 100 RBI plateau. Of all the great players in franchise history, Suhr is perhaps the most underrated—but make no mistake, still one of the best.

WORST PIRATES TO WEAR THE NUMBER: (W-L-ERA)

Ed Albosta (0–6-6.13)

After breaking in with the Dodgers in 1941, pitcher Ed Albosta entered the Army during World War II and missed three major league seasons. When he returned in 1946, he pitched for the Pirates, where he was winless in six decisions with a 6.13 ERA. He would not return to the majors after that, ending his career 0–8. Baseball-reference.com projects a player's average per season stats for his career over a 162-game schedule. For Albosta, his average per season won-loss record over the course of a 162-game schedule projects to 0–20 ... 'nuff said.

Dennis Moeller (1–0-9.92)

While he replaced Barry Bonds as number 24 on the Pirates roster, Moeller proved quickly he was no Bonds. He won his only decision in 1993, but his main accomplishment is that he avoided having his ERA reach above ten.

Paul LaPalme (14–33-4.99)

A knuckleball specialist who shut out the Braves in his first major league start in 1951, Paul LaPalme had one of the great minor league seasons in 1946 after he returned from World War II service. He went 20–2 with Bristol. His success would not translate to the Pirates, however: over four seasons combined he couldn't match his number of wins in 1946 with Bristol.

OTHER NOTABLE PIRATES TO WEAR THE NUMBER

Arky Vaughan, Omar Moreno, and Zane Smith

In the middle of his career in the Steel City, Hall of Famer Arky Vaughan wore the number 24 for one season, in 1936. Omar Moreno's first two seasons in the majors had him wearing the number. Zane Smith put it on when he was reacquired by the Bucs in 1996, his final major league season.

Ed Bahr

After being discharged from the Army in 1945 due to a bad back, Ed Bahr pitched in only two major league seasons, in 1946 and '47, with the Pirates. While his career was brief it was effective, as he split time between the starting rotation and the bullpen with an 11–11 mark and 3.37 ERA.

Bob Chesnes

Like Ed Bahr, Bob Chesnes began his major league career after a stint in the Armed Forces. He had a wonderful rookie season in 1948, leading the Bucs in wins with a 14–6 record. It was definitely his high point, as he was 10–16 over the next two campaigns with a 5.81 ERA. They would be his last big league years.

Hank Borowy

During the World War II years, Hank Borowy was one of the best pitchers in the game. He had an outstanding 67–32 record, with a sub-three ERA at 2.66 that included a 21-win season in 1945. After the war, his effectiveness diminished as his record dipped to 41–50 and his ERA shot up by almost two runs a game to 4.43, which included a 1–3 mark with the Pirates in 1950.

Jim Nelson

Pitching in only two major league seasons, in 1970 and '71, both for the Pirates, Jim Nelson had two memorable moments in his career: winning a ring as a member of the Pirates when they won the World Series in 1971, and, more importantly, was the fact that Danny Murtaugh chose him to start the final game ever at Forbes Field on June 28, 1970, making Nelson the last winning pitcher in the facility's sixty-one-year history, when he defeated the Chicago Cubs, 4–1.

John Lamb

More famous as the brother-in-law of legendary Pirates pitcher Steve Blass, John Lamb pitched in parts of three major league seasons for the team between 1970 and '73. His career might have been longer if not for a broken skull he suffered in 1971 during spring training, when he was hit with a line drive by teammate Dave Cash. He would be winless in two decisions in his career in Pittsburgh, with a 4.07 ERA.

Paul Popovich

West Virginia University's Paul Popovich was a good-field no-hit short-stop with the Cubs and Dodgers for nine seasons before ending his career with the Bucs. He played two seasons in Pittsburgh, 1974 and '75 and, true to his reputation, he could field and couldn't hit, racking up only a .211 average.

Bobby Tolan

Playing most of his career in both right and center fields, Bobby Tolan was a speedy outfielder with the Cardinals and Reds; he led the circuit in steals in 1970 with 57. He also showed flashes of power, smacking 37 homers combined in 1969 and '70. Tolan, who tortured the Pirates in the 1970 NLCS with a .417 average and a homer in the three-game sweep, came to the Steel City toward the end of his career in 1977, hitting .203 in 74 at bats.

Mike Easler

Nicknamed the "Hit Man," Mike Easler was a natural hitter who eclipsed the .300 plateau in his Pittsburgh Pirates career with a .302 average over six seasons. His best year was his first as a regular, in 1980, when he batted .338 with 21 homers. After he was traded to the Red Sox for John Tudor in in 1984, he continued his impressive offensive prowess with a career-high 27 homers and 91 RBIs that first season.

John Tudor

Even though they gave up an effective hitter in Mike Easler, the Bucs in trade got a fine pitcher in John Tudor. He was 12–11 with a solid 3.27 ERA in his one year in Pittsburgh. Pirates management should have let well enough alone by keeping him, but they wanted more offense, so they sent Tudor to St. Louis for . . . George Hendrick. Tudor went on to

Pedro Alvarez (photo courtesy of the author)

win 21 games for the Cards in 1995 with a 1.93 ERA and a second-place finish in the Cy Young race, while Hendrick just irritated Pirates fans with his lackadaisical play.

Tom Gorzelanny

A top prospect with the Pirates early in the first decade of the twenty-first century, Tom Gorzelanny made a name for himself in 2007 with a 14–10 mark and 3.88 ERA. Bouts of wildness ended his effective performances with the Bucs, and he was sent to the Cubs in 2009, a trade that brought the Pirates a player by the name of Josh Harrison. Despite his control issues, Gorzelanny currently remains in the majors as a pitcher for the Tigers.

Pedro Alvarez

The second overall pick in the 2008 amateur draft, Pedro Alvarez has often upset the Pirates Nation, first with his poor defensive play at third that became an issue in 2014 when he often couldn't control his throws, and then continuing his poor defense after he moved to first. He also struck out many times when the team needed him most. But, man, when he gets hold of the ball it's a beautiful thing. A streak hitter who has the ability to lift an offense all on his own, Alvarez led the National League in home runs in 2013 with 36 (tied with Arizona's Paul Goldschmidt), and had cracked 30 homers or better twice in six seasons. While the Bucs waived Pedro Alvarez after the 2015 campaign before he had the opportunity to enter his last year of arbitration in 2016, it was certain that, although he did frustrate fans, he had been an important part in the resurgence of this franchise.

#25: THE POWERLESS WONDER

ALL TIME NO. 25 ROSTER	YEAR
Gregory Polanco	(2014–2015)
Kyle Farnsworth	(2013)
Daniel McCutchen	(2012)
Derrek Lee	(2011)
Kevin Hart	(2009)
Adam LaRoche	(2008–2009)
Sean Casey	(2006)
Carlos Maldonado	(2006)
Xavier Nady	(2006)
Luis Figueroa	(2001)
Mendy Lopez	(2001)
Enrique Wilson	(2000–2001)
Ivan Cruz	(1999–2000)
Mark Smith	(1997–1998)
Trey Beamon	(1996)
Steve Pegues	(1994–1995)
Will Pennyfeather	(1992–1994)
Kirk Gibson	(1992)
Bobby Bonilla	(1987–1991)
Jose DeLeon	(1984–1986)
Lee Tunnell	(1982)
Pascual Perez	(1980–1981)
Bruce Kison	(1971–1979)
Johnny Jeter	(1970)
Bo Belinsky	(1969)
Bob Robertson	(1967)
Tommie Sisk	(1963–1968)
Al Jackson	(1961)
Harry Simpson	(1959)
Roman Mejias	(1955, 1957–1958)
Jack McMahan	(1956)
Bob Garber	(1956)
Cal Hogue	(1954)
Bill Macdonald	(1950, 1953)
Bob Friend	(1951–1952)
Hugh Casey	(1949)
Ken Gables	(1947)
Johnny Lanning	(1945–1946)
Joe Vitelli	(1944–1945)
Harry Shuman	(1942–1943)
Nick Strincevich	(1941–1942)
Mace Brown	(1940–1941)
Bill Brubaker	(1936–1939)

NUMBER RETIRED: None

HALL OF FAMERS TO WEAR THE NUMBER: None

FIRST PERFORMANCE WITH THE NUMBER

7/2/1932- Pinch-hitting for reliever Erv Brame in the ninth inning, Tommy Thevenow was unsuccessful in a 5–4 loss to the Cardinals.

FIRST HOME RUN WITH THE NUMBER

4/30/1936- In his first appearance of the 1936 campaign, Bill Brubaker was the star of a 6–5 win against the Phillies, hitting his first home run of the season, a three-run shot, while also singling in four at bats.

FIRST VICTORY BY A PITCHER WITH THE NUMBER

4/23/1940- Sporting the number 25 for the first time as a Pirate, veteran hurler Mace Brown won his first game of the season out of the bullpen, allowing a hit while working the ninth inning for starter Danny MacFayden. Down 2–1, the Bucs plated two in the bottom of the ninth as Hall of Famer Paul Waner knocked in both with a pinch-hit single to defeat the Cubs, 3–2.

Tommy Thevenow	(1932–1935)
COACHES	
Pete Mackanin	(2003–2005)

BEST PIRATES TO WEAR THE NUMBER: (HR-RBI-AVE) (W-L-ERA)

Bobby Bonilla (114–500-.284)

They lost him inexplicably to Chicago in the rule V draft in 1986, then made up for the mistake by dealing their star-crossed hurler Jose DeLeon to the White Sox. Bonilla wasn't much of a fielder, being rotated between third base and right field, but they needed his lethal bat in the lineup, where he became one of the greatest hitters in franchise history. The switch-hitter smashed home runs twice from both sides of the plate in the same game for the Bucs, the first Pirate to do so (he did it six times in his major league career), and reached the upper deck at Three Rivers Stadium. After being selected to four All-Star Games, winning three Silver Slugger Awards, and finishing second in the MVP race twice in his six seasons with the Bucs, he signed a huge contract with the Mets in 1992. After being resigned by the team, New York bought out his $5.9 million contract in 2000, agreeing to pay him $1.2 million a year until 2035, making it one of sports' worst contracts ever.

Bruce Kison (81–63-3.49)

Bruce Kison had a memorable rookie season in 1971; the highlight was in the first night World Series game in history, when he tossed 6 1/3 one-hit innings in relief to help the Pirates even up the series at two games each with a dramatic 4–3 win over the Orioles. He went on to win 81 games in his nine-year Pittsburgh career, and was one of the few Bucs to play on both the 1971 and '79 world championship squads.

Adam LaRoche (58–213-.265)

Adam LaRoche was a streaky hitter who nonetheless gave the Pirates a good left-handed option at first base. As streaky as he was, LaRoche was consistent for the year, hitting 21 and 25 home runs in his two full seasons in a Pirate uniform and 85 and 83 RBIs, while coming up with .270 and .277 averages. He had the opportunity to play with his brother, Andy, in 2008 and part of 2009, when, as part of another Pittsburgh rebuilding program, he was traded to Boston for no one of consequence. (As it turned out they did get someone of consequence receiving Hunter Strickland. Unfortunately Strickland never played for the Bucs but has become a shut down reliever in San Francisco).

WORST PIRATES TO WEAR THE NUMBER: (W-L-ERA) (HR-RBI-AVE)
Jack McMahan (0–0-6.08)

Jack McMahan was only twenty-three when he began his major league career in 1956 with the Pirates, and pitched poorly in the process. He was dealt to the Kansas City A's at mid-season, and his major league career ended at that same young age.

Kirk Gibson (2–5-.196)

A star wide receiver at Michigan State who decided to play baseball, Kirk Gibson first became a legend with the Detroit Tigers, winning the MVP in the 1984 ALCS before hitting a memorable homer in the fourth game in their World Series sweep of the Padres, then with the Dodgers, for whom he won the NL MVP in 1988 and hit one of the game's most memorable long balls to win the first game of the Series that season. All those great memories were just that when he came to the Pirates in 1992, as he couldn't even break the Mendoza Line before he was released in May.

Jose DeLeon (17–38-4.02)

Jose DeLeon began his career in dramatic fashion in 1983, with a 7–3 mark his rookie season, showing dominance at times as it appeared he was going to be a certain star for the Bucs.

Two years later, he was a 19-game loser with one of the poorest records in modern major league history, at 2–19. DeLeon was dealt to the White Sox in 1986 for Bobby Bonilla and had a thirteen-year career, eventually becoming a reliever. While his career wasn't as bad as some Pirates, having a 2–19 record in a season makes one a prime candidate for this list.

OTHER NOTABLE PIRATES TO WEAR THE NUMBER

Tommy Thevenow

It would be incorrect to call Tommy Thevenow a hitless wonder; he did at least have a .247 career average. But to call him perhaps the most quintessential powerless wonder in baseball history, well, you may have something there. Thevenow lasted fifteen years in the majors as an infielder, and hit two home runs in his third campaign. After his last homer he would go 3,347 at bats over the entire remainder of his career without hitting another! He played six of his final eight seasons with the Pirates, between 1931 and '35, and again in his final year in '38 batting .251, but having 1,730 at bats without a long ball.

Bill Brubaker

An infielder for nine years with the Bucs in the 1930s, Bill Brubaker had one big season with Pittsburgh, 1936, when he knocked in 102 runs, but led the NL with 96 strikeouts. His other claim to fame: he was the grandfather of Dennis Rasmussen.

Harry Shuman

Harry Shuman was a little-used reliever for the Pirates and Phillies during the World War II seasons between 1942 and '44 who had the distinction of having no decisions in a career that spanned 30 games.

Joe Vitelli

A minor league pitcher whose career appeared to be over after entering the Army in 1942, pitcher Joe Vitelli got a rare opportunity to live his dream at thirty-six years of age. The McKees Rocks native was hired by the Pirates as a batting practice pitcher in 1944, and eventually had the opportunity to pitch in four games that season. He was effective in seven innings with a 2.57 ERA. The next season he entered one game, as a pinchrunner, and eventually quit the Bucs when they wouldn't use him on the mound, feeling that the team only did that so they wouldn't have to pay him more; a bitter end to a fine story.

Ken Gabels

After spending time in the Army during World War II, pitcher Ken Gabels made his major league debut with the Bucs in 1945. sporting a fine 11–7 record. He would win only two more games over the next two seasons; his major league career ended in 1947.

Hugh Casey

Most famous in major league history for a boxing match he had with the legendary Ernest Hemingway after a night of drinking while Brooklyn trained in Havana in 1942, reliever Hugh Casey was more than just a rough and tumble person. Losing three years in his major league career while serving in the Navy during World War II, Casey twice led the NL in saves with the Dodgers, and was 4–1 during the first part of his final season in 1941 for the Bucs before being released in August. He tragically shot and killed himself two years later while involved in a paternity suit.

Bob Friend and Bob Robertson

Bob Friend wore number 25 for his first two seasons in a Pirates uniform. Bob Robertson was also number 25 as a rookie in 1967.

Bill MacDonald

He announced his presence in the major leagues in a big way, shutting out the Phillies in his first career start in 1950. Winning eight games his rookie season, MacDonald spent the next two years in the Army during the Korean War. He would return to pitch in only four more games in the big leagues, in 1953.

Roman Mejias

A fourth outfielder for the Pirates in the 1950s, hiting .245 over six seasons, Roman Mejias played a key role in the infamous Harvey Haddix almost-perfect game in 1959. Haddix did what no man ever had by tossing twelve perfect innings before losing the contest in the thirteenth. If not for Mejias, he would never have gone twelve innings for his spot in history, nor gotten a place in history at all. Mejias made a shoestring catch to preserve the gem, but he also had a chance to win the game in regulation rounding second after a hit, before hesitating while trying for third base. Had he not hesitated he would have been safe easily. Instead, he was thrown out and the next batter hit the ball deep enough to have scored Mejias with what would have been the game's lone run, which ironically allowed Haddix to have his sad place in history, sending the game into extra innings.

Harry Simpson

It took Harry Simpson a long time to get to the major leagues, spending four years in the Army during World War II, then with the Philadelphia Stars of the Negro League for three more years. He finally made it to the majors in 1951 with the Indians, and was selected to the All-Star Game in 1956 when he hit 21 homers and knocked in 105 for the A's. He spent his last season in 1959 with the Bucs, hitting .267 in 15 at bats.

Bob Garber

Bob Garber's stay in the majors was brief. The twenty-seven-year-old pitched decently in two contests in 1956 with a 2.25 ERA in four innings, but never pitched again.

Al Jackson

Most people will brag about being a 20-game winner, but very few can say they lost 20 . . . twice. After starting his career with the Pirates in 1959, and before returning in 1961 when he won his only decision in 11 contests, Al Jackson would be selected by the Mets in the 1962 expansion draft, and not only lost 20 that season but repeated his 8–20 mark in 1965.

Tommie Sisk

A hybrid starter/reliever in his seven seasons in a Pirates uniform in the mid- to late 1960s, Tommie Sisk twice won more than ten games with Pittsburgh, including a career-high 13 in 1967.

Bo Belinsky

To say that Bo Belinsky lived an interesting life would be an understatement. After being signed by
Pittsburgh in 1956, he ended up beginning his time in the big leagues
with the Los Angeles Angels in 1962
and had a magnificent early career
with a no-hitter against Baltimore
in his fourth start. His baseball career would never reach those lofty
heights again, but his dating career
was of the Hall of Fame variety. He
went out with such Hollywood icons
as Tina Louise, Ann-Margaret, and
Connie Stevens. He pitched for the
Bucs in 1969 and was winless in
three decisions.

Bo Belinsky (photo courtesy of the
Pittsburgh Pirates)

Pascual Perez

After a substandard 2–8 start to his career with the Pirates in 1980 and
'81, Pascual Perez, famed for losing his way to Fulton County Stadium
and arriving late to a game after getting his driver's license, went to
Atlanta where he found success going 29–16 combined in 1983 and
'84. Perez went on to win 67 games in eleven seasons that included a
five-inning rain-shortened no hitter with Montreal. Tragically, he was
killed in 2012 after thieves broke into his Dominican Republic home,
hitting Perez in the head and stabbing him.

Steve Pegues

Steve Pegues didn't have much of a major league career; he hit .266
in parts of two seasons, but if you're wondering who held the Arizona
Fall League's record for hits in a season he's your man, with 68 in
1992.

Mark Smith

With Mark Smith it always looked as if he could hit a home run every time he came up, but in reality he hit only 11 in 321 at bats during his two-year Pirates career. Nevertheless, one of them was a dramatic tenth-inning, three-run pinch-hit shot to preserve the Francisco Cordova/Ricardo Rincon no-hitter in 1997.

Mendy Lopez

While his major league career lasted seven seasons, including two with the Bucs in 2001 and '02, when he hit .217, he never was more than a little-used utility player with only 422 at bats in his career. He went on to win the MVP of the Mexican League in 2006, and currently manages in the Pirates' system heading their Dominican League team.

Sean Casey

A Mt. Lebanon native who starred for the Cincinnati Reds, where he was nicknamed "the Mayor," Sean Casey came to play with his hometown team, hitting .296 in 213 at bats during the 2006 campaign. Like many other Pirates in their memorable losing era who had some success, he was traded at the deadline to the Tigers, which turned out to be fortuitous for him. In Detroit, he played in his only World Series, batting .529.

Derrek Lee

Derrek Lee came to Pittsburgh in 2011, at the end of his fifteen-year major league career that included 331 home runs. He was a late-season addition who did well, hitting seven homers in 101 at bats, for a .337 average. He retired following the season, rather than sign a contract to play for what was a bad Pirates team.

Gregory Polanco

He was supposed to be the second coming of Roberto Clemente when he started his time in the big leagues in 2014. At the beginning Polanco looked to be all that and more, with an eleven-game hitting streak to begin his career. But he started to fail miserably after that, eventually being replaced by Travis Snider, and was sent back to AAA. The year 2015 started no better, but finally, after the All-Star break, Polanco began to reach his potential, becoming an effective lead-off hitter who has a gun in right field, just like the Hall of Fame right fielder with whom he hopes one day to be deservingly compared.

#26: THE FORKBALL

ALL TIME NO. 26 ROSTER	YEAR
Tony Sanchez	(2014–2015)
Felix Pie	(2013)
Rod Barajas	(2012)
Dusty Brown	(2011)
Ronny Paulino	(2006–2008)
Jose Hernandez	(2006)
Chris Duffy	(2005)
J.J. Davis	(2002–2004)
Brian Smith	(2000)
Jason Phillips	(1999)
Steve Cooke	(1992–1997)
Dennis Lamp	(1992)
Jeff Robinson	(1992)
Neal Heaton	(1989–1991)
Junior Ortiz	(1985–1989)
Amos Otis	(1984)
Alfonso Pulido	(1984)
Jim Bibby	(1978–1983)
Mike Edwards	(1977)
Ed Ott	(1974–1975)
Roy Face	(1953, 1955–1968)
Gail Henley	(1954)
Clem Koshorek	(1952)
Bill Koski	(1951)
Elmer Singleton	(1947–1948)
Hank Gornicki	(1946)
Johnny Gee	(1943–1944)
Tommy O'Brien	(1943)
Joe Sullivan	(1941)
Oad Swigart	(1939–1941)
Pep Young	(1933–1939)
Howdy Grosskloss	(1932)
COACHES	
Joe Kerrigan	(2009–2010)

NUMBER: None

HALL OF FAMERS TO WEAR THE NUMBER: None

FIRST PERFORMANCE WITH THE NUMBER

7/2/1932- Howdy Grosskloss had an unsuccessful pinch-hitting attempt, batting for reliever Larry French, in a 5–4 loss to the Cardinals.

FIRST HOME RUN WITH THE NUMBER

5/25/1935- While the Pirates defeated the Boston Braves at Forbes Field, 11–7, and Pep Young hit the only home run of the day for the Bucs the first for a number 26 (a three-run shot), the day belonged to the great Babe Ruth, who upstaged Young and his teammates by hitting the last three home runs of his legendary career.

FIRST VICTORY BY A PITCHER WITH THE NUMBER

6/29/1941- After being acquired from the Boston Braves, Joe Sullivan came into a tied game in the eighth inning for starter Lefty Wilkie. He pitched a perfect eighth as the Bucs plated one in the top of the ninth and held on for a 3–2 win. It was Sullivan's third win of the year and first with the Pirates; future star Rip Sewell got the save.

BEST PIRATES TO WEAR THE NUMBER: (HR-RBI-AVE) (W-L-ERA)

Roy Face (100–93-3.46)

Probably the second greatest rule V draft pick in franchise history behind Roberto Clemente, Roy Face was a below-average starter who became a pioneer thanks to a forkball he learned to throw with the Bucs. As one of the first true great late relief specialists in major league history, Face led the league three times in saves and had one of the great seasons of all time in 1959. He went 18–1 with a record .947 winning percentage, victorious in twenty-two consecutive games between 1958 and '59; no relief pitcher has ever won more games in a year, before nor since.

Pep Young (photo courtesy of the Pittsburgh Pirates)

The 1962 Fireman of the Year was traded to the Tigers in 1968; before he left Face got to pitch to one batter in his last contest, which set a record for most games pitched with one team, 802.

Pep Young (32–347-.262)

Timing was not always one of Pep Young's best traits. A starting second baseman for the Pirates between 1935 and '38, Young hit his

Roy Face (photo courtesy of the Pittsburgh Pirates)

first major league home run in 1935, the same day that Babe Ruth hit numbers 712, 713, and 714 (and last) home runs of his legendary career. While Young's timing could have been better, it's a fact that most baseball fans will remember the day a player got his first round tripper; in this case, no one would probably have noticed.

Jim Bibby (50–32-3.53)

A tall hulky hurler who would sweat like few athletes could, Jim Bibby was signed by the Bucs as a free agent in 1978. The brother of former NBA star Henry Bibby, Jim had hurled a no-hitter with the Rangers in 1973, and won 19 games a year before being signed by Pittsburgh as a free agent in 1978; he was just what the Bucs' rotation needed. A Vietnam War veteran, Bibby was 12–4 during the Pirates' world championship run in 1979 and then started two games in the World Series, pitching effectively.

In 1980, he was one of the few Pirates who exceeded their 1979 production, with a phenomenal 19–6 campaign in which he led the senior circuit in winning percentage for a second consecutive season, and finished third in the Cy Young race. It would be his final successful season in a Bucs uniform, as a torn rotator cuff for all intents and purposes ended his major league career.

WORST PIRATES TO WEAR THE NUMBER: (W-L-ERA) (HR-RBI-AVE)
Elmer Singleton (6–8-5.54)

It was apparent that Elmer Singleton loved the game of baseball; he played twenty-four seasons of professional ball, eight of which came in the majors. For two seasons in the late 1940s the reliever showed that love wasn't enough to be a success, as he stumbled just like so many Pirates pitchers of the time period did.

Bill Koski (0–1-6.67)

Playing in 1951, his only major league season, Bill Koski had a 2.000 WHIP in 26 innings, which did not warrant another opportunity. In the

Baseball-reference.com bullpen he made the statement that, "Honus Wagner would sit in the dugout once in a while, but I didn't even know who he was . . . just an old-time player. I'd come off the mound and he'd talk to me, telling me to be more aggressive out there or something . . . But I look back now and wonder how many guys even got to meet him?" Everybody needs a highlight and this was his.

Amos Otis (0–10-.165)

Amos Otis had a wonderful sixteen-year major league career during which he accumulated over 2,000 hits. Hoping to get from Otis whatever he had left, the Pirates signed him as a free agent in 1984; they soon found he had nothing left.

JJ Davis (1–7-.163)

In 2000, JJ Davis was a slugger who was the ninety-seventh best prospect in baseball. By the time his Pirate career had ended in 2004, he was just another failed product of the worst system in baseball.

OTHER NOTABLE PIRATES TO WEAR THE NUMBER
Howdy Grosskloss

There wasn't a lot to Pittsburgh native Howdy Grosskloss's major league career — three abbreviated seasons between 1930 and '32, when he hit .261 — but it was outside of baseball that he made his mark. A star football player at Amherst College, Grosskloss received a medical degree from Yale and taught at some of the most prestigious medical schools in the country, including the University of Pittsburgh. He was also one of the oldest players of all time, passing away on July 15, 2006, three months after his 100th birthday.

Oad Swigart

In a major league career that lasted all of ten games in 1939 and '40, Oad Swigart won exactly one game, an eight-hit shutout of the Boston Braves on September 21, 1939. While his career was brief on the field, in Pirates history it is eternal, as he was the first Pittsburgh Pirate to be drafted into the service during World War II. He spent four years between 1941 and '45 in the military, playing baseball for the morale of the troops. When he returned in 1946 it was in an unsuccessful attempt to make the Bucs roster in spring training.

Tommy O'Brien

Tommy O'Brien was the quintessential World War II–era player, good enough to play in the majors when the majority of talent was in the service, but not good enough when they came back. The outfielder, who went to the University of Tennessee on a football scholarship, hit .301 with the Bucs between 1943 and '45 as a reserve outfielder. He was out of the majors until 1949, when he reappeared with the Red Sox and played two more years, hitting only .200.

Johnny Gee

Johnny Gee wasn't much of a pitcher for the Bucs, posting a 5–8 mark over parts of four seasons, but what made him special was the fact that Gee was a hell of a basketball player at Michigan, eventually playing for the Syracuse Nationals in the National Basketball League. Being 6'9" also made Gee the tallest person to play in major league baseball until Hall of Famer Randy Johnson emerged with the Expos.

Clem Koshorek

Clem Koshorek was the anti-Johnny Gee. Playing in two seasons in 1951 and '52, the World War II veteran was a full foot-and-a-half shorter. At 5'4" he was one of the shortest players in the game.

Gail Henley

While he played in only one major league season, in 1954, Gail Henley would have the honor of being a major leaguer to have a career .300 batting average, going nine-for-30 in his brief time in the big leagues.

Ed Ott and Chris Duffy

Ed Ott wore uniform number 26 his first two seasons in the majors. Chris Duffy donned 26 his rookie year, when he hit .341 for the team.

Neal Heaton

A second-round draft pick by the Cleveland Indians in the 1981 draft, Neal Heaton was an All–Star with the Pirates in 1990 because of an exceptional half season, when he pitched to a 10–4 record. After going to the mid-summer classic, he came down to earth with a 2–4 mark and only won seven more games in his major league career. At least he will always have those three months in 1990 that put the words All-Star next to his name.

Dennis Lamp

Winner of more than ten games four times in his sixteen-year major league career, Dennis Lamp pitched his final big league season with the Pirates in 1992, when he was 1–1 with a 5.14 ERA in twenty-one relief appearances.

Steve Cooke

One of a long line of potential pitching superstars with the Pirates during their twenty-year streak of losing baseball, Steve Cooke went 10–10 his official rookie season in 1993, making the Topps All-Rookie team. A 13–26 record for the remainder of his career showed that his potential was not realized.

Jose Hernandez

A slugger who hit more than 20 home runs three times in his fifteen-year big league career, and 163 homers in total, there were two constants in Jose Hernandez's career: he struck out a hell of a lot, leading the league twice in that category while accumulating a 30.1 per cent strikeout rate in his career; and he played with many teams, nine to be exact, which included his two stints with the Pirates in 2003 and '06.

Ronny Paulino

Oh Ronny, what we thought we had in you after you hit .310 in your rookie season of 2006, a year when the Pirates thought their catching woes had ended. It was just a mirage, unfortunately, as Paulino spent two more unsuccessful years with the Bucs before heading to Florida. Since then his career continued to fall; he has been suspended twice for PED use, and currently catches in the Mexican Leagues.

Rod Barajas

The first in a line of free-agent catchers the Bucs have utilized to help their pitching staff to be more successful, Rod Barajas was a beefy option who was the least successful of the three. While Russell Martin and Francisco Cervelli have helped the Pirates to reach the upper echelon of the National League, Barajas was a disappointment, hitting only .206 in 2012 while throwing out only 6 six percent of the runners who tried to steal against him. Maybe the proper description of Barajas is that he was the catcher who showed the Pirates the importance of a great defensive catcher, so they went out and got Martin and Cervelli.

Tony Sanchez

The first-round choice of the team in the 2009 amateur draft, Tony Sanchez was a great catcher at Boston College, and was a future hope that the team could utilize home-grown talent behind the plate instead of finding it from other organizations. While Sanchez has shown glimpses of success offensively with the team, defensively he has not proven to be what they are looking for. As a result, he has found himself behind Elias Diaz in the minor league depth chart. With Reese McGuire also coming up, it seems that Sanchez will not be that home-grown talent the Pirates had hoped he would be. The fact he was DFA'd before the 2016 campaign is probably a good sign of that the Bucs think this way.

#27: RUBBER BAND MAN

ALL TIME NO. 27 ROSTER	YEAR
Jung Ho Kang	(2015)
Jayson Nix	(2014)
Jeff Karstens	(2009–2012)
Ty Taubenheim	(2008)
Shane Youman	(2006–2007)
Josh Fogg	(2002–2005)
Alex Hernandez	(2001)
Adam Hyzdu	(2000)
Tim Laker	(1998)
Steve Parris	(1995–1996)
Lonnie Smith	(1993)
Jeff Richardson	(1992–1993)
Steve Buechele	(1991)
Mark Huismann	(1990–1991)
Mark Ryal	(1990)
Miguel Garcia	(1987–1989)
Sam Khalifa	(1986–1987)
Johnnie LeMaster	(1985)
Kent Tekulve	(1975–1985)
Jerry Reuss	(1974)
Dave Augustine	(1974)
Bob Johnson	(1971–1973)
Bruce Dal Canton	(1970)
Bob Robertson	(1969)
Ron Kline	(1968–1969)
Jim Shellenback	(1967)
Bob Oliver	(1965)
Earl Francis	(1961–1964)
Spook Jacobs	(1956)
Cholly Naranjo	(1956)
Dick Littlefield	(1954–1956)
Eddie O'Brien	(1953)
Pete Reiser	(1951)
Mel Queen	(1950)
Ray Poat	(1949)
Bob Muncrief	(1949)
Lenny Levy	(1948)
Art Herring	(1947)
Cookie Cuccurullo	(1944–1945)
Hank Gornicki	(1942–1943)
Ray Harrell	(1940)
Joe Bowman	(1937)
COACHES	
Joe Jones	(1999–2000)

NUMBER RETIRED: None

HALL OF FAMERS TO WEAR THE NUMBER: None

FIRST PERFORMANCE WITH THE NUMBER

4/29/1937- In the sixth game of the season, the Pirates battled the Cubs to a 5–5 tie as the eighth inning came to a close. Reliever Joe Bowman came into the game in the ninth and tossed five shutout innings. The Pirates plated a run in the top of the thirteenth for a 6–5 win, with Bowman getting the victory.

FIRST HOME RUN WITH THE NUMBER

8/27/1942- In a contest in which he had a complete-game two-hit shutout against the Braves, pitcher Hank Gornicki also had the rare accomplishment of being the first pitcher to hit a home run by a Pirate while wearing a specific uniform number, the first and only one of his career, to go along with a single, two runs, and two RBIs during the 5–0 victory.

FIRST VICTORY BY A PITCHER WITH THE NUMBER

4/29/1937- Please see the first performance for information on the first victory.

BEST PIRATES TO WEAR THE NUMBER: (HR-RBI-AVE) (W-L-ERA)

Kent Tekulve (70–61-2.68)

Mocked by scouts after his career at Marietta College because of his strange running style, at some point the Bucs decided that pitchers don't need to run and made a very advantageous signing. Nicknamed "rubber band man" after a popular song due to his tall, lanky stature and side-arm delivery, Kent Tekulve became one of the greatest relievers in Pirates history, as well as a key component and the last man on the mound in their memorable 1979 World Series run. When he retired he had pitched in more games than any other relievers, (1,050) and has since become a treasured member of the team's pre-game broadcasts. He received a heart transplant in 2014, but has recovered remarkably well to continue his spot on the show.

Jung Ho Kang (15–58-.287)

Having Jung Ho Kang on the "best" list after just one season shows not only the lack of great 27s in Pirates history, but the potential of what his career can become. His signing was a shock after he hit 40 home runs in the Korean League in 2014, then mocked when the Pirates put him on the major league roster out of spring training, instead of giving him more seasoning for the American game in AAA. Kang has proved all

his critics wrong with an incredible rookie season. He was the NL Rookie of The Month in July. His .379 average and 13 extra-base hits were the most by a Pirates rookie in a month since the legendary Paul Waner in the final month of Waner's spectacular rookie campaign of 1926. Unfortunately, Kang's promising season came to a disappointing end after an aggressive slide by the Cubs' Chris Coghlin, who ripped ligaments in

Jung Ho Kang (photo courtesy of Christina Bortak)

Kang's knee and broke his leg. He should be ready to go early in 2016, though, to continue his ride up the "best of 27" list.

Josh Fogg (39–42-4.79)

There was some confusion about whether to put Josh Fogg on the "best" or "worst" list; he made it on the best not only due to the lack of great players who wore the number 27, but because he was actually a pretty good pitcher on some bad Pirates teams, garnering at least a .500 record in three consecutive seasons. His career ended in Pittsburgh when he signed a free agent contract with the Rockies in 2006. While the high altitude of Colorado helped raise his career ERA to over 5.00, when he had a chance to pitch in his only World Series in 2007 he allowed six runs and ten hits in only 2 2/3 innings during a game three start.

Kent Tekulve (photo courtesy of the Pittsburgh Pirates)

WORST PIRATES TO WEAR THE NUMBER: (W-L-ERA) (HR-RBI-AVE)

Roy Harrell (0–0-8.10)

After his four pretty unsuccessful years as a reliever in the majors, the Pirates decided to take a gamble on pitcher Roy Harrell in 1940, picking him up on waivers. It was a gamble that was not sound; he allowed five hits and three runs in 3 1/3 innings before the team traded him to Portland in the PCL.

Art Herring (1–3-8.44)

Herring was an eleven-year veteran who had his career in the majors split into three playing periods between 1929 and 1934, then again in

1939, before having a major league renaissance in 1944 when he pitched until the age of forty-one in 1947 when, as a Pirate, he had by far his worst campaign in the big leagues. Strangely enough, because of that scattered time in the majors, he held a weird record of having fifteen years in between doubles, hitting one in 1931 and then not again until '46.

Spook Jacobs (0–1-.162)

After a successful rookie campaign with the Philadelphia A's in 1954 at the age of twenty-eight, Jacobs played two more seasons in the majors, the final one in 1956 with the Bucs, when he proved that the only thing big league about him was his nickname. For some reason unbeknownst to most, he threw out the first pitch before a game at Veterans Stadium in Philadelphia in 2002.

OTHER NOTABLE PIRATES TO WEAR THE NUMBER

Hank Gornicki

A starter/reliever with the Pirates during war years in 1942 and '43, when he was 14–19, Hank Gornicki was drafted into the Army in 1944. Gornicki suffered from leg issues and pneumonia in the service and was discharged in 1945. He returned to the team in 1946, but tossed only - 12 2/3 innings in his final major league campaign.

Cookie Cuccurullo

Better known by his unique name, Cookie Cuccurullo was a decent reliever for the Bucs during World War II. With a 4.55 ERA and 1.582 WHIP over three seasons, perhaps decent was a generous word, but the name still makes him worthy for inclusion in this book.

Ray Poat

A chemist after his career ended, Ray Poat won 22 games in five years with the Indians and Giants before coming to the Bucs in 1949. He lost his only decision for the team before hurting his arm, which ended his career; then a chemist was born.

Pete Reiser

Pete Reiser was a rough-and- tumble player who was a star early in his career with Brooklyn, being selected to the All-Star Game three times, and finishing in the top ten in the National League MVP race three times. His aggressive style of play, which helped him to be a star, got the best of him as he would continually run into the outfield fence in pursuit of high flies. The probable concussions led to dizziness, which contributed to the end of a once-promising career a year after he hit .271 for the Bucs in 1951.

Bob Muncrief

Bob Muncrief was an awesome hurler with the St. Louis Browns during the World War II seasons, going 58–41 for the St. Louis Browns between 1941 and '45. After the war years he was not as good, with a 32–41 mark that included 1–5 for the Pirates in 1949.

Eddie O'Brien, Bob Robertson, Luke Walker, and Jerry Reuss

Former college basketball superstar Eddie O'Brien wore uniform number 27 in his rookie season. Robertson wore 27 in 1969, his second year with the Bucs, as did Luke Walker in 1966. Jerry Reuss won 16 games as number 27 during his first year in Pittsburgh in 1974.

Dick Littlefield

Winner of 15 games for the Bucs between 1954 and '56 while splitting time between the starting rotation and bullpen, nine-year veteran Dick Littlefield was most important in Pirates history as one of the trading chips the team used to acquire Bill Virdon from the Cardinals.

Earl Francis

Turning down a football scholarship at West Virginia State College to play professional baseball, Earl Francis began his career with the Bucs in 1960, pitching effectively out of the bullpen until he hurt his arm. He came back and, in 1963, became the first African American pitcher to start an opening game for the franchise. A year later, unfortunately, his time in Pittsburgh was over. He pitched in two games for St. Louis in 1965, which would be his final two major league games.

Bob Oliver

Hitless in two at bats for the Pirates during his first year in the big leagues in 1965, Bob Oliver went on to become a decent power hitter with the Royals and Angels, hitting 94 home runs in eight seasons, and was the first Royals player ever to hit a grand slam.

Bob Johnson

A member of the Pirates' starting rotation during their world championship season in 1971, Bob Johnson started game three of the NLCS, tossing eight innings and allowing no earned runs in a 2–1 victory. Unfortunately, Johnson was terrible in their loss to the Orioles in game two of the World Series.

Johnnie Lemaster

The ultimate good-field no-hit shortstop, mostly for the San Francisco Giants in his twelve-year career, Johnnie Lemaster made his next-to-last stop in the majors with the Pirates, where he hit .155 in 1985. Hitting only 22 long balls in his career, Lemaster had the honor of hitting an inside-the-park home run for his first homer in 1975, and hit his last major league homer while with the Bucs.

Sammy Khalifa

The first-round pick for the Pirates in 1982, Sam Khalifa was supposed to be the Pirates' future at shortstop. After his three-year career between 1985 and '87, when he hit .219, he proved his future was over.

Miguel Garcia

Not only was it bad enough that Miguel Garcia was winless in two decisions in his three years in Pittsburgh, he will always be a reminder of a horrible deal the Pirates made with the Angels in 1987, receiving him and Billie Merrifield in exchange for Johnny Ray.

Lonnie Smith

A speedy star who went to the World Series with four different teams — the Phillies, Cardinals, Royals, and Braves — the only man in major league history to do so, Lonnie Smith came to Pittsburgh in his next-to-last major league season. Although thirty-seven years of age at the time, in 1993, Smith hit .286 for the Bucs.

Tim Laker

A little-used backup catcher for most of his eleven seasons in the majors, with a .226 career average, Tim Laker played for the Bucs in 1998 and '99, where he had a spike in his average, hitting .364 in 33 at bats. Currently a minor league coach, Laker had purchased PEDs on four occasions according to the famed Mitchell Report, although with a .226 average he wasn't exactly a poster child for the Steroid Era.

Adam Hyzdu

A god in Altoona, where he is the only player in Curve history to have his number retired, Adam Hyzdu had a less-than-stellar major league career with a .229 average, although he can proudly say he was a member of the first Red Sox team since 1918 to win a world championship in 2004.

Jeff Karstens

Part of the Xavier Nady trade with the Yankees that brought Ross Ohlendorf, Jose Tabata, and Daniel McCutchen with him, Jeff Karstens was arguably the best part of the deal, with 23 victories in five injury-plagued seasons.

#28: THE FOREVER PIRATE

ALL TIME NO. 28 ROSTER	YEAR
Paul Maholm	(2006–2011)
Ron Villone	(2002)
Ryan Vogelsong	(2001)
John Vander Wal	(2000–2001)
Al Martin	(1992–1999)
Jeff Banister	(1991)
Carmelo Martinez	(1990–1991)
Randy Kramer	(1989–1990)
Denny Gonzalez	(1984, 1987–1988)
Sixto Lezcano	(1985)
Bob Owchinko	(1983)
Wayne Nordhagen	(1982)
Dick Davis	(1982)
Bill Robinson	(1975–1982)
Steve Blass	(1966–1975)
Ozzie Virgil	(1965)
Bobby Shantz	(1961)
Paul Giel	(1959–1960)
R C Stevens	(1959)
Danny Kravitz	(1958)
Chuck Churn	(1957)
Paul Martin	(1955)
Ben Wade	(1955)
Walker Cooper	(1954)
Johnny Lindell	(1953)
Ted Wilks	(1951–1952)
Vic Lombardi	(1948–1950)
Steve Nagy	(1947)
Cal McLish	(1946)
Vinnie Smith	(1941, 1946)
Dick Lanahan	(1940–1941)
COACHES	
Gerald Perry	(2003–2005)
Jeff Banister	(2012–2014)

NUMBER RETIRED: None

HALL OF FAMERS TO WEAR THE NUMBER: None

FIRST PERFORMANCE WITH THE NUMBER

4/16/1940- After the Pirates broke out to a 6–0 lead against the Cardinals in the 1940 opener, pitchers Bob Klinger and Johnny Lanning struggled in the sixth as St. Louis cut the lead to 6–4. Reliever Dick Lanahan entered the game in the seventh and shut down the Cardinal offense, allowing only a hit and two walks in three shutout innings for his first save of the season.

FIRST HOME RUN WITH THE NUMBER

4/15/1953- Returning after a three-year hiatus from the majors as an All-Star outfielder, Johnny Lindell went to the mound. He walked 10 and allowed four hits in a complete-game 4–2 loss to the Dodgers, although he was all the offense the Pirates had, smacking a two-run homer in the third, which temporarily gave Pittsburgh a 2–1 lead.

FIRST VICTORY BY A PITCHER WITH THE NUMBER

7/21/1940- When starter Danny Mac Fayden was ripped for two runs in the first inning, manager Frankie Frisch called on reliever Dick

Lanahan to try and stop the Boston Braves. Lanahan was superb for 7 1/3 innings, giving up a single run and four hits as Pittsburgh overcame the early 2–0 deficit to win, 5–3. It was Lanahan's first victory of the season after three losses.

BEST PIRATES TO WEAR THE NUMBER: (HR-RBI-AVE) (W-L-ERA)
Steve Blass (103–76-3.63)

By the time Steve Blass completed his eighth major league season he had won 100 major league games, finished second in the Cy Young race, and was on the mound in the seventh game of the 1971 World Series, pitching the Bucs to the world championship; then there was that pesky disease that was named after him. 1973 was a bad year for Blass, losing his beloved teammate Roberto Clemente in a tragic plane crash in the off-season, then completely losing his control soon after. He never regained it, and every time a pitcher or fielder has lost control of his throws since then it's been dubbed "Steve Blass Disease." While this could have led to a disastrous future for some, Blass made the most of it, first dealing with the malady with class, then carving out an outstanding life for himself as the long-time color man for the Pirates' broadcasts. In the Pirates organization since 1960, has Blass made himself a lifetime Pirate—fifty-six years and going strong.

Bill Robinson (109–412-.276)

A failed prospect with the Yankees, Bill Robinson hoped to forge a career with the Pirates when they obtained him for pitcher Wayne Simpson; mission accomplished. A super sub at times, if you will, Robinson surpassed 20 home runs on

Bill Robinson sitting on home plate as Omar Moreno crosses over him. (Photo courtesy of the Pittsburgh Pirates)

three occasions and 100 RBIs in 1977. He was a pivotal part of the Bucs' 1979 world championship, and while he wasn't the next Mickey Mantle, as New York's pinstripe nation thought he would be, he was still a player the Pirates Nation will remember as a damn good player.

Al Martin (107–381-.280)

A good, consistent player for the Bucs, who hit double-digit home runs in all but one full season in Pittsburgh, Al Martin became a national news story after he left the team, with a domestic violence charge that reported he was potentially married to more than one woman at the same time . . . which in most of the United States would be a felony. Luckily, Martin claimed that he didn't think the ceremony in Las Vegas was legally binding. If that wasn't interesting enough, he also claimed to have played football at USC, which again took a poor twist for Martin, since there was no record of him playing there. Further research revealed that his stats for the Pirates were, in fact, real—which is why he remains on this list.

WORST PIRATES TO WEAR THE NUMBER: (W-L-ERA)
Bob Owchinko (0–0-INF)

The pride and joy of Eastern Michigan University, Bob Owchinko enjoyed a decent career as a pitcher before he came to the Pirates in 1983. He didn't even last an inning with the team, allowing two hits and a home run to future Pirate Andy Van Slyke in a 7–6 loss to St. Louis. He never retired a batter, making his ERA something every pitcher likes to see next to his name . . . INF for infinity . . . the highest career ERA in Pirates history.

Paul Martin (0–1-14.14)

He was a rarity, never spending any time in the minor leagues, but after seven mostly poor games with the Pirates in 1955 Paul Martin hurt his arm, which ended his professional baseball career.

Cal McLish (0–0–10.50)

Debuting in 1944 at the age of only eighteen, Cal McLish had a poor rookie season, going 3–10. He spent a year in the military before returning to a Pittsburgh uniform. He pitched only three games for the Pirates over two seasons, but did poorly, allowing seven runs in six innings. McLish eventually found his way, winning 92 games over his fifteen-year career, including 19 wins for the Indians in 1959.

Cal McLish (photo courtesy of the Pittsburgh Pirates)

OTHER NOTABLE PIRATES TO WEAR THE NUMBER

Vinnie Smith

There were five years between Vinnie Smith's major league seasons with the Bucs. He hit .303 in 1941 before heading into the military during World War II, where he played the game to help the morale of the troops, becoming Bob Feller's favorite catcher. After he was discharged he came back in 1946 and hit only .190 in his final big league season. Smith eventually made it back to the majors as an umpire, and was behind home plate during Harvey Haddix's incredible "twelve-inning perfect game" in 1959 that he lost in the thirteenth inning.

Steve Nagy

A teammate of Chuck 'the Rifleman" Connors at Seton Hall, as well as of Jackie Robinson with the Montreal Royals in 1946, Steve Nagy was a little-used reliever for the Pirates in 1947, when he was 1–3 with a 5.79 ERA. He played one more season three years later in 1950, going 2–5 in nine starts with Washington.

Vic Lombardi

Vic Lombardi was a member of the Brooklyn Dodgers Hall of Fame, winning 35 games in his first three major league seasons, before being traded to the Pirates following the 1947 campaign. A World War II vet who served in the military for only a couple of months before being discharged with bad vision, Lombardi pitched well with the Bucs his first season, bad vision and all (he did wear glasses for a time while playing). He spent the majority of his last two seasons with Pittsburgh in the bullpen, where he fashioned a 5.31 ERA.

Ted Wilks

After a fabulous rookie season in 1945 with the Cardinals where he was 17–4, Ted Wilks pitched in ten big league campaigns, but never reached that success again. He found himself with the Pirates for part of the 1950 and '51 seasons, when he was an effective reliever with an 8–10 mark in 92 games and an impressive 1.219 WHIP.

Johnny Lindell

Johnny Lindell was thirty-six years old when he played with the Pirates in 1953, hitting .286 in 91 at bats after three seasons out of the major leagues. Before that he was a star in the Bronx during the war years, especially in 1944 when he hit 18 homers, knocking in 103 RBIs. The great thing about Lindell was that before he became an All-Star outfielder he was an exceptional pitcher in the minors, going 23–4 with the Newark Bears in 1941. And now for the rest of the story: when he was with the Bucs he went back from the outfield to the mound. Unfortunately, at 5–16 the unusual return to the mound could not be deemed a success.

Ben Wade

After winning 11 games in his rookie season for the Dodgers in 1952, Ben Wade was relegated to the bullpen for the rest of his five-year career, the last of which was with the Bucs in 1955, when he had an 0–1 record with a 3.21 ERA.

Paul Giel

College football fans remember Paul Giel as one of the greatest football players the University of Minnesota ever produced. The All-American halfback finished runner-up in 1953 for the Heisman Trophy and was inducted into the College Football Hall of Fame. Baseball fans don't really remember Paul Giel the pitcher who, while undefeated with the Bucs at 2–0 in two seasons and capturing a championship ring in 1960, had a 7.30 ERA for the club.

Chuck Churn

Other than having a very rhythmic name, Chuck Churn is one of the few Pittsburgh Pirates in the franchise's history to also play professional baseball in . . . Uniontown. Other than having no decisions in five contests during his brief Pirate career in 1957, Churn's only noteworthy trivia is the fact that he was the last pitcher Enos Slaughter would face while Chuck pitched with the Dodgers . . . oh yeah, and he pitched for Uniontown.

Danny Kravitz

A backup catcher with the Bucs at the end of the 1950s who hit .236, Danny Kravitz had the honor of playing with the soon-to-be world champion Pirates in 1960. Unfortunately, he was traded early on to the Kansas City A's for Hank Foiles and never got the chance to enjoy much of that memorable season.

Bobby Schantz

One year after he was rescued from being the losing pitcher of game seven in the 1960 World Series for the Yankees, when Ralph Terry saved the sixteen-year vet and 1952 AL MVP from that embarrassment by dishing up the Mazeroski home run in the ninth, Bobby Schantz became a Pittsburgh Pirate for one season. He was 6–3 with a 3.32 ERA for the Bucs in 1961.

Ozzie Virgil

The man who broke the color barrier for the Detroit Tigers in 1958, Ozzie Virgil had a very undistinguished nine-year major league career. He played for the Bucs in 1965, hitting .265. After his retirement he became a long-time major league coach for the Giants, Expos, Padres, and Mariners.

Wayne Nordhagen and Dick Davis

A decent outfielder and designated hitter for the White Sox and Blue Jays, Wayne Nordhagen was dealt to the Bucs in a three-way deal in 1982 that saw Philadelphia give Toronto Dick Davis, Pittsburgh deal Bill Robinson to the Phillies, and the Bucs get Nordhagen. Although he had two hits in four at bats in the only game he played for Pittsburgh, it was discovered that Nordhagen had a bad back; he was returned to Toronto ten days later in exchange for Dick Davis, who hit .182 for the Pirates in his last major league season and would eventually go to Japan, where he was arrested on marijuana possession charges. All in all, a pretty forgettable deal in every way, except for the fact that all three people involved in the trade wore number 28 for the Bucs.

Sixto Lezcano

A great outfielder for the Milwaukee Brewers, who not only hit 102 home runs, but also knocked in 101 RBIs in 1979 while winning a Gold Glove, Sixto Lezcano ended his career in a forgettable manner in 1985, hitting .207 in 116 at bats.

Carmelo Martinez

Carmelo Martinez played sparingly in his two abbreviated seasons with the Pirates after a decent career in San Diego. Despite that fact he almost became a hero in Pittsburgh history, knocking in the only run with a double (the only hit for the Bucs that evening) in the 2–1 loss to the Reds in game six of the 1990 NLCS. In the eighth inning, with a runner on first, he hit a long shot to right field that appeared to be headed for a potential game-winning home run that would have sent the Series to a seventh and final game. Instead, a defensive replacement, the tall Glen Braggs, reached up and brought it in for the disappointing out.

Paul Maholm

The 2003 first-round draft pick by the Pirates out of Mississippi State, Paul Maholm came back from a broken orbital bone after being hit by a line drive in the minors to become one of the few contributing first-round picks made by Bucs between 1992 and 2007. While he won only 53 games in seven seasons in a Pittsburgh uniform, Maholm was often the best pitcher on some bad teams. No player has worn his number since he left in 2011 (coach Jeff Bannister did from 2012 through 2014), which leaves many to wonder whether or not they will retire it in his honor. If they did it would be only the second strangest number retirement next to Billy Meyer's.

#29: ARNIE PALMER IN BASEBALL SPIKES

ALL TIME NO. 29 ROSTER	YEAR
Francisco Cervelli	(2015)
Ernesto Frieri	(2014)
Bryan Morris	(2013–2014)
Kevin Correia	(2011–2012)
Octavio Dotel	(2010)
Don Kelly	(2007)
Nyjer Morgan	(2007)
Jody Gerut	(2005)
David Ross	(2005)
Kevin Young	(1995, 1997–2003)
John Hope	(1996)
Randy Tomlin	(1990–1994)
Mark Ross	(1990)
Billy Hatcher	(1989)
Felix Fermin	(1987–1988)
Onix Concepcion	(1987)
Rick Rhoden	(1979–1986)
Jim Fregosi	(1977–1978)
Ken Macha	(1977)
Jim Minshall	(1975)
Ken Brett	(1974)
Milt May	(1970–1973)
Lou Marone	(1969–1970)
Al Oliver	(1968)
Juan Pizarro	(1967–1968)
Don Schwall	(1963–1966)
Clem Labine	(1960–1961)
Bennie Daniels	(1960)
Earl Francis	(1960)
Red Witt	(1958)
Nellie King	(1956–1957)
Dale Long	(1955)
Johnny Hetki	(1953–1954)
Jim Dunn	(1952)
Junior Walsh	(1949–1951)
Bill Werle	(1949)
Don Gutteridge	(1948)
Preacher Roe	(1944–1947)
Johnny Lanning	(1940–1943)
COACHES	
Tony Beasley	(2010)

NUMBER RETIRED: None

HALL OF FAMERS TO WEAR THE NUMBER: None

FIRST PERFORMANCE WITH THE NUMBER

4/16/1940- In the opener against the Cardinals, the Bucs won 6–4. Johnny Lanning finished the sixth inning for Bob Klinger, tossing 1/3 of an inning while giving up a hit.

FIRST HOME RUN WITH THE NUMBER

5/5/1955- After returning to Pittsburgh in 1955, Dale Long crushed a home run in the fifth inning of a game against the Cardinals to give Pittsburgh a temporary 1–0 lead. St. Louis came back to win 5–1, as the homer by Long was one of only three hits by the team that day.

FIRST VICTORY BY A PITCHER WITH THE NUMBER

6/7/1940- After Mace Brown allowed four runs in the second inning against the Phillies, Johnny Lanning entered the game and tossed 7 1/3 innings of shutout three-hit ball. The Bucs came back to win the game 10–4, with Lanning getting his first victory in a Pirate uniform.

BEST PIRATES TO WEAR THE NUMBER: (HR-RBI-AVE) (W-L-ERA)

Kevin Young (136–583-.269)

Persistence is a great value in life, and for first baseman Kevin Young it was the reason he stands among this list as the king of uniform number 29s. A prized prospect, Young was nothing more than a disappointment with the Bucs his first five seasons; he had a huge hole in his swing. He ended up going to Kansas City in 1996, but was reacquired by the Pirates a year later. Finally, in 1997, the hole was closed. Young hit .300 with 18 homers that year, and went on to top 20 homers three times and 100 RBIs twice. It was a great "feel good" story, until he was named in the Mitchell Report for reportedly buying PEDs between 2000 and 2003. Oh well, perhaps all feel good stories need a twist.

Rick Rhoden (79–73-3.51)

A fine pick-up by the 1979 Pirates from the Dodgers, Rick Rhoden spent most of the season on the mend from rotator cuff surgery. Rhoden came back to be one of the team's best hurlers through 1986, a season when he finished fifth in the Cy Young race. As good a pitcher as he was, Rhoden was also a tremendous hitter, winning three Silver Slugger Awards with a .238 career average and starting a game as a DH for the Yankees in 1988. After Rhoden retired, he continued to excel as a championship golfer and became arguably the greatest celebrity golfer ever.

Randy Tomlin (30–31-3.43)

Concocting a pitch called the "Vulcan change," which is a pitch for which the ball is held between the fingers in a way that resembles Spock's famous hand signal, Randy Tomlin was a fine hurler with the team during the championship era in the early '90s. Starting his career with a 2.85 ERA in 1990 and '91, Tomlin had his best major league season in '92, when he won a career-high 14 games for the Bucs.

WORST PIRATES TO WEAR THE NUMBER: (W-L-ERA)

Ernesto Frieri (1–1-10.13)

The Pirates sent beloved reliever and star Jason Grilli to the Angels for their one-time closer, Ernesto Frieri. Every time Frieri took the mound he would just remind the Bucs he was no Grilli . . . even after Grilli slumped . . . pitching in fourteen mostly painful contests.

Don Gutteridge (0–0-.000)

After eleven seasons as a middle infielder with the Cardinals, Browns and Red Sox, Don Gutteridge was hitless in four at bats for Pittsburgh in his final major league season. In a way, he was kind of a hometown boy in name only: Gutteridge was born in Pittsburg . . . well, Pittsburg, Kansas . . . where his birthday is considered a city holiday every year, and everything there is named after him.

Don Kelly (0–0-.148)

A Mt. Lebanon native and Point Park University alum, Don Kelly had a poor first season for the Pirates in 2007. He went on to play for the Tigers, where he became a very important super sub for former Bucs manager Jim Leyland, and hit .364 in his first post-season series against the Yankees in 2011.

OTHER NOTABLE PIRATES TO WEAR THE NUMBER

Johnny Lanning

A North Carolina State alum who started his career in 1936 with the Boston Braves, Johnny Lanning was dealt to the Bucs in 1939. He won 11 games for the team in 1941 and 33 over his six years with the team. Lanning missed the 1944 campaign and most of '45 while serving in the Armed Forces during World War II.

Preacher Roe

Starting his major league career with St. Louis in 1938 at the age of twenty-two, it would be six years until Preacher Roe made it back to the show, pitching in 1944 with the Bucs. He would be a solid war years hurler, going 27–24 in 1944 and '45 before an off-season brawl that resulted in him receiving a fractured skull that led to a poor 1946 campaign. He ended up being traded to the Brooklyn Dodgers, where he resurrected his career, with a 93–37 record for the Bums over seven seasons, including a 22–3 mark in 1951.

Junior Walsh

A World War II vet, Junior Walsh had a less-than-stellar time in the big leagues, where he spent all five years in a Pirate uniform with a 5.88 ERA. He was at his best, not on the real diamond but in Hollywood, as an extra in the movie, *Angels in the Outfield*.

Johnny Hetki

A reliever for most of his eight-year career in the show, Johnny Hetki spent his last two seasons in the Steel City, finishing 77 games in 1953 and '54, including a NL high 46 the latter season.

Nellie King

A decent reliever in his four-year major league career with the Bucs, where he was 7–5 with a 3.38 ERA, Nellie King went on to be a Pittsburgh icon as the longtime color man to Bob Prince in the Bucs' broadcasting booth. He was involved in the infamous firing of both in 1975 that is still a bitter memory for the Pirates nation. King later became a long-time SID at Duquesne University, and was the color man on their basketball broadcasts.

Red Witt

Red Witt had a phenomenal rookie season in 1958, with a 9–2 mark and 1.61 ERA in fifteen starts for the Bucs. With a bright future in front of him, arm injuries would all but end it as he won only two more big league games.

Clem Labine (photo courtesy of the Pittsburgh Pirates)

Clem Labine

Clem Labine was a memorable reliever for the Brooklyn Dodgers in the 1950s, with a 13–5 record in the lone world championship season in 1955. He was dealt to Pittsburgh late in his career, in 1960, pitching two seasons for a won-loss of 7–1 and a 3.15 ERA. Labine was a member of the 1962 expansion New York Mets, finishing his career in the majors with an 11.25 ERA.

Don Schwall

Another alum of the baseball hotbed that is Eastern Michigan, Don Schwall won the Rookie of the Year Award with the Boston Red Sox in 1961, despite his rather high 1.550 WHIP (thankfully, the electorate in 1961 had no idea what a WHIP was). He was acquired by Pittsburgh in 1963 for Dick Stuart and became a good middle-reliever, winning 22 games over four seasons.

Billy O'Dell

After twelve mostly successful big league seasons with the Orioles, Giants, and Braves, left-hander Billy O'Dell began his Pirates career in 1966 in a trade by the Braves for Don Schwall. The two-time All-Star, who also suffered from Addison's disease, had a fine first season out of the Pirates bullpen with a 2.78 ERA in 71 innings. He had his worst campaign a year later, when his ERA shot up by over three runs to 5.82. It would prove to be the thirty-four-year-old's final season in the show.

Juan Pizarro

Juan Pizzaro had been a successful starter with the Chicago White Sox, going 61–38 with a 2.93 ERA and two All-Star games before the Pirates picked him up in 1967. He pitched mostly out of the bullpen in his one-plus years in a Pittsburgh uniform, winning nine games. After being sold to Boston in 1968 he returned to the Bucs in 1974, where he finished his major league career with a 1.88 ERA in seven games.

Al Oliver

Al Oliver wore number 29 in his first two major league seasons.

Pedro Ramos

Known for his penchant for losing games, Ramos once led the American League over four consecutive seasons in losses, topping out at 20 in 1961 with the Twins. He came to the Bucs late in his career, in 1969, when he, of course, lost his only decision.

Milt May

Coming up with the Pirates for his first four big league seasons, Milt May made his presence known as a rookie in 1971 during game four of the World Series before a national TV audience. The contest was the first night game in Series history as May pinch-hit for Bruce Kison in the seventh inning and singled in the game-winning run, plating Bob Robertson for the 4–3 victory.

Jim Minshall

Jim Minshall's career was just a blip on the screen, lasting only six games for the Pirates in 1974 and '75, but what a six-game career it was. He allowed only one hit and no runs in those contests, setting a record for most games pitched without allowing a run for a career. The boys at Elias had to work hard figuring out that one.

Ken Macha

A hometown boy from nearby Monroeville, as well as the University of Pittsburgh, Ken Macha proved to be a better manager than player, winning two division titles with the Oakland A's.

Jim Fregosi

Like Ken Macha, Jim Fregosi was a fine manager in the majors, winning two division titles and the 1993 NL pennant with the Phillies. But Fregosi was unlike Macha in one respect: he was also a damn good player for eighteen seasons. Fregosi's last two came with the Bucs in 1977 and '78, when he hit .263 in 76 at bats.

Onix Concepcion

After six decent seasons with the Kansas City Royals, Onix Concepcion went to the Pittsburgh Pirates in 1987 and became a record-setting hitter. He has the franchise's all-time career best batting average, singling in his only at bat for a perfect 1.000 average.

Felix Fermin

A slick fielding shortstop with the Indians in the 1990's, Felix "the cat" Fermin began his career with the Pirates in 1987 and would be important to the franchise as the bait that helped them lure Jay Bell away from Cleveland. Later on in his career, he would again be bait, being dealt to Seattle for a shortstop who became one of their all-time greats, Omar Vizquel.

Billy Hatcher

In 1989 the Pirates acquired speedster Billy Hatcher, to see if he could ignite their offense. He failed to, hitting only .244. Hatcher was dealt to the Reds shortly before the 1990 campaign, where he not only came back to haunt the Bucs in the NLCS, with a .333 average against them, but was spectacular in Cincinnati's upset sweep of the A's in the World Series, where he had a record .750 average.

David Ross

The ultimate great defensive, no-hit catcher who had a .229 career average, including .222 for the Bucs in 2005, David Ross became a spokesperson for Pittsburgh's own UPMC Health, as he went to their facilities to recover from concussions suffered throughout his career.

Octavio Dotel

For fifteen seasons Octavio Dotel was an excellent reliever, garnering 59 wins and 109 saves. But one e of his best seasons was *not* with the Pirates in 2010 when, despite the fact he had 21 saves, he had a 4.28 ERA.

Kevin Correia

It was a love-hate relationship between the Pirates Nation and Kevin Correia. A starter on their final two awful teams in 2011 and '12, Correia was either great or bad, with a 24–22 record on losing teams, but a less-than-stellar 4.49 ERA.

Francisco Cervelli

The New York Yankees have a habit of giving up on catchers too soon, and the Pittsburgh Pirates have a habit of taking advantage of that fact. First it was Russell Martin, then Chris Stewart. Their third catching project was the oft-injured Francisco Cervelli, the Venezuelan-born Italian who never could stay healthy long enough with New York to show them exactly what he was: a fabulous catcher. In Pittsburgh he did stay healthy, not only keeping his average around .300 all season, but also showing the fans in Pittsburgh just how important framing pitches can be. Perhaps, finally, the Yankees will figure out a way to understand their catchers aren't that bad.....then again, the Pirates Nation probably hopes they don't.

#30: EEPHUS

NUMBER RETIRED: None

HALL OF FAMERS TO WEAR THE NUMBER: None

FIRST PERFORMANCE WITH THE NUMBER

6/30/1932- Catcher Earl Grace was three for five with two RBIs in the Pirates' 9–6 victory against the St. Louis Cardinals.

FIRST HOME RUN WITH THE NUMBER

7/2/1932- Two days after debuting the number 30, Earl Grace cracked the digit's first home run, his fifth of the season, in a 5–4 loss to the Cards.

FIRST VICTORY BY A PITCHER WITH THE NUMBER

6/6/1940- After starter Bob Klinger blew up against the Boston Braves, allowing four runs and five hits in an inning of work, Rip Sewell came on in relief and tossed the remaining eight innings, surrendering only two more runs on ten hits. After being down 5–0, Pittsburgh scored one in the second and six more in the third inning to hang on for a 7–6 victory, with Sewell getting his first win of the year.

BEST PIRATES TO WEAR THE NUMBER: (HR-RBI-AVE) (W-L-ERA)

Rip Sewell (143–97-3.43)

Don Cardwell (photo courtesy of the Pittsburgh Pirates)

Rip Sewell was coming off his best season with the Bucs in 1940, going 16–5, when he went hunting in Florida and accidentally shot his foot; disaster would turn out to be the birth of Sewell's memorable career. He first re-learned to walk, then would have to teach himself balance off the mound. In the process he developed a blooper pitch with a softball-like arc that was named the "Eephus." It became his calling card; he not only learned to pitch again, but became one of the game's greats during the war years, winning 21 games on two occasions. After never allowing a home run with the pitch, it all came to an end when he tossed one to Ted Williams in the 1946 All-Star Game; that ended the streak with an exclamation point!

Jason Thompson (93–354-.259)

A great slugger with the Detroit Tigers in the 1970s, Jason Thompson was picked up by the Bucs in 1981 for Ed Ott and the below-mentioned Mickey Mahler from the Angels in 1981. He ended up being a pretty good power hitter for the Pirates, too, hitting 93 homers in five seasons that included a monster 1982 campaign in which Thompson belted 31 home runs and 101 RBIs.

Vinegar Bend Mizell (21–16-3.94)

After winning 69 games with the St. Louis Cardinals over seven seasons, Vinegar Bend Mizell was the key pick-up by general manager Joe L. Brown for the Pirates' 1960 championship run. Mizell solidified Pittsburgh's starting rotation with a 13–5 mark that season before getting ripped apart in game three of the World Series, allowing four runs in one-third of an inning. After he retired following his time with the expansion 1962 Mets, Mizell was elected to the U.S. House of Representatives in 1968, and served in both the Reagan and George H.W. Bush administrations.

WORST PIRATES TO WEAR THE NUMBER: (W-L-ERA)

Frank Papish (0–0-27.00)

Nicknamed "Pap," Frank Papish was a decent pitcher with the White Sox in the mid-1940s before ending his time in the majors with the Bucs in 1950. While he tossed only 2 1/3 innings for the team, they were incredibly bad innings, with eight hits and seven runs allowed, for a "sparkling" 5.143 WHIP.

Con Dempsey (0–2-9.00)

His career lasted only three games in 1950; side-arm hurler Con Dempsey couldn't get past the fourth inning in his two starts, giving up seven runs in seven innings.

Mickey Mahler (0–0-63.00)

A career record of 14–32 in eight major league seasons would be enough to put Mickey Mahler on most "worst" lists, but four hits, three walks, and seven runs in one inning of work for the Bucs that included a three-run homer to future enemy of the Pirates Nation George Hendrick in 1980 gets him on this one.

OTHER NOTABLE PIRATES TO WEAR THE NUMBER

Earl Grace

Earl Grace was a solid hitting catcher for the Bucs, hitting .275 over five seasons with the team between 1931 and '35 before being traded to the Phillies for the next number 30, Al Todd.

Al Todd

Replacing Earl Grace as the resident 30 on the team was catcher Al Todd. He was a step up defensively. With a .307 average in 1937, Todd had a .284 average in his three seasons in a Pirates uniform. 1937 also saw Todd knock in 86 RBIs, which makes him the answer to the question, "Which catcher had the most RBIs in a single season for the Bucs?"

Johnny O'Brien, Nellie King

College basketball star Johnny O'Brien wore uniform number 30 during his rookie season in 1953. Broadcasting icon Nellie King donned it his first two major league seasons.

Dave Cash

The heir apparent to Bill Mazeroski at second base, Dave Cash looked to be the answer, hitting .285 between 1969 and '73. Unfortunately for the Bucs, he was dealt to the Phillies for Ken Brett. It was in Philadelphia that Cash really took off, becoming a three-time All-Star with a .296 average before signing a free-agent contract with the Expos in 1977. Currently, he holds the all-time record for plate appearances in a single year by a right-handed hitter with 766, which he set in 1975.

Ken Brett

The brother of the great George Brett, Ken spent two of his fourteen major league seasons in Pittsburgh, where he was 22–14. Like Rick Rhoden, Brett was one of the era's greatest hitting pitchers, with ten lifetime home runs and a .262 average. His hitting prowess included a .310 campaign with four homers and 15 RBIs for the Bucs in 1974.

Rick Langford

Losing his only decision for the Pirates during his first season in the big leagues, Rick Langford was dealt to the A's as part of the Phil Garner deal. He won 73 games for the A's over ten seasons, including 19 in 1980, when he led the AL in innings pitched with 290. He also held the major league record, while with Oakland, of 230 consecutive games for a pitcher without an error.

Benny Distefano

A good power-hitting prospect for the Bucs in the 1980s, much was expected of Benny Distefano in the show, especially after he hit .345 in 29 at bats in 1988. That stat shows just how deceiving 29 at bats can be, as he never could reach that lofty potential, finishing with a .228 average in the big leagues and a lowly seven homers.

Midre Cummings

The major piece of the John Smiley trade to the Twins in 1992, Midre Cummings was supposed to make Pirates fans forget about Barry Bonds. Instead, he barely made them forget Doug Frobel, managing only a .217 average over five seasons. While he went on to play in the majors for eleven years by becoming a serviceable reserve, in Pittsburgh his disappointing play keeps Barry Bonds's legacy alive.

Warren Morris

Warren Morris was a College World Series icon, where his two-run homer in the bottom of the ninth with two outs for LSU won the 1996 National Championship. He enjoyed a fabulous rookie season in Pittsburgh, hitting .288 with 15 homers for the Bucs in 1999, and finishing third in the Rookie of the Year voting. He never came close to that performance again, and was out of the majors after the 2003 campaign.

J.R. House

One in a long line of projected future stars who turned out to be major disappointments for the Pirates in the mid-1990s to mid-2000s, J.R. House looked to be a stud catcher for the team. Unfortunately, he never panned out, hitting only .167 in five abbreviated major league seasons. A high school football star in West Virginia, House decided to attend WVU in 2005 when his baseball career seemed dead. He didn't live up to his football potential, either, never making it above a third-team quarterback for the Mountaineers.

Jeanmar Gomez

Suffering in his first three major league seasons with the Cleveland Indians, Jeanmar Gomez became an effective middle reliever and spot starter for the Pirates during the first two years of their resurgence in 2013 and '14. He was 5–2 with a 3.28 ERA in 78 appearances with the Bucs over that period, before signing with the Phillies.

#31: A CASE OF TRAGIC PERFECTION

NUMBER RETIRED: None

HALL OF FAMERS TO WEAR THE NUMBER: None

FIRST PERFORMANCE WITH THE NUMBER

7/4/1932- In the second game of a July 4 doubleheader against the Cubs, Chicago and Pittsburgh were tied at five heading into the bottom of the eleventh. Pinch-hitting with one out, catcher Tom Padden singled. He would eventually score the winning run on an infield single by Arky Vaughan.

FIRST HOME RUN WITH THE NUMBER

8/26/1935- During a 10–2 victory over the New York Giants, catcher Tom Padden hit his first major league home run in his fourth season as a Pirate, while going two for four on the afternoon.

FIRST VICTORY BY A PITCHER WITH THE NUMBER

5/1/1941- In his last year in a Pirates uniform, hurler Russ Bauers won one ball game, a 15–2 complete-game victory over the Phillies; he allowed five hits and two walks, striking out three.

BEST PIRATES TO WEAR THE NUMBER: (W-L-ERA)
Dave Giusti (47–28-2.94)

The Pirates and Braves both are on the field after Harvey Haddix lost his perfect game in the 13th inning, 1-0. (Photo courtesy of the Pittsburgh Pirates)

Having been a decent starter with the Houston Astros, Dave Giusti was picked up by Joe L. Brown from the St. Louis Cardinals after the 1969 campaign. Danny Murtaugh decided his starting days were over, inserting him instead as a closer . . . and what a closer he was. Developing a palmball, Giusti led the National League in saves in 1971, capturing the circuit's Fireman of the Year Award. He went on to save 133 games, and must be included in any conversation of greatest relievers in franchise history.

Harvey Haddix (45–38-3.73)

Harvey Haddix was a runner-up for Rookie of the Year Award in 1953 with St. Louis, where he was a 20-game winner, a three-time All-Star, and part of arguably the greatest trade in Pirates history, coming along with Smoky Burgess and Don Hoak from the Reds in 1959. While it had been a fine career for Harvey Haddix to that point, no one could have guessed that, on May 26, 1959, he would not only pitch the greatest game ever hurled, but be part of one of the great heartbreaks that evening. After tossing 12 perfect innings against the Milwaukee Braves, he lost not only the perfect game, and then the no-hitter, in the 13th inning, but the game itself, 1–0. It was a case of tragic perfection. Haddix went on to win 45 games over five years for the Bucs, plus two in the 1960 World Series, including game seven, when he was on the mound in the ninth inning. In the history of the game, though, there would be no more important achievement than his 1959 ruptured masterpiece.

Ray Miller

The Pittsburgh Pirates had one of the game's greatest pitching coaches at the time in Ray Miller. The man who once managed the Twins and Orioles did wonders with what was often a mediocre pitching staff, and played a pivotal role on the team's three eastern division championship clubs between 1990 and '92.

WORST PIRATES TO WEAR THE NUMBER: (HR-RBI-AVE) (W-L-ERA)

Roy Jarvis (1–4-.160)

After returning from the Navy in World War II, Roy Jarvis spent two seasons with the Bucs in 1946 and '47. The catcher did not make a great impression, hitting .160 in 49 at bats to end his major league career.

Roger Bowman (0–7-5.60)

Winning 131 minor league games, pitcher Roger Bowman fell 131 short of matching that in the Steel City, losing all seven decisions in 1953 and '55.

Chase Sanford (0–3-.143)

Other than the fact that he and Chase d'Arnaud were two Chases who each tripled for his first big league hit, Chase Sanford had a brief unexciting career with the Bucs.

OTHER NOTABLE PIRATES TO WEAR THE NUMBER

Tom Padden

In six seasons with the team the Pirates' first number 31, Tom Padden, never had more than 302 at bats, but he was a good hitter with a .272 career average that included a .321 mark in 1934. His Bucs career ended in 1937; six years later he re-emerged with the Phillies and Senators for one last campaign, in 1943.

George Susce

A Pittsburgh native who spent eight years in the majors, where he was a seldom-used catcher, George Susce played with his hometown team in 1939, hitting .227. He is touted as having the most at bats among St Bonaventure alum. Considering the fact that he only had 268, it speaks volumes about baseball at St Bonaventure. After he retired, he became a long-time major and minor league coach.

Vic Janowicz

While the Pirates had a runner-up for the Heisman Trophy in Paul Giel they would do one better when they grabbed 1950 Heisman Trophy winner Vic Janowicz. Like Giel, he wasn't much of a baseball player, averaging .214 for 1953 and '54. Janowicz eventually went back to the game at which he was more successful, playing for the Washington Redskins. His sports career ended in 1956, when he was involved in a serious car accident.

Lino Donoso

Playing for the New York Cubans in the Negro National League in 1947, Cuban pitcher Lino Donoso made it to the majors in 1955 at the age of thirty-two and compiled a record of 4–6 over two seasons.

Al Holland and Ed Whitson

Al Holland and Ed Whitson were good young prospects with the Pirates in the mid-1970s. Both were sent to San Francisco for Bill Madlock in 1979, who helped the Bucs win a world championship. The two hurlers went on to become effective pitchers, with Holland saving 78 games in ten seasons with a 2.98 ERA, and Whitson winning 126 games over fifteen years.

Yamid Haad

Hitless in his only at bat as a Pittsburgh Pirate, Yamid Haad has the distinction of being the first member of the Altoona Curve to be promoted to the majors.

Omar Olivares

After eleven major league seasons, pitcher Omar Olivares played his final year with the Bucs in 2001, intending to help patch up a severely injured pitching staff. He went 6–9 with a 6.55 ERA . . . not an effective patch.

Daryle Ward

The first player to hit a ball into the river on the fly at PNC Park, Daryle Ward unfortunately accomplished the feat as a member of the Houston Astros in 2002. He came to Pittsburgh two years later and hit 27 home runs in two seasons. Ward is also the last Pirate to date who hit for the cycle, which he did on May 26, 2004, against the Cards.

Jose Tabata

Every so often Jose Tabata flashed his potential, hitting .299 in his rookie season of 2010. Pirates management thought enough of him to ink Tabata to a six-year $14.5 million contract; in retrospect, his off-field antics proved to be more newsworthy than anything he'd done on the field. In 2009 he married a forty-three-year-old woman who told him she was pregnant, then proceeded to kidnap a child. After his rookie season his attitude came into question, and he was often put on waivers with no takers. Eventually, the long and interesting tenure of Jose Tabata in Pittsburgh came to an end when he became the Dodgers' problem in a trade for Mike Morse.

#32: THE DEACON

ALL TIME NO. 32 ROSTER	YEAR
J.A. Happ	(2015)
Vin Mazzaro	(2013–2014)
Chad Qualls	(2012)
Brad Lincoln	(2010–2012)
Phil Dumatrait	(2008–2009)
Shawn Chacon	(2006–2007)
Kip Wells	(2002–2005)
Francisco Cordova	(2001)
Dan Miceli	(1993–1996)
Denny Neagle	(1992–1993)
Timothy Jones	(1977)
Doc Medich	(1976)
Ed Ott	(1975–1976)
Daryl Patterson	(1974)
Jim Sadowski	(1974)
Kent Tekulve	(1974)
Chris Zachary	(1973)
John Morlan	(1973)
Tom Dettore	(1973)
Bob Miller	(1971–1972)
Jim Nelson	(1971)
Vern Law	(1954–1967)
Roger Bowman	(1953)
Cal Hogue	(1953)
Hal Gregg	(1948)
Roger Wolfe	(1947)
Jim Russell	(1942–1946)
Ken Heintzelman	(1940–1942)
Ray Berres	(1938–1939)
Bill Schuster	(1937)
Hal Finney	(1932–1934, 1936)
MANAGER	
Gene Lamont	(1997–2000)
COACHES	
Bill Posedel	(1949–1950)
Joe Lonnett	(1979–1984)
Steve Demeter	(1985)
Gene Lamont	(1986–1991)

NUMBER RETIRED: None

HALL OF FAMERS TO WEAR THE NUMBER: None

FIRST PERFORMANCE WITH THE NUMBER

7/1/1932- Catcher Hal Finney debuted the number 32 in style, with no plate appearances, as he was a late defensive substitute for Earl Grace in a 5–3 loss to the Cardinals.

FIRST HOME RUN WITH THE NUMBER

8/26/1933- With the score tied in the sixth inning against the New York Giants, Hal Finney was called on to pinch-hit for starting pitcher Ralph Birkofer. He responded with his only major league home run, a three-run shot giving the Bucs the lead on their way to a 7–2 win.

FIRST VICTORY BY A PITCHER WITH THE NUMBER 6/8/1940-

Replacing ineffective starter Max Butcher in the second inning, Ken Heintzelman pitched six solid innings, allowing seven hits and two earned runs while striking out five. It was good enough to propel the Pirates to a 6–5 win against the Phillies as he captured his first victory of the season.

Vern Law (photo courtesy of the
Pittsburgh Pirates)

BEST PIRATES TO WEAR THE NUMBER: (HR-RBI-AVE) (W-L-ERA)

Vern Law (162–147-3.77)

One of the greatest pitchers ever to lace up his spikes for the Pittsburgh Pirates, Vern Law dazzled National League opponents for sixteen seasons in a Pirates uniform, but it was one special campaign that has made him a Pittsburgh icon. Missing two years while in the Armed Forces during the Korean War, Law, who was nicknamed the Deacon due to his position in the Mormon Church, came into his own in 1959 with 18 victories before winning 20 games one year later, plus two in the 1960 World Series. For his efforts he became the first Bucco to win the Cy Young Award. Injuries would plague him over the next couple of seasons, but he rebounded for 17 wins with a 2.15 ERA in 1965, and was awarded the Comeback Player of the Year Award.

Law retired two years later, but when looking back on that memorable 1960 campaign he always said with a smile that if Danny Murtaugh hadn't taken him out of game seven in the 1960 World Series (the Pirates were winning 4–2 at the time in the sixth) they would have won easily, and Bill Mazeroski wouldn't have had the chance to be a hero in the ninth.

Jim Russell (40–288-.277)

A fine outfielder with the Pirates during the World War II era, Jim Russell, who had the honor of playing for the nearby Beaver Falls Browns in the minors, had his best year in 1944 when he hit .312 for the Bucs. He had a couple of "firsts" in his career that made him memorable: the first Pittsburgh player to hit a pinch-hit grand slam, and the first player in the history of the game to hit a home run in one contest from both sides of the plate, which he did with the Braves in 1948 (he repeated the feat two years later while playing for Brooklyn).

J.A. Happ (7–2-1.85)

The Pirates Nation wanted the likes of David Price at the trading deadline in 2015; instead, they got a hurler named J.A. Happ. A nine-year veteran who pitched well for the Phils in 2009 with a record of 12–4, he was only 43–55 the rest of his time in the majors before coming to Pittsburgh. After allowing four runs on nine hits in 4 1/3 innings in his Bucs debut, Happ missed a turn in the rotation. When he returned, the results were spectacular. He ended the season 7–2 with a 1.85 ERA, and turned out to be arguably the best pitching pickup of 2015. Kudos to you, Neil Huntington, for not listening to the Pirates Nation.

WORST PIRATES TO WEAR THE NUMBER: (W-L-ERA) (HR-RBI-AVE)
Hal Finney (1–27-.203)

Hal Finney had languished as a little-used back-up catcher throughout his four-year Pirates career between 1931 and '34. When he returned to the Bucs in 1936, he set a major league record that lasted for seventy-five years: most at bats in a season without a hit, 35.

Roger Wolfe (1–4-8.70)

A former 20-game winner, having fashioned a 20–10 record with the Washington Senators in 1945, Roger Wolfe ended his major league career in 1947 when the seven-year vet had his worst big league season.

Daryl Patterson (2–1-7.29)

A member of the 1968 world champion Detroit Tigers, Daryl Patterson came to the Pirates in 1974 after four seasons out of the majors. He pitched poorly, with a 2.095 WHIP in 26 2/3 innings of work. It would be his last major league season.

OTHER NOTABLE PIRATES TO WEAR THE NUMBER
Bill Schuster

A member of the Pacific Coast League Hall of Fame, Bill Schuster had a brief stay in Pittsburgh, going three for six in 1937. While poor, it also was an experience he would remember for a lifetime, because he had the opportunity to room with Bucco great Honus Wagner, a coach with the team at the time, during that abbreviated tenure.

Ken Heintzelman

World War II vet Ken Heintzelman found himself on the losing side of more games than he won in his thirteen-year major league career, but after winning 37 games in eight seasons in Pittsburgh he went to Philadelphia, where he enjoyed a career campaign in 1949, going 17–9 and finishing ninth in the MVP race.

Hal Gregg

An 18-game winner during the final war season in 1945 while pitching with the Dodgers, Hal Gregg was also known for his seven spectacular innings of relief in game four of the 1947 World Series, the game in which the Yankees' Bill Bevens had his no-hitter broken up in the ninth. Gregg came to Pittsburgh in 1948 and became a little-used reliever for three seasons.

Bob Miller

Thirty-two-year-old reliever Bob Miller was a mid-season pickup for the Bucs during their world championship run in 1971. He was lights out down the stretch, with a 1.29 ERA in 16 games. Miller was effective again for Pittsburgh in 1972, going 5–2, and his ERA was still spectacular at 2.65. He returned to San Diego in 1973, where he ended his seventeen-year major league career. Miller's career was not only long, it was also a well-traveled one: the hurler played for ten teams over that time period.

Tom Dettore

Tom Dettore had a brief four-year career in the show, including his rookie year with the Bucs, when he was 0–1 with a 5.96 ERA. Two years later he played a role in major league history with the Cubs when he pitched 3 2/3 innings of relief, allowing seven earned runs in a 22–0 defeat of Chicago. That day he also allowed two of Rennie Stennett's record-setting seven hits, a single in the third and a double in the fifth.

Kent Tekulve and Ed Ott

Kent Tekulve wore the number 32 during his rookie campaign. Ed Ott wore it in his second and third seasons in Pittsburgh, in 1975 and '76.

Jim Sadowski

A born and bred Pittsburgher who was the area's Athlete of the Year while with Pittsburgh Central in 1969, Jim Sadowski lost his only major league decision, allowing a three-run bottom-of-the-12th inning home run to the Astros' Doug Radar on August 8, 1974. The long ball turned a 6–5 Bucs lead into an 8–6 loss.

Doc Medich

Doc Medich was a University of Pittsburgh grad, from which he received his medical degree. Before that he was a star with the New York Yankees, winning 49 games in three seasons, after which he returned to his hometown in 1976. The Aliquippa native did not have a celebrated return to Pittsburgh, racking up only an 8–11 mark. Medich was not worth the price they paid for him, giving up Willie Randolph, Dock Ellis, and Ken Brett. Medich went on to be traded to the A's, and would win a total of 124 games in his eleven-year career. After retirement his life spiraled out of control; he was charged with writing bad prescriptions and suffered from substance abuse.

Dan Miceli

Playing the first four seasons of his fourteen-year major league career with Pittsburgh, Dan Miceli was a microcosm of relievers with the Bucs during their twenty-year hiatus from winning baseball. He showed signs of success, but was never quite consistent enough to maintain it, He registered 8–15 in those seasons with a 5.41 ERA. Miceli was the closer in 1995 when he saved 21 games, although a 4.66 ERA and 1.534 WHIP shows he wasn't one of the best.

Kip Wells

Part of the Todd Richie trade to the White Sox late in 2001, Kip Wells was a former first-round pick who proved to be one of, if not *the* best, hurler in the Bucs rotation in 2002 and '03, putting together a combined 22–23 record with a 3.43 ERA. It all went to hell after that; he lost 18 games in 2005, and had surgery to remove a blood clot from his arm a year later, which cost him most of the year. Despite the surgery, Texas traded for Wells in 2006. He played until 2012, when he ended his career in the majors with 103 losses and a .401 winning percentage.

Brad Lincoln

The first pick in the 2006 amateur draft by the Pittsburgh Pirates, Brad Lincoln always appeared to have star potential, but it wasn't until 2012 when he actually began to become at least a contributing major league player. One of the team's best relievers, with a 2.73 ERA in 59 1/3 innings in a year when it looked like they might finally break their string of losing seasons, Lincoln was instead traded in mid-season to the Blue Jays for Travis Snider. The team collapsed, and so did their middle relief after he left. Lincoln has not been effective since; he spent the 2015 campaign with the Bucs' AAA affiliate in Indianapolis.

Vin Mazzaro

Like Brad Lincoln, Vin Mazzaro was a top prospect who struggled in the majors until he became a reliever with the Pirates. After four subpar seasons with the Royals and A's, Mazzaro came to Pittsburgh and was one of their better relievers in the magical 2013 campaign, with an 8–2 record and 2.81 ERA. He also tossed a perfect five innings of relief against Milwaukee on June 30, the most perfect innings by a Pirates reliever in ninety-four years. He was also similar to Lincoln in the fact that his success was a one-year phenomenon; he spent most of 2014 in the minors, and currently is in the Atlanta Braves organization.

Gene Lamont

Gene Lamont had the unfortunate task of replacing Jim Leyland as manager in 1997, and was probably the best manager the Bucs had in their twenty-year losing odyssey. He will always be remembered by the Pirates faithful for leading a group of young players in the Freak Show season of 1997, a club that many thought would challenge the 1962 New York Mets and their 120 losses for the title of being the worst team in major league history. Instead, they surprisingly challenged for the central division title until late in September, when their magic ran out.

#33: HONUS

NUMBER RETIRED: HONUS WAGNER (1952)

HALL OF FAMERS TO WEAR THE NUMBER: HONUS WAGNER (1936)

FIRST PERFORMANCE WITH THE NUMBER: None

FIRST HOME RUN WITH THE NUMBER: None

FIRST VICTORY BY A PITCHER WITH THE NUMBER: None

BEST PIRATES TO WEAR THE NUMBER

Honus Wagner (1933–1951)

Honus Wagner was the unquestioned greatest Pirate of all time; unfortunately, he did not wear a number when he achieved that distinction.

Honus Wagner (photo courtesy of the Pittsburgh Pirates)

Long after he retired, Pirates President Barney Dreyfuss heard that the Bucs legend had been hit hard by the Depression and hired him as a coach for the team in 1933. He was not a tactical magician nor much else as a coach, but he was very colorful and the fans and players alike loved him. He wore the number 33 for the first time in 1940, and kept it on until 1949. In 1951 he left the organization and, appropriately, the next year had his number as a coach retired, the first Pirate to be so honored.

WORST PIRATES TO WEAR THE NUMBER: None to speak of!!

OTHER NOTABLE PIRATES TO WEAR THE NUMBER

Jewel Ens (1935–1939)

Jewel Ens was a manager with the Bucs from 1929 to 1931, with a winning percentage of .517. He came back as a coach for the team in the latter half of the 1930s, when he was the last man before Honus to wear the number.

Jewel Ens (photo courtesy of the Pittsburgh Pirates)

George Gibson

George Gibson, a former great catcher with the franchise, was in his second tenure as manager of the team in 1932 after being replaced ten years earlier by Hall of Famer Bill McKechnie. He could have been the best, winning 56 percent of his games in two-plus seasons and finishing second twice before being replaced by Pie Traynor in 1934, but it would be inconceivable to name him as the best over Honus Wagner, so, unfortunately, he had nowhere else to go.

#34: BATMAN

NUMBER RETIRED: None

HALL OF FAMERS TO WEAR THE NUMBER: PIE TRAYNOR (1948)

FIRST PERFORMANCE WITH THE NUMBER

9/14/1946- Rookie Junior Walsh entered the game in the seventh inning of his first major league contest, a 9–3 thrashing at the hands of the Boston Braves. He threw two innings, giving up three hits, a run, and a walk.

FIRST HOME RUN WITH THE NUMBER

6/5/1955- Pitcher Bob Purkey hit the first home run by a number 34, smacking a third-inning blast to give the Bucs a 1–0 lead. It would be the only run for Pittsburgh, as they lost to the Reds that day, 5–1.

FIRST VICTORY BY A PITCHER WITH THE NUMBER

4/25/1948- It wasn't a thing of beauty, but Junior Walsh got his first major league victory, pitching four innings of relief while allowing three runs on three hits and an equal number of walks in a 13–10 win over the Reds.

BEST PIRATES TO WEAR THE NUMBER: (W-L-ERA)

Al McBean (65–43-3.08)

He was Frenchy Fuqua in baseball cleats, flashy on the diamond with his unhittable sinker, and flashy off it with his fashionable wardrobe. More important than his fashion sense, Al McBean helped give the Bucs an awesome bullpen in the 1960s. After a brief spell as a start-er in 1962, when he was 15–10, the first major league pitcher ever to come from the Virgin Islands be-came a lights out reliever, saving 51 games between 1963 and '65. The final season of that period he was named *The Sporting News* Fireman of the Year, one of only three Pirates to be so honored in the history of the franchise. It was a year when he saved 19 contests with a 2.29 ERA. After leaving the team in 1969, he returned for one last season in the show a year later, when he bowed out with a career-high 8.10 ERA.

Johnny Gooch (photo courtesy of the Pittsburgh Pirates)

A.J. Burnett (35–26-3.34)

His career appeared to be over when the Pittsburgh Pirates took him off the Yankees' hands before the 2012 season, but A.J. Burnett proved to be a steal, and one of the main reasons the Bucs ended their twenty-year streak of losing seasons. He spent two years with the club and was a great influence on a young pitching staff. Burnett went unsigned after the 2013 campaign and inked a deal with the Phillies, where once again he had a poor season, losing a National League high 18 games while pitching with a sports hernia. With the end of his career loom-ing, he decided to play one more season, coming back to the city that was made for him: Pittsburgh. He once again found a fountain of youth here and, despite the fact he had a mid-season arm injury, the man dubbed Batman was 9–7 with a 3.18 ERA. Whether or not he really does hang up his spikes, his contribution to making the Pirates Nation viable again will always be celebrated.

Nellie Briles (36–28-2.98)

A 19-game winner with the St. Louis Cardinals in 1968, who had led the NL in winning percentage a year earlier, Nellie Briles quietly came to the Pirates in 1971 as part of the Matty Alou trade. After splitting his time between the bullpen and starting rotation in their championship season of 1971, he stabilized the starting rotation over the next two years, winning 28 games in the process. While all the success above was nice, it was his performance in the World Series that makes Briles special. In 1967 he was almost unhittable in two games, but it was his two-hit shutout of the Orioles in game five of the 1971 Fall Classic that will etch his name in Pirates history forever. One of the saddest days for the Pirate Nation came in 2005, when he passed away on a golf course at a team alumni event. He may have been here only three seasons, but they were enough to leave a permanent mark on the city.

WORST PIRATES TO WEAR THE NUMBER: (W-L-ERA)

Chris Bootcheck (0–0-11.05)

After five less-than-stellar seasons with the Angels, Chris Bootcheck made his Pirates debut in 2009. Thirteen games later he sported an 11.05 ERA, which was not enough for him to continue his Pirates career, but certainly enough to land him the top spot as the all-time worst to wear number 34.

Ed Wolfe (0–0-7.36)

Ed Wolfe's major league career lasted all of three games in 1952, when he walked five and gave up seven hits in 3 2/3 innings. After refusing a demotion to the Mexican League in 1955, Wolfe retired from professional baseball.

Ross Baumgarten (0–5-6.55)

After a solid season with the White Sox in 1979, where he was 13–8, Ross Baumgartner followed it up with a 2–12 campaign; he'd never regain his effectiveness. Two years later, he ended his big league career when he came to Pittsburgh in 1982 and was winless in five decisions.

OTHER NOTABLE PIRATES TO WEAR THE NUMBER

Bob Purkey

A Steel City boy through and through, who attended South Hills High School, pitcher Bob Purkey played three years for the Bucs before he finally found his way with an 11–14 record in 1957. His reward was to be traded to the Cincinnati Reds for Don Gross; it was not Joe L Brown's finest moment. Purkey continued to improve with the Reds, going 103–76 in a Cincinnati uniform that included a career season in 1962, when he was 23–5 for a NL-high .821 winning percentage. A practitioner of the knuckleball, Purkey returned to his hometown in 1966, finishing his career with a 1.37 ERA in ten games for the Pirates.

Curt Raydon

It looked as though rookie Curt Raydon would have a wonderful career with the Pittsburgh Pirates when he ran up an 8–4 record and 3.62 ERA in 1958. Unfortunately, a cyst on his finger and a sore arm would render 1958 Raydon's lone season in the majors.

John Milner

After losing his luster with the Mets following two 20-plus home run seasons in 1973 and '74, John Milner was dealt to the Bucs before the 1978 campaign in a complicated four-team deal that saw Al Oliver leave the Steel City and Burt Blyleven also join the Bucs. While Milner wasn't spectacular for most of his time in a Pirates uniform, in 1979 he hit 16 homers as a part-time player. One of them was a memorable grand slam in the bottom of the ninth of a doubleheader against the Phillies that helped propel the Bucs to the eastern division crown.

Mike Bielecki

One of the best pitching prospects in the game during the early 1980s, Mike Bielecki could never capture that magic in a Pirates uniform, going 10–17 over four seasons. After moving on to the Cubs he eventually lived up to that potential, winning 18 games in 1989 and forging a fourteen-year major league career.

Rick Reed

Read the bio for Mike Bielecki above and you can copy it for Rick Reed. Not as prized a prospect, Reed was equally ineffective in his first four seasons with the Bucs, going 4–7. Later in his career he figured things out, winning 51 games for the Mets between 1997 and 2000, and then going 15–7 for the Twins in 2002.

Danny Jackson

A solid southpaw who finished as runner-up for the Cy Young Award in 1988 when he was 23–8 for the Cincinnati Reds, Danny Jackson was a mid-season pickup for the Bucs in 1992 to help stabilize their starting rotation for the stretch drive, on the way to their third consecutive eastern division crown. He was solid if unspectacular, going 4–4 with a 3.36 ERA in his only season in a Pirates uniform.

Alejandro Pena

After disappointing the Pirates Nation in 1991 and '92 as an opposing pitcher who stifled the Pittsburgh offense in two NLCS games, Alejandro Pena decided to join the Bucs in 1993. As luck would have it, the long-time reliever hurt his elbow and was out the entire season. He came back in 1994, but was unable to stifle other teams' offenses with a 5.02 ERA.

Esteban Loaiza

As was the case for most of the great losing era of Pirate baseball, when they had a great prospect pitcher whom they gave up on too early only to see him become successful with another franchise, Esteban Loaiza was just that kind of pitcher. He showed flashes of potential with the Bucs, where he was 27–28 in four seasons, but Loaiza was shipped off to Texas in 1998. He would eventually become a 20-game winner with the White Sox in 2003, with a 21–9 mark, finishing as runner-up in the Cy Young race and garnering his first All-Star Game appearance, all with another team, of course.

Kris Benson

Sportswriter Peter Gammons once said that the Pirates' 1996 first-round draft pick, Kris Benson, would win a Cy Young Award; it was the kiss of death, unfortunately. While Benson would show flashes of the talent that made him such a high pick, capturing 14 games his rookie season, most of the news he would eventually make usually had to do with his publicity-hungry wife.

Benito Santiago

Catcher Benito Santiago had enjoyed a fabulous nineteen-year major league career when he joined the Pittsburgh Pirates in 2005. The former Rookie of the Year and three-time Gold Glove Award winner was forty years old when he hit .261 in 23 at bats in what turned out to be his last season in the majors.

Roberto Hernandez

One of the game's greatest relievers, saving 326 games over his seventeen-year big league career, Roberto Hernandez was forty-one years of age when he hooked up with the Bucs in 2005. Although past his prime he still had a good 2.93 ERA in 43 innings; his 1.628 WHIP told another story. Halfway through his Pirates season he was dealt to the Mets, along with Oliver Perez, for Xavier Nady.

John Grabow

As John Grabow's Pirates career developed, he eventually became a very effective left-handed option out of the bullpen, where he was

20–15 with a 4.09 ERA over seven seasons. He was dealt to the Cubs in 2009, together with Tom Gorzelanny, in a trade that brought Josh Harrison to the Steel City. Grabow's development stalled out in Chicago, ending his time in the bigs following the 2011 season.

#35: A SMILE AND A BARBEQUE

NUMBER RETIRED: None

HALL OF FAMERS TO WEAR THE NUMBER: HONUS WAGNER (1936), PIE TRAYNOR (1948), FRANKIE FRISCH (1947)

FIRST PERFORMANCE WITH THE NUMBER

3/19/1934- Starting behind the plate in the third game of the year for the Pittsburgh Pirates, Pat Veltman had a single and an RBI in five at bats during a 14–4 victory over the Cardinals.

FIRST HOME RUN WITH THE NUMBER

4/21/1960- In an 11–5 victory over the Philadelphia Phillies, reliever Fred Green hit his first major league homer to lead off the bottom of the sixth for the Bucs, giving them their last run in the one-sided win.

FIRST VICTORY BY A PITCHER WITH THE NUMBER

4/30/1947- Coming over from the Yankees before the season, Tiny Bonham entered the game in the sixth inning in relief of Hugh Mulcahy and Elmer Singleton, with Pittsburgh ahead, 5–4. He pitched the final four innings magnificently, allowing

Manny Sanguillen crosses first base ahead of the throw. (Photo courtesy of the Pittsburgh Pirates)

only one hit while striking out two. The Bucs won the contest, 11–4, but since Mulcahy didn't go five innings he wasn't eligible for the victory and it was given to Bonham.

BEST PIRATES TO WEAR THE NUMBER: (HR-RBI-AVE) (W-L-ERA)

Manny Sanguillen (59–527-.299)

Go to behind centerfield at PNC Park and you will come across a barbeque restaurant with a smiling ex-Pirate by the name of Manny Sanguillen there to greet you. He will talk to you about the time when he was considered among the best catchers in the game, along with the legendary Johnny Bench. Arguably the greatest catcher in team history, Sangy hit over .300 four times for the Bucs, and in his day had a cannon for an arm. He had an electric personality to boot, one that still comes across at his barbeque pit, which every patron who enters PNC Park should make it a priority to experience.

Mark Melancon (9–8-1.75)

There was an angry roar in the Pirates Nation when successful closer Joel Hanrahan and minor league star Brock Holt were dealt to the Red Sox for Ivan DeJesus, Jerry Sands, Stolmy Pimentel, and a struggling reliever by the name of Mark Melancon. Injuries have most likely ended Hanarahan's career, while Melancon has been one of the greatest relievers in Pittsburgh's history, saving 100 contests over three seasons, including a team record 51 in 2015, the ninth highest total in major league history. The Pirates Nation no longer roars in anger, but in support of one of the best closers in the game.

Jim Gott (8–10-3.59)

Coming from the Giants midway in the 1987 campaign, reliever Jim Gott's enthusiastic demeanor was a sparkplug for the franchise's spectacular finish that year. The following season, his 34 saves helped them continue the turnaround. An elbow injury cost Gott almost all of the 1989 campaign before he moved to the Dodgers. He finished his career with a return to the Bucs in 1995, going 2–4 with a 6.03 ERA. Even though his Steel City career ended poorly, Gott's effect on this team in the late 1980s was a big reason for their eventual success in the 1990s.

WORST PIRATES TO WEAR THE NUMBER: (W-L-ERA) (HR-RBI-AVE)

Pat Veltman (0–2-.107)

For the first five seasons catcher Pat Veltman played in the majors he batted only ten times. When he came to the Bucs in 1934 he was given a whopping 28 at bats. The fact that he only had three singles in those 28 at bats explains why he never got any more. Well, at least he had the same name as the doctor in *Ghostbusters.* No, that was Dr. Venkman, so never mind.

Matt Morris (3–8-7.04)

Matt Morris, along with Daniel Moskos, were the fathers of the current successful Pirate franchise. Had it not been for David Littlefield inexplicably trading for a pitcher who appeared to be finished — and assuming the $10 million-plus he was owed the next season, making him the highest-paid Pirate — he might not have been let go, and Neal Huntington might not have been hired, so thank you Matt Morris for your contribution to our current success.

Woody Main (4–13-5.14)

After bravely serving for three years in the Marines during World War II, pitcher Woody Main played parts of four seasons with the Pirates, amassing a.235 winning percentage.

OTHER NOTABLE PIRATES TO WEAR THE NUMBER

Tiny Bonham

A star pitcher with the Yankees during the World War II era, when he was 21–5 in 1942, Tiny Bonham — and, yes, he was nicknamed "Tiny" sarcastically as he was 6'2", 215 lbs — pitched his final three major league seasons in Pittsburgh between 1947 and '49, compiling a 24–22 record. Bonham's career didn't end because he was pitching poorly; it ended when he tragically died late in the 1949 campaign from com-

Tiny Bonham (photo courtesy of the Pittsburgh Pirates)

plications following an emergency appendectomy.

Honus Wagner, Pie Traynor, and Frankie Frisch

Three Hall of Famers donned the number 35, with Honus Wagner wearing it in 1938 when he was a coach, Pie Traynor in his last seasons as Pirates manager, and his replacement, Frankie Frisch, who was a Hall of Fame second and third baseman with the Giants and Cardinals before managing the Bucs for seven seasons, the majority of that time during the war years.

Max Surkont

After having a Max Surkont Day celebrated in Milwaukee, where he was 11–5 with the Braves in 1953, he was part of a six-player haul by the Bucs for Danny O'Connell a year later. Surkont lost 18 games that season and was 16–32 in three seasons with the team. Needless to say, there was no Max Surkont Day in Pittsburgh.

Fred Green

Fred Green pitched in 83 games for the Pirates over four seasons., More than half of them — 45 to be exact — came in their world championship campaign in 1960, when Green was an outstanding reliever. Sporting an 8–4 mark with a fine 3.21 ERA, his effective play came to an end in the World Series against the Yankees, when he gave up ten runs in four innings of work.

Wilbur Wood

After his first five seasons with the Red Sox and Pirates, including 1–3 for the Bucs over two seasons, Wilbur Wood was dealt to the White Sox in a trade for Juan Pizarro. It was a bad deal by Joe L Brown, as Wood went on to win 20 games four times with Chicago. Wood, who was a knuckleball aficionado, also had the distinction of winning and losing 20 games in a single season with a 24–20 mark in 1973 for the Sox.

Gary Alexander

Gary Alexander had one tremendous season, hitting .304 with 27 home runs and 84 RBIs for the Oakland A's and Cleveland Indians in 1978. He never came close to that output again, finishing his major league career with the Bucs in 1981, when he had a .213 average in 47 at bats.

Walt Terrell

A grizzled veteran right hander who won 79 games with the Tigers through seven seasons, Walt Terrell was signed in 1990 by the Bucs, who hoped he'd be a great addition to their starting rotation. He went only 2–7 with a 5.88 ERA before being released.

Dave Clark

Dave Clark proved to be a great bench option for the Pirates between 1992 and '96, when he hit .278. He has since become a long-time major league coach, spending some time with the Bucs.

Marc Wilkins

A solid middle-relief option out of the bullpen in the late 1990s and early 2000s, right-hander Marc Wilkins was 19–14 over six seasons with three saves.

Randall Simon

Picked up by the Bucs from the Tigers before the 2003 campaign, first baseman Randall Simon was known for an incident in which he playfully hit the Milwaukee Brewer Sausage mascot with a bat, which caused him to be arrested by Milwaukee police. The incident overshadowed his exploits on the diamond, which included 13 home runs in parts of two seasons.

Brad Eldred

A legendary minor league player who once had 50 RBIs over 27 games in the Bucs system, Eldred led the Pittsburgh Pirates to hope that he would be one of the best power hitters in the game. They even turned down an offer of Ryan Howard from the Phils for Kris Benson because of it. Eldred started out fine, with 12 homers in 190 at bats his rookie season, but hit only three more over the next three years. He eventually became a star in Japan, smacking 37 long balls for Hiroshima in 2014.

#36: LIKE FATHER, LIKE SON

ALL TIME NO. 26 ROSTER	YEAR
Edinson Volquez	(2014)
Phil Irwin	(2013)
Justin Morneau	(2013)
Yamaico Navarro	(2012)
Garrett Olson	(2011)
Ryan Ludwick	(2011)
Wil Ledezma	(2010)
Luis Cruz	(2009)
Jeff Karstens	(2008)
Juan Perez	(2006–2007)
Craig Wilson	(2001–2006)
Billy Taylor	(2001)
Javier Martinez	(1998)
Jason Johnson	(1997)
Mark Johnson	(1995–1997)
Kevin Young	(1992–1994)
Joe Redfield	(1991)
Jeff Richardson	(1991)
Dave Rucker	(1988)
Brian Fisher	(1987)
Marvell Wynne	(1983–1985)
Junior Ortiz	(1983)
Matt Alexander	(1979–1982)
Odell Jones	(1977–1978)
Ramon Hernandez	(1971–1976)
Dick Colpaert	(1970)
Fred Cambria	(1970)
Gene Garber	(1969–1970)
Carl Taylor	(1968)
Dennis Ribant	(1967)
Frank Bork	(1964)
Tom Butters	(1962–1964)
Jack Lamabe	(1962)
Ron Blackburn	(1959)
Joe Trimble	(1957)
Luis Arroyo	(1956)
Fred Waters	(1955)
Bob Hall	(1953)
Bob Addis	(1953)
Cal Hogue	(1952)
Mel Queen	(1951–1952)
Joe Muir	(1951–1952)
Woody Main	(1948, 1950)

NUMBER RETIRED: None

HALL OF FAMERS TO WEAR THE NUMBER: HONUS WAGNER (1936), HEINIE MANUSH (1964)

FIRST PERFORMANCE WITH THE NUMBER

4/22/1938- Coming over from the Dodgers late in the 1938 campaign, Hall of Famer Heinie Manush unsuccessfully pinch-hit for reliever Jim Tobin in an 11–10 loss to the Cardinals.

FIRST HOME RUN WITH THE NUMBER

6/25/1944- One of the most controversial home runs in team history occurred when Spud Davis cracked a pinch-hit two-run homer in the bottom of the ninth to tie the game against the Cardinals at 5. The ball apparently went through the right field screen into the stands instead of over the screen, prompting St. Louis to protest the contest, claiming that the ball must go over the fence to be an official home run. It would be the last play of the game, as it was the second half of a twin bill, and Pennsylvania Blue Laws at the time dictated that a sporting contest not be played after 7:00 PM on a Sunday; fortunately for the Bucs, the clock struck seven after the home run.

Jim Bagby	(1947)
Spud Davis	(1942–1945)
Heinie Manush	(1938)
COACHES	
Honus Wagner	(1933–1939)
Jewel Ens	(1938)
Mike Kelly	(1940–1941)
Bruce Kimm	(1989–1990)

FIRST VICTORY BY A PITCHER WITH THE NUMBER

6/27/1947- It was a horrible start, to be honest, by new Pirate Jim Bagby, allowing 14 hits, six runs, and a walk in seven innings. Thankfully, the Bucs' offense was impressive, led by Frankie Gustine's two hits and three RBIs . . . as well as Bagby's own offensive performance, which included two hits and an RBI. Pittsburgh defeated the Cubs, 12–8, giving the former Indian and Red Sox player his first win of the year.

BEST PIRATES TO WEAR THE NUMBER: (HR-RBI-AVE) (W-L-ERA)

Ramon Hernandez (23–12-2.51)

After struggling in his first two major league seasons, left-handed reliever Ramon Hernandez got a chance to pitch with the Pirates in 1971. After an almost unhittable trial in 12 1/3 innings that championship year, he stuck with the team for six seasons. Hernandez combined with closer Dave Giusti to provide the Bucs an incredible lefty/righty one-two punch in the bullpen reminiscent of Tony Watson/ Mark Melancon, if you will, in the team's championship era in the first half of the 1970s

Craig Wilson (94–282-.268)

Coming over from the Toronto Blue Jays as part of the Orlando Merced/ Carlos Garcia deal in November of 1996, Craig Wilson was a young prospect years away from the big leagues. When he was finally brought up in 2001, Wilson proved to be more than worth the loss of Merced and Garcia, and became a decent power-hitting first baseman/outfielder. Hitting .310 in his rookie season, Wilson had a career year in 2004 with 29 homers and 82 RBIs. He never seemed to be a favorite of David Littlefield's, who traded him to the Yankees two years later for Shawn Chacon. A team doesn't lose for twenty years in a row without making many bad trades, but at least in this case Wilson had a bobblehead made of him while he was here.

Mark Johnson (30–104–.239)

Mark Johnson's inclusion on the "best" list shows more the lack of talented players who wore number 36, rather than the fact that he belongs here. A slugger who just couldn't get to the next level, Johnson hit 30 home runs in 783 at bats with the Bucs over three years. After dropping to four long balls in 1997, the Pirates finally realized he wasn't going to be the next Willie Stargell and put him on waivers.

Luis Arroyo (photo courtesy of the Pittsburgh Pirates)

WORST PIRATES TO WEAR THE NUMBER: (W-L-ERA) (HR-RBI-AVE)

Mel Queen (19–36-5.33)

Father of the successful reliever in the 1960s by the same name, Mel Queen was a World War II vet whose path crossed with the Pirates during the beginning of one of the worst eras in franchise history. Never having a good season with the Bucs, Queen's 5.33 ERA and 1.645 WHIP in five years showed he wasn't the type of pitcher who was going to lead them out of their doldrums.

Bob Hall (2–13-5.39)

A Swissvale native, pitcher Bob Hall was part of a forgettable rotation with the Pirates in 1953; he won only two of his 15 decisions. The World War II veteran who served in the US Coast Guard ended his major league career that season. He was struck by a car and tragically killed in 1983 in St. Petersburg, Florida, where he worked as a traffic director for a construction company.

Joe Redfield (0–0-.111)

Third baseman Joe Redfield was signed as a free agent in 1991 by the Bucs. After being called up in late June, Redfield managed two singles in 18 at bats and never saw the light of day in the show again.

OTHER NOTABLE PIRATES TO WEAR THE NUMBER

Honus Wagner and Jewel Ens

The great shortstop wore number 36 for most of his first seven years as a coach for the team. Former manager Jewel Ens wore it for a season in 1938, when he was a coach.

Jim Bagby

A good pitcher for the Red Sox and Indians, winning 92 games over nine seasons, Jim Bagby Jr. — the son of the man by the same name who won 31 contests with the 1920 Cleveland Indians — ended his major league career in the Steel City in 1947. He was 5–4 in 37 games that year, mostly out of the bullpen. Interestingly, his father had also ended his career with the Bucs, playing one season, in 1923.

Joe Muir

To be a cop or not be a cop, that was the question. After two subpar years with the subpar Bucs in 1951 and '52, the twenty-nine-year-old Joe Muir had two dreams: to be a baseball player, or to be a policeman in Maryland. You couldn't be a recruit for the State Police in Maryland if you were thirty or older. Muir had to make a choice; perhaps staying with a godforsaken team as the Pirates were at that time made the decision easier for him: he became a policeman.

Ron Blackburn

From a 3–2 record over his two big league seasons in the Steel City, Ron Blackburn had very few highlight memories, except for the first batter he faced: home run king Hank Aaron, who beat out an infield single.

Jack Lamabe

Jack Lamabe had a fine rookie season with the Pirates in 1962, when he was 3–1 with a 2.88 ERA in 46 games, which spurred a seven-year major league career. After he retired, he became head coach for both Jacksonville University and the perennial NCAA baseball powerhouse, LSU. Unfortunately, he coached the Tigers before their dynasty days, finishing with a 134–115 record over four seasons.

Tom Butters

In his four seasons with the Pittsburgh Pirates, the bulk of reliever Tom Butters's on-field activity came in 1964, when he was 2–2 with a 2.38 ERA in 64 1/3 innings. His career ended abruptly from injuries suffered in an auto accident, but his next journey in life brought him to Duke University, where he was baseball coach before taking on the job of athletic director in 1977. He served twenty-one years in the post, which would have made him the AD responsible for hiring Mike Krzyzewski and Steve Spurrier.

Dennis Ribant

Like Deion Sanders before him, pitcher Dennis Ribant, who played for the Bucs in 1967, was also a minor league hockey player who played two seasons with Hamilton in the Ontario Hockey Association with the likes of Penguin Lowell McDonald, Blackhawk great Pit Martin, and one of Canada's great hockey legends, Paul Henderson.

Odell Jones

Odell Jones was a fine pitching prospect with the Bucs who could never translate that success to the majors. Playing parts of four seasons in Pittsburgh, where he compiled a 9–12 record, Jones then had his moment in the sun with the Brewers in 1988, when he tossed 8 1/3 innings of no-hit ball against the Indians before giving up a hit.

Marvell Wynne

The starting center fielder with the Bucs in the mid-1980s when times were lean, Marvell Wynne was a speedy player who showed an occasional glimpse of power for the team. As fast as he was, the .247 career hitter was not an efficient base stealer with Pittsburgh, swiping 46 bases in 80 attempts for a less-than-stellar .575 success rate, before heading off to San Diego.

Jeff Richardson

Jeff Richardson was a middle-infielder in the show for three seasons, including one in Pittsburgh in 1991, when he had a hit and three strikeouts in four at bats. After his career was over he became a successful minor league manager in the Pirates system before taking over as successful head coach at Louisiana Tech.

Jason Johnson

Pitching three games for the Bucs in his first major league season in 1997, Jason Johnson left the team and eventually became a decent starter for the Orioles, winning ten games twice in his eleven-year major league career.

Billy Taylor

Finishing his time in the majors with the Bucs in 2001 by pitching in one game, Billy Taylor had a good career as a closer before that with the A's, where he saved 99 contests over a four-year period between 1996 and '99.

Wil Ledezma

Going 0–3 with the Bucs in 2009 in his next-to-last major league season, Wil Ledezma is the answer to the trivia question, "Who owns the major league record for most consecutive starts with never going more than six innings?" That answer is "31."

Ryan Ludwick

A heavy-hitting first baseman who had a monster season with the Cards in 2008, with 37 homers and 113 RBIs, Ryan Ludwick came to the Bucs for the stretch drive in 2011. It would be a disappointing performance in which he hit only two homers in 133 at bats. Signing with the Reds after the season, he reestablished his power with 27 homers in the bandbox where the Cincinnati Reds play.

Justin Morneau

One of the game's great players in the first decade of the twenty-first century, Justin Morneau won the MVP Award in 2006 with the Twins, and finished second in that category two years later. With his career seemingly over in 2013, he was dealt to the Bucs late that year for the end of the Pirates' magical season. He hit only .260 with little power, but Pirates fans were upset that the team didn't sign him going forward, especially after they watched him hit .319 for the Rockies a year later.

Edinson Volquez

A pitcher who seemed long on talent, but not on performance, after he had gone 17–6 with the Reds in 2008, Edinson Volquez became another project for the pitching whisperer, Ray Searage, in 2014. Proving once again that he could revive anyone, Searage did his magic and Volquez not only went 13–7 with a 3.04 ERA, but got the start in the Wild Card game against the Giants. He, unfortunately, reverted to his old ways in the contest as the Bucs lost, 8–0.

Luis Arroyo

The great reliever who faced the Bucs in the 1960 World Series, Arroyo wore number 36 in his first season in a Pirate uniform in 1956.

#37: IS THERE REALLY A GREATEST NUMBER 37?

ALL TIME NO. 37 ROSTER	YEAR
Arquimedes Caminero	(2015)
Justin Wilson	(2013–2014)
Juan Cruz	(2012)
Lyle Overbay	(2011)
Charlie Morton	(2010)
Raul Chavez	(2008)
John Wasdin	(2007)
Yurendell de Caster	(2006)
Mike Johnston	(2004–2005)
Jeff Suppan	(2003)
Nelson Figueroa	(2003)
Bruce Aven	(2000)
Brant Brown	(1999)
Rafael Belliard	(1983–1985)
Alberto Lois	(1978–1979)
Miguel Dilone	(1974–1978)
Fernando Gonzalez	(1972–1973)
Bill Short	(1967)
Bob Purkey	(1966)
Tommie Sisk	(1962)
Larry Foss	(1961)
Jim Umbricht	(1959–1961)
Don Gross	(1959)
Bob Smith	(1957–1959)
Bob Kuzava	(1957)
Bob Garber	(1956)
Al Grunwald	(1955)
Bob Schultz	(1953)
Clem Koshorek	(1953)
Ed Stevens	(1950)
Harry Gumbert	(1949–1950)
Hal Gregg	(1949–1950)
Ray Poat	(1949)
Elmer Riddle	(1948)
Alf Anderson	(1946)
Dick Conger	(1941–1942)
Bill Clemensen	(1939–1941)
Vince DiMaggio	(1940)
Fern Bell	(1940)
Aubrey Epps	(1935)
Burleigh Grimes	(1934)
COACHES	
Johnny Gooch	(1938)

NUMBER RETIRED: None

HALL OF FAMERS TO WEAR THE NUMBER: BURLEIGH GRIMES (1964)

FIRST PERFORMANCE WITH THE NUMBER

8/8/1934- In the first performance of his third tenure with the Bucs, Burleigh Grimes was anything but effective in relief of Bill Swift, allowing nine hits, four walks, and seven earned runs in only 4–2/3 innings during a 14–3 defeat by the Cubs.

FIRST HOME RUN WITH THE NUMBER

6/12/1940- After coming over from the Reds in an early-season trade, Vince DiMaggio, in his only season wearing the number 37, hit a solo home run in a 5–4 loss to the Dodgers.

FIRST VICTORY BY A PITCHER WITH THE NUMBER

9/10/1934- In relief of Waite Hoyt and Heinie Meine, Hall of Famer Burleigh Grimes tossed two innings of relief for the Bucs against the Giants, giving up a run and three hits. The Bucs scored five in the top of the ninth to make Grimes the winner, 9–7.

Rogers McKee	(1947)
Ron Schuler	(1986)
Tommy Sandt	(1987–1996, 2000–2002)
Joe Jones	(1997–1998)

BEST PIRATES TO WEAR THE NUMBER: (HR-RBI-AVE) (W-L-ERA)

Burleigh Grimes (48–42-3.26)

After 269 wins, Burleigh Grimes came to the Bucs in his final major league season, 1934, showing it was time for him to retire. His 1–2 record and 7.24 ERA technically could have made him the worst Pirate to wear the number 37. We could have also taken into consideration his first two major league seasons, when he was 5–19 in Pittsburgh. Instead, taken into account was the fact that he pitched for the Bucs in 1928 and '29, a third trip to the Steel City in his nineteen-year career when the team didn't wear numbers, and Grimes won 42 games, including a league-high 25 in 1928, to rate him as the best ever in this category.

Rafael Belliard (1–72-.218)

Rafael Belliard was the definition of a slap hitter, once setting a major league record for most at bats without a double: 286. While he hit only .218 during his nine seasons in a Pirates uniform, he was a very slick-fielding shortstop.

Including his eight years in an Atlanta Braves uniform, Belliard played seventeen seasons in the majors and had the dubious distinction of having the fewest number of win shares in major league history, among players who were in more than 1,000 games . . . a stat conceived by SABRmetrician Bill James. Either that means win shares are a meaningless stat, or "pac-man" was an ineffective major leaguer. In the world of number 37s, he was effective enough to be on this list.

Bob Smith (4–6-3.74)

A middle-reliever with the team between 1957 and '59, Bob Smith got

Vince DiMaggio (left) waits at home to greet Bill Elliott after a home run. (photo courtesy of the Pittsburgh Pirates)

the call seventy-five times in his career (sixty-seven out of the bullpen and eight starts) in a Pirates uniform. He was an effective reliever who is lucky that not many greats wore the number 37 in Pirates history, which allows him a spot on this list.

WORST PIRATES TO WEAR THE NUMBER: (W-L-ERA) (HR-RBI-AVE)

Bill Clemensen (1–1-5.77)

Bill Clemensen pitched in parts of three seasons with the Bucs, in a career that was interrupted by a four-year stay in the US Army Air Corps during World War II. He showed some promise in 1941 before he left, but when he returned to the Bucs in 1946 it was apparent his major league career was over.

Bob Kuzava (0–0-9.00)

A ten-year major league vet who played with eight teams, Bob Kuzava was with the Bucs in his final major league season in 1959, giving up two runs in two innings of work. The World War II veteran did have one day in the sun against the White Sox while with the Yankees, when he went into the ninth with a no-hitter before losing it after one out.

Miguel Dilone (0–0-.145)

He wore the number 37 longer than any other player in Pirates history, and while he was a great base-stealing option, with 23 stolen bases in 26 attempts during his Pittsburgh tenure, he averaged only .145 in 69 at bats, making the most tenured number 37 one of the worst.

OTHER NOTABLE PIRATES TO WEAR THE NUMBER

Aubrey Epps

He lived the dream for one day, one game. Even though Audrey Epps's time in the show was brief, he made the most of it. The date was September 29, 1935 against the Reds in Crosley Field, when Epps started behind the plate. He went three for five with a triple and three RBIs during a 9–6 loss to Cincinnati. Epps returned to Scranton in 1936 and hit .332, but never got another chance in the big leagues, retiring from professional baseball after the 1941 campaign.

Fern Bell

Fern Bell's career was a tad longer than Epps's, but not by much. He had one full season in 1939, hitting .286 in 262 at bats. Going hitless in three at bats in 1940, Bell was sent to the minors. Three years later Bell would enter the Navy. fighting in the Pacific during World War II. He would never return to the big leagues.

Elmer Riddle

A great pitcher with the Reds during the war years, Riddle had a NL-best .826 winning percentage and 2.24 ERA in 1941, before leading the league in wins with 21 two years later. He ended his career in Pittsburgh in 1948 and '49. Riddle won 12 games the first season, before going 1–8 his final year.

Harry Gumbert

Harry Gumbert won 143 games over his fifteen-year career, playing his final two years in the Steel City with a 1–4 mark and 5.83 ERA.

Ed Stevens

A big first baseman with adequate power, Ed Stevens took over the position from Hall of Famer Hank Greenberg in 1948. He hit a career-high ten homers that season, but showed he didn't have Greenberg's power, with only four more in his last two big league seasons.

Al Grunwald

A former first baseman, Al Grunwald was converted to pitcher by the Pirates. His debut in 1955 showed that might have been a mistake as he allowed a cycle in his first inning of work (a single, double, triple and homer). He remains the only pitcher in major league history to have such a start in his first inning pitched.

Jim Umbricht

Jim Umbricht was a two-sports star at the University of Georgia, where he also excelled at basketball. After a three-year tenure with the Bucs, where he was 1–2 with a 5.12 ERA, he went to Houston and became an outstanding reliever over the next two years. The story became tragic at that point: he developed a malignant tumor in his leg, then lymphoma. He passed away before the start of the 1964 campaign, and has had his number for the Astros, which was 32, retired. The franchise also has its yearly MVP award named after him.

Bob Priddy

A native Pittsburgher who went to McKees Rocks High, Bob Priddy was 2–2 with a 3.86 ERA in parts of two seasons with the Pirates. He went on to have a nine-year career with six teams, mostly out of the bullpen.

Fernando Gonzalez

Fernando Gonzalez was a utility infielder with Pittsburgh for four seasons in the early 1970s, hitting .257 for the Pirates and .235 over his six-year major league career.

Alberto Lois

Never more than a pinch-runner who scored six runs in 1979 without ever coming to the plate, Alberto Lois had a tragic end to his baseball career. After a Dominican League game, he was driving a truck that was hit by a train. The accident injured his eye and, unfortunately, killed six of his passengers.

Brant Brown

After dropping a fly ball for the Cubs at the end of the 1998 pennant race, which was the reason they lost an important game to Milwaukee,

8–7, promising young Brant Brown was dealt to the Pirates for John Lieber. He seemingly never got over the error, as he hit .232 in his one Pirate season and never topped .200 again.

Mike Johnston

Winless in his two-year major league career with the Bucs, Mike Johnston nonetheless was courageous, having made the majors despite having Tourette's syndrome.

John Wasdin

Somehow, John Wasdin's big league career lasted twelve seasons, despite the fact that he gave up 135 homers in 793 1/3 innings and sported a 5.28 career ERA. With the Pirates he only allowed one homer in his final major league season, in 2007, pitching 19 2/3 innings; but he still struggled with an ERA of 5.95.

Lyle Overbay

A feared hitter seemingly everywhere else he played throughout his fourteen-year career, that was not the case in Pittsburgh in 2011, when Overbay amassed a .227 average with only eight long balls before being released.

Justin Wilson

An outstanding prospect who became a good reliever for the Bucs in 2013 with a 6–1 record, 2.08 ERA, and 1.059 WHIP, Justin Wilson suffered a year later when his ERA more than doubled. The southpaw was dealt to the Yankees after the season, Pittsburgh receiving in return catcher Francisco Cervelli, who turned out to be a fan favorite.

Arquimedes Caminero

He can easily whip a fastball over the 100 MPH plateau, but until reliever Arquimedes Caminero got some advice from pitching coach Ray Searage he was at times batting practice for major league hitters. The former Marlin had a tough time, especially in July of 2015 when opposing batters left him with a 7.59 ERA and three home runs allowed in 10 2/3 innings. But the extra coaching worked; a month later he won three games and was unscored upon in 15 innings.

#38: ROOKIE OF THE YEAR

ALL TIME NO. 38 ROSTER	YEAR
Joakim Soria	(2015)
Chris Volstad	(2015)
Stolmy Pimentel	(2013–2014)
Xavier Paul	(2011)
Erik Kratz	(2010)
Chris Leroux	(2010)
Craig Hansen	(2008–2009)
Jason Bay	(2003–2008)
Adam Hyzdu	(2001–2003)
Don Wengert	(2001)
Ramon Martinez	(2001)
Chris Peters	(1996–1999)
Jim Gott	(1995)
Roberto Ramirez	(1994–1995)
Bob Patterson	(1989–1992)
Scott Little	(1989)
Vicente Palacios	(1987–1988)
Rafael Belliard	(1986–1987)
Manny Sarmiento	(1982–1983)
Luis Tiant	(1981)
Bob Moose	(1967–1976)
Jim Shellenback	(1966–1967)
Diomedes Olivo	(1960, 1962)
Don Gross	(1958, 1960)
Dick Hall	(1959)
Al Jackson	(1959)
Hank Foiles	(1956)
Len Yochim	(1951, 1954)
Frank Barrett	(1950)
Cal McLish	(1948)
Billy Cox	(1941)
Joe Schultz	(1939–1941)
Ed Fernandes	(1940)
Ed Holley	(1934)
COACHES	
Zack Taylor	(1947)

NUMBER RETIRED: None

HALL OF FAMERS TO WEAR THE NUMBER: None

FIRST PERFORMANCE WITH THE NUMBER

7/13/1934- Relieving for starter Red Lucas, Ed Holley allowed a run on a hit and three walks in 1 2/3 innings during a 7–6 loss to the Giants.

FIRST HOME RUN WITH THE NUMBER

5/23/1956- In a 6–0 victory over the Cardinals, catcher Hank Foiles hit his first homer of the year, a sixth-inning two-run shot off Willard Smith that gave Pittsburgh a five-run lead.

FIRST VICTORY BY A PITCHER WITH THE NUMBER

9/4/1950- After the Cubs took a 3–1 lead in the seventh inning, Frank Barrett came into the game in relief of Cliff Chambers. He retired Hank Bauer on a ground-out, and then was replaced by Junior Walsh after one-third of an inning in the top of the eighth. Luckily, the Pirates had scored three of their own in the bottom of the seventh, making Barrett the first winner by a number 38.

Diomedes Olivo (photo courtesy of the Pittsburgh Pirates)

BEST PIRATES TO WEAR THE NUMBER: (HR-RBI-AVE) (W-L-ERA)

Jason Bay (139–452-.281)

Until 2004, the one award no Pittsburgh Pirate had ever won was the National League's Rookie of the Year. That streak came to an end in 2004, when young Jason Bay proved to be even better than advertised after they acquired him from the Padres the year before. The Canadian native hit 26 homers and knocked in 82 as he finally secured a Rookie of the Year Award for the franchise. He went on to play in Pittsburgh for six mostly fabulous seasons, knocking in over 100 on two occasions. In what would turn out to be their final rebuilding job before the team finally broke out of its twenty-year losing streak, Bay was dealt in a three-way trade to the Boston Red Sox that saw Boston send Manny Ramirez to the Dodgers. Bay had a fabulous 2009 campaign with the Sox, smacking a career-high 36 home runs and 119 RBIs.

Bob Moose (76–71-3.50)

Bob Moose was a local boy who made good as Export, PA's star hurler, playing for Franklin High School before becoming a successful starter with the Bucs. His best season was in 1969, when he not only topped all NL pitchers with an .824 winning percentage, but also tossed a no-hitter against the world champion Mets. After having a blood clot removed from his shoulder in 1974 he missed most of the season, and then returned as a reliever for the next two years. His story had a tragic end, though, as he was killed in an auto accident on his twenty-ninth birthday.

Bob Patterson (25–21-3.97)

Bob Patterson was a good left-hander out of the Pittsburgh bullpen during their three consecutive eastern division championships in the early 1990s. He appeared in 207 games in a Pirates uniform, and had sub-three ERAs for the only times in his thirteen-year career, in 1990 and '92.

WORST PIRATES TO WEAR THE NUMBER: (W-L-ERA)

Ed Holley (0–3-15.43)

An adequate starter for the Philadelphia Phillies in the early 1930s, until he collapsed with a 1–8 mark in 1934 which prompted his sale in the middle of the season to the Bucs, Ed Holley never recovered. He lost all three decisions, with a 15.43 ERA and 2.786 WHIP, in 9 1/3 innings in a Pirates uniform. Predictably, it was the end of his four-year major league career.

Don Wengert (0–2-12.38)

After floating around the majors for six unspectacular seasons, mostly out of the bullpen, Don Wengert made his last stop in 2001 at PNC Park, suffering through his worst year with a 12.38 ERA and a career-high 2.438 WHIP.

Len Yochim (1–2-7.62)

A great pitcher in the minors, southpaw Len Yochim never succeeded in the big leagues, pitching for the Bucs in two seasons. After he retired he did contribute to the club as a long-time scout and East Coast scouting director.

OTHER NOTABLE PIRATES TO WEAR THE NUMBER

Joe Schultz

A little-used catcher for his first three major league seasons with the Bucs, hitting .231 in 52 at bats before heading to the St. Louis Browns for six years, Joe Schultz eventually was immortalized in the best-selling book by Jim Bouton, "Ball Four", as the first manager of the Seattle Pilots.

Don Gross

A decent southpaw out of the bullpen for the Pirates in 1958 and '59 after coming over from the Reds, Don Gross had a chance to pitch with the Bucs during their 1960 championship campaign, but only appeared in five contests and was in the minors by June.

Diomedes Olivo

It took a long time for pitcher Diomedes Olivo to reach his dream of playing in the majors after a long and distinguished career in his native Dominican Republic, but at the age of forty-one, in 1960, he pitched in four games for the world champion Pirates. He was the second oldest rookie in major league history, behind the great Satchel Paige. After winning the International League Pitcher of the Year Award in 1961, Olivo returned to the majors in 1962 in a more prominent role, appearing in 62 games with a 5–1 record and 2.77 ERA.

Luis Tiant

In 1981, superstar Cuban pitcher Luis Tiant came to Pittsburgh for his eighteenth major league season at the age of forty. He was 2–5 for the Bucs with a fine 3.92 ERA, before ending his career a year later with the Angels.

Manny Sarmiento

A reliever for the Cincinnati Reds for his first four seasons, Manny Sarmiento started 17 games for the Pirates in 1982. He won nine games, then had a fine season out of the bullpen a year later in his final major league season.

Scott Little

His career in the show lasted all of four at bats in 1989, with a single, before Scott Little found his calling as a longtime successful minor league manager, including a stint in the Pirates organization.

Chris Peters

Spending all but one of his six seasons in the majors with the Pirates, southpaw Chris Peters, who grew up in nearby McMurray and went to Peters Township High School, went from the bullpen to the starting rotation. Peters was 17–21 with the Bucs before heading to the Expos in 2001. He returned to work for the hometown franchise in 2015 as a left-handed batting practice pitcher.

Ramon Martinez

A star with the Dodgers, where he twice finished in the top five for the Cy Young Award and was a 20-game winner in 1990, Ramon Martinez, brother of the great Pedro, was signed by Pittsburgh as a hopeful boost to their starting rotation as they opened PNC Park in 2001. The team had lost three starters when they inked Martinez, but he pitched poorly in four starts. Given the option to go to the bullpen, Martinez decided to retire instead.

Stolmy Pimentel

When he was brought in from the Boston Red Sox as part of the Joel Hanrahan trade, Pittsburgh thought they had a diamond in the rough who would be a staple in their starting rotation. They could never harness his talent as he stayed on the roster in 2014. After a great four-inning performance in the opener that season, he pitched poorly the rest of the year. They finally gave up on him and DFA'd Pimentel before the 2015 campaign, when he was picked up by Texas.

Joakim Soria

A former closer for most of his eight-year major league career during which he saved 43 games with the Royals in 2010, and 202 in his career, Joakim Soria was a mid-season acquisition from Detroit in 2015. He helped turn what was a weakness into a strength, as the Bucs' bullpen was arguably the strongest in the National League in the final months of the pennant race. Giving the team a strong seventh- inning option, Soria had a 2.03 ERA in twenty-nine appearances for Pittsburgh.

#39: THE COBRA STRIKES

NUMBER RETIRED: None

HALL OF FAMERS TO WEAR THE NUMBER: None

FIRST PERFORMANCE WITH THE NUMBER

4/22/1941- In the middle of blowing a 7–4, lead against the Cards, Lefty Wilkie came into the game with two outs in the ninth and promptly gave up a hit to the only batter he faced, before being replaced by Bob Klinger. Pittsburgh would lose the game in 12 innings, 9–8.

FIRST HOME RUN WITH THE NUMBER

7/28/1959- Pitcher Bennie Daniels had the rare honor of being a pitcher who hit the first home run wearing a particular number, as he hit a two-run shot in a 9–4 loss to the Dodgers.

FIRST VICTORY BY A PITCHER WITH THE NUMBER

5/21/1941- The Braves broke out to a quick first-inning 4–0 lead, knocking Pirates starter Ken Heintzelman out of the game. Russ Bauers pitched well in relief for five innings, but Boston still had a 4–2 lead when Lefty Wilkie entered the contest. In four scoreless innings he surrendered only two hits, as the Bucs rebounded to win, 8–4, giving Wilkie the win.

BEST PIRATES TO WEAR THE NUMBER: (HR-RBI-AVE) (W-L-ERA)

Dave Parker (166–758-.305)

Dave "The Cobra" Parker had it all: power, hitting for average, and brilliant defensively. He was one of the greatest talents ever to don a Pirates uniform. His impressive accomplishments are as follows: winner of the 1978 MVP Award; three times among the top three in the MVP race; three Gold Gloves; twice the NL batting champion; and the MVP of the 1979 All-Star Game, when he received the award for his two incredible outfield assists. His talent was in line to put

Bob Veale preparing to throw a pitch in spring training. (Photo courtesy of the Pittsburgh Pirates)

him among the top three or four in the history of the franchise when injuries and drug usage curtailed his plans and embittered the Pirates Nation toward him. He went on to overcome his issues, but did so in Cincinnati, Oakland, and Milwaukee, rather than in the city where he began his legacy. Fortunately, time heals all wounds and he has been forgiven by Bucco fans. He sadly announced that he has Parkinson's Disease, but still makes his rounds in the Steel City, where fans can meet the man who remains one of the top ten Pirates of all time.

Bob Veale (116–91-3.06)

Perhaps the hardest-throwing pitcher in Pirates history, Bob Veale not only led the league in strikeouts in 1964 with 250, but eclipsed the 200 strikeout plateau four times. Veale still holds the franchise records both for strikeouts in a season with 276, and in a single game, when he mowed down 16. The bespectacled southpaw made hitters nervous when it was extremely humid and his glasses would fog up.

It especially frightened Lou Brock, who called him one of the most intimidating pitchers he faced. The fact that Veale led the league in walks four times showed that he had a tendency to be wild, so batters had reason to be afraid. Regardless of his occasional wildness, Veale had a magnificent Pirates career.

Jason Grilli (3–11-3.01)

It appeared as if Jason Grilli's major league career was over at the age of thirty-two, in 2009. Two years later he returned to the show with the Bucs, and in 2013 became one of the faces of this surprising franchise as the closer who saved 33 games for the team and found his face on the cover of *Sports Illustrated*. The Pirates Nation adored "Grilled Cheese," but a trip to the disabled list late that season, and again in 2014 for arm issues, ended his remarkable story in the Steel City. He ended up in Atlanta in 2015, where he had 24 saves by July when a ruptured Achilles tendon ended the thirty-eight-year-old's season, and possibly his career.

WORST PIRATES TO WEAR THE NUMBER: (W-L-ERA) (HR-RBI-AVE)

Jeff Granger (0–0-18.00)

A first-round pick by the Royals in the 1993 draft, Jeff Granger never lived up to his lofty status in Kansas City; then completed his career in 1997 with the Pirates. Giving up ten runs in five innings of work, Granger was sent down to the minors never to return.

Bob Addis (0–0-.000)

Serving in Guam, and then with the occupation forces in China during World War II, Bob Addis made it to the majors in 1950 with the Braves, and then Cubs, having his best seasons in 1951 and '52 when he hit a combined .287. Addis was part of the Ralph Kiner trade in 1953, and spent his final part of his last big league season in a Pirates uniform, where he was hitless in three at bats.

Bennie Daniels (8–16-5.84)

Pitching his first four seasons in Pittsburgh, the last of which was on the 1960 world champions for whom he had a 7.81 ERA, Bennie Daniels eventually moved to Washington, where he had more success, winning 37 games in a Senators uniform.

OTHER NOTABLE PIRATES TO WEAR THE NUMBER

Lefty Wilkie

Bill Burwell (photo courtesy of the Pittsburgh Pirates)

Lefty Wilkie was a star pitcher in the Army, registering a 23–3 mark while serving during World War II in Germany. With the Bucs he had been a solid southpaw reliever in 1941 and '42, compiling an 8–11 record. He returned after being discharged in 1946, and had a 10.57 ERA in his final big league campaign.

Jack Hallett

Jack Hallett spent two years in the Navy during World War II after pitching in relief for the White Sox and Pirates, having earned a 1.70 ERA for the Bucs in 1943. When he returned in 1946, he had his best major league season with a 5–7 mark and an ERA of 3.29 in 35 appearances. It was his last season in a Pirates uniform; he spent one more year in the show, with the Giants in 1948.

Bill Burwell

A longtime pitching coach with the Bucs who was in that position during the magical 1960 campaign, Bill Burwell won his only decision in 1928 as a pitcher with the Pirates. In 1947 he was named manager, replacing Billy Herman, who left the club with one game remaining in a disappointing season. Burwell lived the dream of being a major league manager at that point . . . for exactly one game. The Bucs won the contest, giving Burwell a perfect record in his career as a manager.

Jake Theis

Pitcher Jake Theis's career started in a magnificent way in 1954, when he came into a game with the bases loaded against Brooklyn and proceeded to strike out Jackie Robinson, and force Gil Hodges to hit into a double play. While he was only 3–9 his rookie season, he had an adequate 3.87 ERA. Unfortunately, his major league career lasted only one more game, in 1955, before he was sent back to the minors for good.

Luis Arroyo

After an 11–9 rookie season with the Cardinals, Luis Arroyo spent two seasons in a Pirates uniform mustering a mere 6–14 mark. The Puerto Rican native eventually became a star with the Yankees, especially in 1961 when he was 15–5 with a league-high 29 saves.

Jeff Wallace

A southpaw with the Bucs in the mid- to late 1990s, Jeff Wallace had the opportunity to finish his Pirates career with a perfect record: three wins in three decisions. His other pitching parameters weren't as impressive — a 1.800 WHIP and 4.67 ERA — but, hey, not many hurlers can claim to have a perfect record win-loss in the majors. Jeff Wallace can.

Mike Fetters

Mike Fetters was a closer at one point for the Brewers during his sixteen-year major league career; then he brought his smiling face to Pittsburgh in 2001. He proved to be an effective righty out of the pen, going 2–1 with a 3.75 ERA in 52 appearances over two seasons.

Alberto Reyes

Pitching in the show for thirteen seasons highlighted by an incident in a Tampa bar when he was arrested on a disturbing the peace charge,

Alberto Reyes was impressive, if only for a short time, in a Pirates uniform with an 0.941 WHIP in 17 innings during the 2002 campaign.

Pat Mahomes

A middle reliever who had little success over his eleven-year major league career, Pat Mahomes ended his time in the show with the Bucs, losing his only decision while having the third-lowest ERA in his career: 4.84.

Brandon Moss

Brandon Moss was a good prospect with the Red Sox who came over in the Jason Bay trade. He never reached his potential with the Bucs, but sure as hell has in A's, Indians, and Cardinals uniforms, having blasted 30 homers in 2013, and 110 in his big league career to this point.

Chris Jakubauskas

Chris Jakubauskas had a long name not many could pronounce; it was much longer than his time in the show, which included two-thirds of an inning with the Bucs. It could have been longer, if not for the fact he was hit in the head with a line drive by Lance Berkman, a scary sight that left him with a concussion. Luckily, it wasn't more serious but it marked the end of his Pirates career. After spending time on the disabled list, Jakubauskas was sent back to the minors on a rehab assignment that never ended; he wasn't promoted to the Pirates again.

#40: THE IRISHMAN

NUMBER RETIRED: DANNY MURTAUGH (1977)

HALL OF FAMERS TO WEAR THE NUMBER: None

FIRST PERFORMANCE WITH THE NUMBER

7/2/1932- In a 5–4 loss to the Cardinals, veteran starter Ray Kremer was not at his best going only three innings while giving up five hits and four runs in the defeat.

FIRST HOME RUN WITH THE NUMBER

9/12/1943- Pitcher Jack Hallett hit his first and only major league home run in his first game as a Pirate. It was during the second game of a doubleheader against the Braves that ended after the 11th inning, with the score tied, 2–2. The game was called so that the Pirates could make their train to New York to play the Giants the next day.

FIRST VICTORY BY A PITCHER WITH THE NUMBER

7/15/1932- Unlike his first start with a number on his back, Ray Kremer was at his best on this day as the thirty-nine-year-old tossed a three-hit shutout against the Braves, with left fielder Dave Barbee plating the only run with a fourth-inning double that scored Arky Vaughan.

BEST PIRATES TO WEAR THE NUMBER: (W–L–PCT. for Murtaugh) (W–L–ERA)

Danny Murtaugh (1,115–950-.540)

In his day, Danny Murtaugh was a manager killer for twenty years; no manager survived the Irishman. He came to the team amidst one of its worst losing eras, and immediately turned the young club into contenders, finally scaling the top of the mountain with a world championship in 1960. Murtaugh would retire several times due to health reasons, but GM Joe L. Brown would always lure him back. He retired in 1964, Harry Walker came in, Murtaugh replaced him in 1967. He retired, Larry Shepard came in, Murtaugh replaced him in 1970. He retired in 1972 after

Danny Murtaugh (left) and Bill McKechnie (right). (Photo courtesy of the Pittsburgh Pirates)

leading the team to a second World Series title the year before, Bill Virdon came in, Murtaugh replaced him in 1973. He retired again in 1976 and Chuck Tanner came in. Tragically, heath issues finally took their toll on the great Pirate manager, and he passed away in December 1976 at the young age of fifty-nine. Pirates management decided to make sure the Irishman would always be there in memory by retiring his number 40 in 1977.

Ray Kremer (143–85-3.76)

Coming to the majors late in life — he was a rookie for the Bucs in 1924 at the age of thirty-one — Ray Kremer pitched eight-and-a-half years in Pittsburgh without a uniform number, leading the National League in victories twice with 20, as well as twice in ERA. He was a major cog in the team's two NL Pennants in 1925 and '27, as well as its second World Series title in '25, where he won two contests, including game seven. Kremer entered the game in the fifth inning that day with the team down, 6–3. He pitched magnificently for four innings as the

Pirates came back to win, 9–7. By the time he had donned the number in 1932, he was thirty-nine, and his career was coming to an end—a career that despite its late start is among the best for Pirates pitchers in the history of the franchise.

Red Lucas (47–32-3.77)

A .281 hitter over his fifteen-year career, when he found himself playing in the field every so often, Red Lucas was actually much more effective on the mound, where he won 109 games for the Reds in eight seasons. He was dealt to the Pirates before the 1934 campaign in the Adam Comorosky trade, and had a successful run for the Bucs, winning 47 games, including in 1936, when he put together a 15–4 record.

WORST PIRATES TO WEAR THE NUMBER: (W-L-ERA) (HR-RBI-AVE)

Windy McCall (0–0-9.45)

While he would become a decent reliever with the Giants in the late 1950s, when he came to the Pirates in 1950 after two less-than-stellar seasons with the Red Sox Windy McCall wasn't quite there yet, allowing 12 hits and seven runs in 6 2/3 innings.

Red Nonnenkamp (0–0-.000)

Hitless in his only Pirates at bat in 1933, Red Nonnenkamp became a reserve left fielder for the Red Sox in the late 1930s and actually challenged the rookie Ted Williams for the starting spot in 1939; needless to say, the Sox made the correct call.

OTHER NOTABLE PIRATES TO WEAR THE NUMBER

Culley Rikard

A seldom-used outfielder in his two major league seasons in the early 1940s, Culley Rikard spendt three years in the Army during World War II before returning to the show, where he saved the best for last, hitting .287 in 1947.

Al Gerheauser

The opening day pitcher for the Phils in his rookie season of 1943, Al Gerheauser proved that a won-loss record is not always the best way to judge a pitcher. He was 25–50 in his five-year career, including 7–12 with the Pirates, but his 4.13 ERA shows that he wasn't as bad as his .333 winning percentage may suggest.

The Pirates celebrate by mobbing Dock Ellis (17) after he tossed a no-hitter against the Padres in 1970. (Photo courtesy of the Pittsburgh Pirates)

Dave Wickersham

An Erie native and Ohio University alum pitcher, Dave Wickersham had a fine career going when he was dealt to the Pirates in 1968. By that time he was a converted starter, having won 65 games for the Tigers and A's, including a 19–12 mark for Detroit in 1964. With the Bucs he won his only decision in 11 relief appearances, and garnered a save.

Dock Ellis

The colorful Dock Ellis wore the number 40 in his first two major league seasons, in 1968 and '69.

41: THE HISTORY MAKER

ALL TIME NO. 41 ROSTER	YEAR
Hisanori Takahashi	(2012)
Ryan Doumit	(2005–2011)
Brian Boehringer	(2004)
Jeff D'Amico	(2003)
Jason Christiansen	(1995–2000)
Zane Smith	(1990–1994)
Mark Huismann	(1990)
Scott Little	(1989)
Mike Smith	(1989)
Mike Dunne	(1987–1989)
Jim Winn	(1984–1986)
Jose DeLeon	(1983)
Paul Moskau	(1982)
Andy Hassler	(1980)
Joe Coleman	(1979)
Jerry Reuss	(1974–1978)
Chuck Workman	(1946)
Xavier Rescigno	(1943–1945)
Bob Klinger	(1938–1939)
Guy Bush	(1935–1936)
Heinie Meine	(1932–1934)
MANAGER	
Bill Virdon	(1972–1973)
COACHES	
Babe Herman	(1951)
Clyde Sukeforth	(1952–1957)
Bill Burwell	(1958–1962)
Don Osborn	(1963–1964)
Bill Virdon	(1970–1971)
Rick Sofield	(2013–2015)

NUMBER RETIRED: None

HALL OF FAMERS TO WEAR THE NUMBER: None

FIRST PERFORMANCE WITH THE NUMBER

6/30/1932- Heinie Meine was the first starting pitcher to take the mound when the Pirates initially put numbers on their backs, in a 9–6 victory against the Cardinals. Despite the fact they were victorious, Meine was not the winner, having been taken out of the game after surrendering five runs on six hits and three walks in 4 1/3 innings.

FIRST HOME RUN WITH THE NUMBER

4/22/1946- New Pirate Chuck Workman hit his first home run of the season during a 5–4 loss to the Dodgers. The shot was a solo homer in the fourth off Ralph Branca, the man who would later give up the famed Bobby Thomson homer in the 1951 playoff.

FIRST VICTORY BY A PITCHER WITH THE NUMBER 7/3/1932-

In his next start, Heinie Meine was no more successful against the Cubs in the first game of a double header, but he was still pitching after six with the Bucs ahead, 5–4. At that point rain drenched Wrigley Field, and the remainder of this game, as well as the second contest in the doubleheader, were cancelled. In six innings, Meinie allowed nine hits and two walks in the victory.

BEST PIRATES TO WEAR THE NUMBER: (W-L-ERA)

Clyde Sukeforth

A coach and scout who turned down several opportunities to manage, except in 1947 when he took over the Dodgers for two games, winning both, Clyde Sukeforth was a very important part of baseball history. He was the man who helped scout and convince Jackie Robinson to sign with Brooklyn and break the color barrier. He also had some-

Babe Herman (photo courtesy of the Pittsburgh Pirates)

thing to do with a rule V draft pick the Pirates took from the Dodgers; his name was Roberto Clemente. Sukeforth coached for the team from 1952 to 1957, and spent some time scouting for the Bucs. It's not often a non-manager/player makes a "best of" list, but when Jackie Robinson and Roberto Clemente are on your resume you find your way onto it.

Heinie Meine (66–50-3.95)

His career appeared over after an abbreviated tenure with the St. Louis Browns in 1922 that saw him pitch only a single game. Heinie Meine retired to run a bar, but eventually was convinced to make a comeback; it was lucky for the Pirate Nation that he did. After returning to the majors seven years later in 1929, Meine became a staple in the Pittsburgh rotation in the early 1930s. The thirty-three-year-old set a dubious major league mark in 1930 when he gave up ten consecutive hits to the Dodgers on June 23. A junkballer, Meine made the disappointment of that day disappear a year later when he won a National League–high 19 games while also leading the league in games pitched, as well as innings pitched. He went on to win 66 games in his second major league venture and, yes, there was a bar waiting for him to run after he quit for good in 1934.

Jerry Reuss (61–46-3.52)

Many play for a very short time in the majors happy just to have lived their dream, for lefty Jerry Reuss, he spent more than just the proverbial cup of coffee in the league, playing for 22 seasons. A winner of 220 games in his career, Reuss was one of, if not the best starter for the Pirates in the mid-1970s, winning 61 times including an 18–11 campaign in 1975 when he was selected to pitch in his first All-Star game. Reuss was dealt to the Dodgers in 1978, which made him miss a shot at playing with the world champion Bucs in 1979. Wanting to pitch in four decades, he signed with the Pittsburgh organization and returned in 1990 to accomplish that feat as a September call up.

WORST PIRATES TO WEAR THE NUMBER: (W-L-ERA) (HR-RBI-AVE)

Hisanori Takahashi (0–0-8.64)

A star in Japan before coming to America with the Mets in 2010, where he won ten games, Hisanori Takahashi could not repeat his performance in 2012, when he played with the Bucs briefly, allowing eight runs in 8 1/3 innings.

Mark Huismann (1–0-7.88)

Reliever Mark Huismann may have won his lone Pirates decision, but he did not pitch effectively in his seven games with the Bucs. His time in the Steel City marked the end of his nine-year big league career.

Joe Coleman (0–0-6.10)

A mid-season acquisition in 1979 from the Giants, reliever Joe Coleman spent his last year in the show with the Pirates. A former 20-game winner with the Tigers who pitched his first major league game the age of eighteen, Coleman didn't have a great season, but pitched well in some situations during that memorable year.

OTHER NOTABLE PIRATES TO WEAR THE NUMBER

Guy Bush

Nicknamed the Mississippi Mudcat, pitcher Guy Bush pitched in seventeen major league seasons, including two with the Bucs in 1935 and '36. Winning 12 games in a Pirates uniform, Bush is most noted in Pirates lore as the hurler who gave up Babe Ruth's 714th and final home run at Forbes Field.

Xavier Rescigno

Major League Baseball's first Xavier. Mr. X, as he was known, was a good reliever for the Bucs during the final three seasons of the World War II era. When the players came back from the Armed Forces in 1946, Rescigno's time in the show came to an end. His name resurfaced in the twenty-first century when another Xavier, former Pirate Xavier Nady, came into the league, Rescigno wrote a letter to him, and met the newest member of the Xavier fraternity.

Chuck Workman

With the majority of the players in the Armed Forces during World War II, outfielder Chuck Workman got a second chance in the show as a power-hitting outfielder with 25 long balls for the Braves in 1945. He proved to be nothing more than a wartime player, coming to the Bucs in 1946 and hitting only .221 in his final big league season.

Andy Hassler

A fourteen-year veteran who had a successful run as a middle reliever during the second half of his career, Andy Hassler had a very abbreviated Pirates career. It lasted six games in 1980 before he headed off to California, where he enjoyed arguably his best success.

Bill Virdon (photo courtesy of the Pittsburgh Pirates)

Jim Winn

John Brown University alum Jim Winn was a first-round pick of the club's in the 1981 draft. Injuries and inconsistencies led to a sub-standard four-year career in black and gold with a 7–11 record and 4.47 ERA.

Mike Dunne

Part of the Andy Van Slyke trade with the Cardinals, pitcher Mike Dunne's career got off to a phenomenal start in 1987; he won 13 games with a NL-high .684 winning percentage. His phenomenal first season saw him being named *The Sporting News* Rookie of the Year. He took a nose-dive soon after, with a 12–24 mark the rest of his time in the show.

Zane Smith

A pitcher from the same school that brought us Larry Bird . . . and Tunch Ilkin . . . Indiana State's Zane Smith was a great mid-season acquisition by the Bucs in their 1990 eastern division pennant drive. A ground-ball pitcher extraordinaire, Smith was 6–2 with a 1.30 ERA down the stretch, and went 47–41 in his six-year Pirates career that ended in 1995. Boy, he would have been something to see if he pitched in today's shifting era.

Jason Christiansen

Jason Christiansen was a good southpaw option out of the bullpen for the Bucs in the late 1990s, especially in 1997 and '98, when he was 6–3 with a 2.65 ERA and six saves in 99 appearances. He was sent to the Cards in 2000, for a shortstop by the name of Jack Wilson, and continued to pitch until 2005, when he ended his eleven-year career with the Angels.

Jeff D'Amico

Having a career year with the Milwaukee Brewers in 2000, accumulating a 12–6 mark and 2.66 ERA, Jeff D'Amico signed with the Bucs three years later hoping to rekindle that magic. He led the NL in losses with 16 and had a 4.77 ERA, showing that his 2000 campaign was more of a mirage, as injuries would take their toll on this hurler.

Ryan Doumit

Ryan Doumit wasn't the best defensive catcher in major league history, which is why the Bucs tried him in the outfield and first base, but they wanted his bat in the lineup and did what they could to keep it there. He had some power, hitting more than ten home runs on three occasions, and hit .318 in 2008. Eventually, his Bucco career came to an end in 2011 as they would eventually replace Doumit behind the plate with the likes of Russell Martin and Francisco Cervelli, two guys who were phenomenal behind the plate without sacrificing offense.

Babe Herman

An outstanding major league hitter for a number of teams, Herman donned number 41 as a coach with the Pirates in 1951.

42: ALL FOR JACKIE

NUMBER RETIRED: JACKIE ROBINSON (1997)

HALL OF FAMERS TO WEAR THE NUMBER: None

FIRST PERFORMANCE WITH THE NUMBER

7/1/1932- Coming in relief of starter Steve Swetonic during a 5–3 loss to the Cardinals, Larry French pitched the eighth and ninth innings, keeping St. Louis scoreless on three hits.

FIRST HOME RUN WITH THE NUMBER

4/30/1989- Remarkably, because of the lack of offensive talent wearing the number 42 for the Pittsburgh Pirates, the generally weak-hitting Steve Carter hit the first home run by the number that honors Jackie Robinson for the Bucs. It was a three-run shot off former Pirate Don Robinson in the first inning that plated Bobby Bonilla and Benny Distefano in an 11–1 victory over the Giants.

FIRST VICTORY BY A PITCHER WITH THE NUMBER

7/6/1932- Larry French collected his ninth win of the season, tossing a complete game and allowing eight hits in a 3–1 victory.

BEST PIRATES TO WEAR THE NUMBER: (W-L-ERA)
Larry French (87–83-3.50)

One of the ultimate .500 pitchers in the history of the game, Larry French played for the Bucs for six seasons; in the five full ones in which he was in the starting rotation French won and lost double digits in each season. The southpaw would win 197 games over fourteen seasons that included stints with the Cubs and Dodgers. In 1943, he retired from the game to join the navy during World War II and would remain there for the next twenty-seven years.

Jason Schmidt (44–47-4.39)

Coming over from the Braves in 1996, Jason Schmidt was tabbed to become the new star of what was hoped to be one of the best young rotations in the game. While injuries would curtail his progress at times, he still became a very solid starter with the Bucs. In 1998 he switched to uniform number 22, so the club could honor Jackie Robinson by retiring his number. Part of another rebuilding program, Schmidt was sent to the Giants in 2001, where he became a star, especially in 2003 when he was 17–5 with a league-high .773 winning percentage and NL-low 2.34 ERA.

BEST NON-PIRATE TO WEAR THE NUMBER WHO HAS HIS NUMBER RETIRED BY THE PIRATES: (HR-RBI-AVE)

Jackie Robinson (137–734-.311)

He broke the color barrier in 1947, had a Hall of Fame career, and is the only player in American Professional Sports history to have his number retired by the entire league. Nuf said!

WORST PIRATES TO WEAR THE NUMBER: (W-L-ERA) (HR-RBI-AVE)

Jim Hopper (0–1-10.38)

A returning World War II vet, Jim Hopper's last two games of his career were in 1946; he lost his only start, giving up five runs in 4 1/3 innings.

Gene Mauch (photo courtesy of the Pittsburgh Pirates)

Steve Carter (1–3-.143)

Outfielder Steve Carter never made his mark as a Pirate, hitting only .143 in his two-year career, but he would be a star in Italy as a .431 hitter in their version of the game.

Mickey Vernon (0–1-.125)

Mickey Vernon was actually a wonderful player who, if not for his two seasons in the military, may have entered the Hall of Fame. The two-time batting champion was a coach with the Pirates in 1960 when he was placed on the active roster in September after they expanded. He was a mere one-for-eight in a Pirates uniform, so while that untypical performance put him on this list, make no mistake: when it comes to the list of baseball greats, he certainly will be on that one.

OTHER NOTABLE PIRATES TO WEAR THE NUMBER

Chuck Hartenstein

A "by god" Texas Longhorn, reliever Chuck Hartenstein was a solid reliever who came to the Pirates from the Cubs in 1969. After a solid '69 campaign in which he was 5–4 with a 3.95 ERA in 56 outings, he was put on waivers by the club a year later. It would be seven years before he got another shot in the majors, pitching for the Blue Jays.

Logan Easley

Logan Easley was a top prospect with the Yankees who was traded to the Pirates in the Doug Drabek deal. The excitement of obtaining him dwindled quickly as he managed only a 2–1 record and 5.12 ERA in 27 major league contests.

Gary Varsho

During the Pirates' championship runs in 1991 and '92, Gary Varsho was an important cog off the bench, hitting .273 in 1991. He became a minor league manager after he retired, and spent two games as the Phillies' skipper to end the 2004 season.

Jim Dykes

Jimmy Dykes was a coach with the Bucs in 1959 before moving to Detroit to begin his long career as a major league manager. In twenty-one seasons he won 1,406 games heading up the White Sox, A's, Orioles, Reds, Tigers, and Indians. Although he had a long tenure Dykes never won a pennant, and finished his career below .500, with a .477 winning percentage.

Gene Mauch

One of the great managers in the history of the game, Gene Mauch wore 42 as well as 19 in his lone season as a player for the Bucs.

43: THE WORST ALL-STAR

ALL TIME NO. 43 ROSTER	YEAR
John Holdzkom	(2014)
Ryan Reid	(2013)
Doug Slaten	(2012)
Jose Veras	(2011)
Jack Taschner	(2010)
Sean Gallagher	(2010)
Jesse Chavez	(2008–2009)
Damaso Marte	(2006–2008)
Ray Sadler	(2005)
Raul Mondesi	(2004)
Willis Roberts	(2004)
Mike Williams	(1999–2003)
Paul Wagner	(1992–1997)
Bill Landrum	(1989–1991)
Don Robinson	(1978–1987)
Bruce Dal Canton	(1967–1969)
Don Cardwell	(1965–1966)
Ralph Kiner	(1946)
Jim Weaver	(1935–1937)
Cy Blanton	(1934)
Steve Swetonic	(1932–1933)
COACHES	
Sam Narron	(1952–1964)
Don Leppert	(1970–1976)
Larry Sherry	(1977)

NUMBER RETIRED: None

HALL OF FAMERS TO WEAR THE NUMBER: None

FIRST PERFORMANCE WITH THE NUMBER

7/1/1932- Starter Steve Swetonic was not at his best, allowing five runs and seven hits in seven innings of work during a 5–3 loss to the Cardinals.

FIRST HOME RUN WITH THE NUMBER

4/18/1946- It took only three major league games until Hall of Famer Ralph Kiner hit his first home run, a two-run shot in the eighth inning, which amounted to the entire Pirate offensive output in a 6–2 loss to the Cardinals.

FIRST VICTORY BY A PITCHER WITH THE NUMBER

7/6/1932- Raising his record to 9–2 on the season, Steve Swetonic permitted only two runs in a complete-game 4–2 win over the Giants.

BEST PIRATES TO WEAR THE NUMBER: (W-L-ERA)

Don Robinson (65–69-3.85)

A native of Ashland, Kentucky, before moving to West Virginia, Don Robinson broke into the majors in a big way, winning 14 games in 1978 for the Bucs while being named *The Sporting News* National League Rookie of the Year. He went on to win 65 games in a Pittsburgh uniform while capturing two decisions during the post-season in 1979. Robinson went from being a good starter to a closer with the club, saving 43 games prior to being traded to the Giants before the 1987 campaign.

Mike Williams (15–23-3.78)

In his first go-around with the Bucs Mike Williams was a good closer, saving 69 games over three seasons. He was sent to the Astros in 2001 but returned a year later. It was an odd second tenure, with impressive achievements in what can be otherwise considered poor seasons. After setting the franchise record for saves with 46 in 2002 (one that was broken in 2015 by Mark Melancon), he was selected as an All-Star a year later, a season when he had a 6.14 ERA, which makes him one of the worst All-Star Game selections in major league history. After eclipsing a 6.00 ERA once again a year later, with 25 saves, he was sent to the Phils in mid-season, where he ended his major league career with 144 saves, all but four coming in a Pirates uniform.

Jim Weaver (36–21-3.76)

Coming over from the Cubs with Guy Bush before the 1935 campaign as part of the Larry French and Freddy Lindstrom deal, Jim Weaver enjoyed his best years with the Pirates, winning 14 games in 1935 and '36, before being purchased by the Browns in 1938.

WORST PIRATES TO WEAR THE NUMBER: (W-L-ERA) (HR-RBI-AVE)

Raul Mondesi (2–14-.283)

The stats wouldn't suggest that this slugging superstar would end up on a "worst" list when he came to the Steel City in 2004. The team had to terminate his contract after allowing him to leave for his native Dominican Republic for personal reasons, then being embarrassed when he didn't return. Nine days later, after first refusing to come back, he signed a contract with the Anaheim Angels, where he deserves to be on *their* worst list for hitting only .118 the rest of the way.

Ralph Kiner (photo courtesy of the Pittsburgh Pirates)

Sean Gallagher (2–1-6.03)

Struggling for most of his four-year career, Sean Gallagher's time in the show came to an end in Pittsburgh in 2010, when he posted a 6.03 ERA in 31 appearances.

Paul Wagner (26–40-4.58)

Paul Wagner was probably a better pitcher than his 26–40 record suggests. A prime example was in 1995, a year when he came within one out of placing his name in Pirates history with a no-hitter. Wagner went 8 2/3 innings before <u>Andres Galarraga</u> broke it up with, of all things, an infield single. His season was a microcosm of that game, with a NL-high 16 losses in a 5–16 tough-luck campaign. In juries would eventually curtail his career, and the poor teams he was on helped take him from the above section to this one.

OTHER NOTABLE PIRATES TO WEAR THE NUMBER

Ralph Kiner

The Pirate icon wore 43 in his rookie season, when he won his first home run title.

Don Cardwell

It took almost twenty years after Ralph Kiner donned the number 43 until someone else put on that uniform. Don Cardwell won 102 games in his fourteen-year major league career, including two 13-win campaigns with the Bucs. In his next-to-last major league season, in 1969, he was with the New York Mets, where he pitched magnificently down the stretch, winning four of his last five decisions.

Bruce Dal Canton

A native of California, PA, where he was an alum of the California University of Pennsylvania, Bruce Dal Canton began his eleven-year major league career with the Pirates. The reliever mastered a magnificent 20–8 mark, with a 3.57 ERA, in his four seasons in Black and Gold.

Bill Landrum

In the late 1980s, Bill Landrum inherited the closer role and had a magnificent 1989 campaign in which he saved 26 games, with an outstanding 1.086 WHIP. He was there for two more seasons, helping the team win two eastern division titles.

Ray Sadler

A good prospect with the Cubs, who was then acquired by the Bucs in the Randall Simon trade, Ray Sandler never made an impression in the majors; he had only eight at bats in 2005, and two hits. At least one was a home run against Noah Lowry of the Giants in his final game in the majors.

Damaso Marte

The original Pirate Marte, Damaso was a solid southpaw in the Bucs' bullpen during the mid 2000s where he posted a 3.52 ERA in 210 appearances before being sent to the Yankees.

Jesse Chavez

After struggling for six years as a reliever, including his first two seasons as a Pirate, Jesse Chavez has become a solid starter with the Oakland A's winning 15 games with a 3.83 ERA in 2014 and '15.

Jose Veras

After Veras posted a fine season for the Bucs in 2011, when he had a 3.80 ERA in 79 appearances, the Pirates Nation was not happy when the pitcher was sent to the Brewers after the season for Casey McGehee, especially since McGehee was coming off a season in which the former star had hit a mere .223. Veras did well in Milwaukee, and McGehee wasn't as bad in a Pirates uniform as his .230 average would have suggested. Ironically, McGhee was in turn dealt for a struggling reliever by the name of Chad Qualls, which put the Nation in an uproar again. Since the Pirates used him in an unsuccessfull effort to upgrade a bullpen that had been weakened without Veras, the Pirates Nation had good reason for their irritation.

Ryan Reid

Coming up to the show late in life, Ryan Reid made his first appearance for the Bucs during their magical season of 2013, when he posted a 1.64 ERA in seven appearances. He returned to the minors and, unfortunately, was out of professional baseball in 2015.

John Holdzkom

It's a terrific rags-to-riches story for the former fourth-round pick by the New York Mets in 2006. John Holdzkom's career was going nowhere, so he resorted to playing independent baseball in order to keep his career hopes alive. Luckily, he began to improve and the Bucs signed him to a minor league deal. He flew through the organization, first in Altoona, then Indianapolis, before getting a long-awaited call to the big leagues in September of 2014. He was unhittable with the Bucs in nine appearances, with a sparkling 0.667 WHIP. He even made the post-season roster with the club. His progress, unfortunately, was put on hold as arm injuries derailed his 2015 campaign. Hopefully, it will continue to develop in 2016.

44: MY DEAR WATSON

ALL TIME NO. 44 ROSTER	YEAR
Tony Watson	(2012–2015)
Alex Presley	(2011)
Brandon Moss	(2009–2010)
Evan Meek	(2008)
Josh Sharpless	(2006–2007)
Mark Corey	(2003–2004)
Dennys Reyes	(2003)
Joe Boever	(1996)
Danny Darwin	(1996)
Rick White	(1994–1995)
Ben Shelton	(1993)
Cecil Espy	(1991)
John Cangelosi	(1987–1990)
Tom Prince	(1987)
Jeff Zaske	(1983–1984)
Eddie Solomon	(1980–1982)
Doe Boyland	(1979)
Cito Gaston	(1978)
Larry Demery	(1975–1977)
John Lamb	(1973)
Tom Detore	(1973)
Carl Taylor	(1969)
Luis Marquez	(1954)
Hal Rice	(1953–1954)
George Metkovich	(1952–1953)
Bill Baker	(1946)
Rip Sewell	(1938–1939)
Ken Heintzelman	(1937)
Jack Salveson	(1935)
Bill Harris	(1932–1934)
COACHES	
Frank Oceak	(1959–1964, 1970–1972)
Terry Collins	(1992–1993)
Trent Jewett	(2001–2002)

NUMBER RETIRED: None

HALL OF FAMERS TO WEAR THE NUMBER: None

FIRST PERFORMANCE WITH THE NUMBER

7/1/1932- After starter Larry French was ripped apart by the Cubs in the first inning for four runs, reliever Bill Harris entered the game and pitched eight solid innings, allowing two runs on four hits. The Bucs came back for a 9–6 win as Harris got credit for the victory.

FIRST HOME RUN WITH THE NUMBER

5/10/1939- In the process of shutting out the New York Giants, 5–0, pitcher Rip Sewell helped himself offensively with a solo shot for his first major league home run.

FIRST VICTORY BY A PITCHER WITH THE NUMBER

See above under first performance for information on the first win by a pitcher.

BEST PIRATES TO WEAR THE NUMBER: (W-L-ERA) (HR-RBI-AVE)
Tony Watson (24–8-2.46)

A ninth-round pick out of the University of Nebraska, Tony Watson began his minor league career as a starter on the mound. Thankfully, in

Rip Sewell (photo courtesy of the Pittsburgh Pirates)

Altoona during the 2010 campaign, he was switched to the bullpen, where the southpaw has made a living since. He is considered one of the toughest eighth-inning set-up men in the game today, helping to lead the Bucs to three consecutive post-season appearances with sub-2 ERA's over the past two seasons. A career as a closer could be in the cards in the future, but in the meantime Clint Hurdle can count on Watson as a great option to set up Mark Melancon.

Catfish Metkovich (11–88-.276)

For a little more than two seasons over his ten-year major league career, Catfish Metkovich was a centerfielder/first baseman with the Bucs. He had a solid run with the team, hitting .276, which was enough to claim him as a "best of." Besides his stats, anyone with the name "Catfish"—given to him by the great Casey Stengel for his having cut himself while trying to release a catfish from a hook — always gets consideration for a best of list.

WORST PIRATES TO WEAR THE NUMBER: (W-L-ERA) (HR-RBI-AVE)

Jack Salveson (0–1-9.00)

In his five-year big league career pitcher, Jack Salveson was mostly a solid reliever, except for a brief time in 1935 when he found himself in a Pirates uniform. He pitched poorly in his five games before being dealt to the White Sox in June, where he did, of course, rebound. After he ended his time in the show in real life, he became part of it in the movies, serving as an extra in *The Lou Gehrig Story* and *The Winning Team*, before his most compelling role as a batting practice pitcher in the famed TV series, *Home Run Derby.*

Luis Marquez (0–0-.111)

A pioneer of sorts as the first player of color to be signed by the New York Yankees in 1949, Marquez had earlier played for the Homestead Grays in the Negro League for three seasons, where he hit .335. He could not translate that success to the majors, where he also played in parts of two seasons with the Braves and Cubs before ending his career in Pittsburgh in 1954, batting one-for nine. He was shot and killed in 1988 by his son-in-law.

Dennis Reyes (0–0-10.45)

A middle reliever with eleven teams over fifteen years, Dennis Reyes was not at his best in Pittsburgh in 2003, when 12 less-than-stellar appearances convinced management to release him.

OTHER NOTABLE PIRATES TO WEAR THE NUMBER

Bill Harris

Bill Harris pitched the majority of his contests in the show with the Bucs, between 1932 and '34. He appeared in 83 games, mostly in relief, with a record of 15–15 and a 3.45 ERA. After he retired he became a long-time scout and minor league manager for the Giants, Reds, Senators, and Yankees.

Rip Sewell

Rip Sewell wore number 44 in his first two full major league seasons, in 1938 and '39.

Hal Rice

A starting left fielder for the Bucs in 1953, when he hit .311, Rice fell off a year later with a .173 average, and was shipped off to the Cubs. While he had a solid seven-year career, his biggest contribution was to the nation during World War II. He was given a Battlefield Commission and was injured in battle serving in the South Pacific.

Larry Demery

After two solid seasons with the Bucs, in 1975 and '76, Larry Demery was 17–12 with a 3.05 ERA; things looked up for his career. At the age of twenty-four, in 1977, his ERA ballooned to 5.08, and his time in the show came to an end.

Cito Gaston

After a good ten years in the majors with the San Diego Padres, where he hit .318 in the franchise's second season of 1970, Gaston finished his big league career with the Bucs in 1978, getting a hit in two at bats. He went on to manage the Toronto Blue Jays for twelve years, winning two World Series championships in the Great White North.

Eddie Solomon

Eddie Solomon had a fine ten-year career in the majors that included a great two-year run with the Bucs in 1980 and '81, when he had a 15–9 mark and 2.93 ERA. The year 1982 proved to be his undoing with the Bucs, as a 6.75 ERA in 11 contests prompted a trade to the White Sox. Eddie Solomon's story ended tragically; he was killed in an auto accident in 1986.

John Cangelosi

A popular bench player with the Bucs in the late 1980s, when he hit .243, John Cangelosi ended up sticking around in the majors for thirteen seasons, retiring in 1999. The highlight was his rookie year with the White Sox, when he stole an AL rookie record 50 stolen bases. Today, Cangelosi runs a baseball school in Lockport, Illinois.

Cecil Espy

Cecil Espy was a speedy outfielder with Texas, where he stole 78 bases over two seasons. An important bench player for the Bucs during their final two eastern division championship squads in 1991 and '92,

Espy hit .254 and had two hits in pinch-hitting appearances during the post-season.

Danny Darwin

Enjoying a fine twenty-one-year major league career with 172 wins that included one ERA title with Houston in 1990, where he had a 2.21 mark, Danny Darwin was forty when he came to the Bucs in 1996. He pitched well with a 7–9 mark and 3.02 ERA, before he was traded to Houston for closer Rich Loiselle.

Joe Boever

Joe Boever was a good reliever for twelve major league seasons before pitching his last campaign with the Bucs in 1996. Boever struggled in 13 appearances, losing both decisions with a 5.40 ERA.

Josh Sharpless

A local pitcher from Beaver, PA, where he went to Freedom High School before heading off to Allegheny College, Josh Sharpless looked as though he was going to be a solid reliever after a 1.50 ERA in 14 appearances his rookie season in 2006, but pitched poorly in 2007, never to return to the show again. He claimed that pitching coach Jim Colborn had played with his delivery the next spring season, an accusation that reportedly had also hurt the development of Zach Duke.

Terry Collins

The manager of the 2015 National League champion New York Mets had his roots in the Pirates organization; he spent his first three seasons in the minors after being selected in the nineteenth round by the Bucs in the 1971 draft, then served as a coach for Jim Leyland in 1992 and '93.

45: BADASS

NUMBER RETIRED: None

HALL OF FAMERS TO WEAR THE NUMBER: None

FIRST PERFORMANCE WITH THE NUMBER 6/30/1932-

In the first game in which the Pirates wore numbers on their uniforms, the St. Louis Cardinals and Pittsburgh engaged in a slugfest. Starter Heinie Meine couldn't make it out of the fifth, and rookie Bill Swift came on to close out the frame. Swift went the rest of the way, allowing only a run and four hits for his sixth victory of the year in the historic 9–6 win.

FIRST HOME RUN WITH THE NUMBER 6/17/1936-

Pitcher Bill Swift made it a clean sweep of firsts for a number 45, when he smacked his first major league home run, a two-run shot, in a 14–5 victory over the Dodgers.

FIRST VICTORY BY A PITCHER WITH THE NUMBER

6/30/1932- See above under first performance for information on the first win by a pitcher.

BEST PIRATES TO WEAR THE NUMBER: (W-L-ERA)
John Candelaria (124–87-3.17)

A true badass on the mound, southpaw John Candelaria announced his presence in the majors in an impressive way, striking out a record

14 Reds during the 1975 NLCS. The next year he tossed a no-hitter against the Dodgers on national TV, then had one of the great seasons in Pirates history with a 20–5 mark in 1977 that included a National League-best .800 winning percentage and his lone ERA title at 2.34. He went on to win 124 games with the Bucs, and pitched in the majors for nineteen seasons despite a chronic bad back . . . something that only a true badass could accomplish.

John Candelaria (photo courtesy of the Pittsburgh Pirates)

Bill Swift (91–79-3.57)

Pittsburgh's original badass to wear number 45, Bill Swift made his living out of accuracy; hitting a strike zone better than almost any other Pirates pitcher in the history of the franchise with the 74th best walks-per-nine-inning rate of all-time at 1.929. He won 91 games over eight seasons, and was the model of consistency his first five years, winning more than 11 games each time. He was dealt in 1940 to the Braves, but remains one of the franchise's greatest players.

Gerrit Cole (40–20-3.07)

The latest Pirates badass is off to an incredible start in his Pirates career. Despite the fact he pitched poorly in the 2015 Wild Card game, he won 19 games that year, and 67 percent of his games over his first three seasons. If his unlimited potential continues to grow, the former first overall pick in the amateur draft could go down as not only one of the greatest number 45s in franchise history but also as one of the top hurlers regardless of number.

WORST PIRATES TO WEAR THE NUMBER: (W-L-ERA) (HR-RBI-AVE)

Duaner Sanchez (1–0–16.20)

Duaner Sanchez had an arm of gold that the Pirates hoped to harvest in the early twenty-first century. Instead, the fire-armed righty was an unmitigated mistake, with a 2.520 WHIP. Like many others experienced during the Pirates' era of incapability, Sanchez finally became effective when he went somewhere else as a solid relief option for the Dodgers and Mets.

Dave Roberts (0–0–.125)

1966 was not a good year for the number 45 in Pittsburgh, as both players who wore the number ended up on the "worst" list. First baseman Dave Roberts came over from Houston after two abbreviated seasons. He promptly had two hits in 16 at bats, which ended his major league career.

Gene Michael (0–2–.152)

Gene Michael went on to become a .229 hitter in ten major league seasons, mostly with the Yankees, and was a slick fielding middle infielder after his less-than-stellar first year with the Pirates in 1966. While he enjoyed a long career as a player, it's his time as a manager and general manager with the Bronx Bombers where he made a name for himself on the national scene.

OTHER NOTABLE PIRATES TO WEAR THE NUMBER

Ken Gables

After a being discharged from the Army in World War II, pitcher Ken Gables enjoyed a fine rookie season in 1945, with an 11–7 record. He stumbled out of the pen a year later and, following a horrible outing in 1947, was sent to the minors, never to appear again in the show.

Dave Augustine

If not for an overturned call by an umpire, the name Dave Augustine may have gone down in Pirates history for an heroic home run that might have given them the eastern division title in 1973. In a game against the Mets on September 20 he hit what they thought was a homer in the 13th inning that most likely would have given them a win over New York. Instead, it was ruled that the ball hit the top of the fence and was a double, with Cleon Jones taking the ball and throwing out Richie Zisk at home. The Mets won the contest in the bottom of the frame and finished as division winners with 82 victories. Had Augustine's shot been upheld as a home run, the Pirates would have probably won the game, which would have tied the Mets for the division. He went on to play only one more season, ending his time in the majors without a homer.

Terry Mulholland

A Uniontown native who pitched for Laurel Highland High School, Terry Mulholland was a fine pitcher in the show for twenty seasons. In 2001 he spent a brief period with his hometown team, tossing 22 games, all but one in relief, with a 3.72 ERA.

Ian Snell

Like many others during the Bucs twenty-year streak of futility, Ian Snell was an incredible prospect who stalled out at the major league level. He did have some success, winning 14 games for the Bucs in 2006, but could never put it all together and was out of the show in 2010, after a two-year stint with the Mariners.

Erik Bedard

A free-agent signing by the Bucs in 2012, Erik Bedard did have some good starts with the team, but unfortunately they were few and far between, as the eleven-year vet went 7–14, with a 5.01 ERA, in the last season of the losing Pirates era.

Joe Morgan

No, this wasn't the Hall of Fame second baseman for the Reds, but a coach for the club under Bill Virdon in 1972 and a longtime minor league manager, who spent seven seasons in the Bucs organization leading his teams to three first-place finishes and a league title for York in 1968. He went on to manage the Red Sox from 1988 to 1991, winning two eastern division crowns.

#46: CY MINUS THE AWARD

ALL TIME NO. 46 ROSTER	YEAR
Vance Worley	(2014–2015)
Garrett Jones	(2009–2013)
Jimmy Barthmaier	(2008)
Tony Armas	(2007)
Brian Meadows	(2002–2005)
Damaso Marte	(2001)
Pete Schourek	(1999)
Jermaine Allensworth	(1996–1998)
Gary Wilson	(1995)
Junior Noboa	(1994)
Hector Fajardo	(1991)
Doug Bair	(1989–1990)
Tom Prince	(1987–1989)
Ray Krawczyk	(1985–1986)
Miguel Dilone	(1983)
Reggie Walton	(1982)
Mark Lee	(1980–1981)
Steve Brye	(1978)
Ed Whitson	(1978)
Jim Minshall	(1974)
Chuck Brinkman	(1974)
Ed Acosta	(1970)
Orlando Pena	(1970)
Bill Hall	(1954)
Ed Bahr	(1946)
Cy Blanton	(1935–1939)
Leon Chagnon	(1932–1934)
COACHES	
Trent Jewett	(2000)

NUMBER RETIRED: None

HALL OF FAMERS TO WEAR THE NUMBER: None

FIRST PERFORMANCE WITH THE NUMBER

7/2/1932- In relief of Ray Kremer and Larry French, Leon Chagnon pitched three perfect innings, striking out three in a 5–4 loss to the Cardinals.

FIRST HOME RUN WITH THE NUMBER

5/19/1978- In a 5–3 victory over the Expos, Steve Brye smacked the third home run in the fourth inning, and the second of back-to-back ones behind Phil Garner, to put Pittsburgh up, 5–1. It would be Brye's last major league homer.

FIRST VICTORY BY A PITCHER WITH THE NUMBER

7/4/1932- Two days after pitching a perfect three frames in his debut as number 46, Leon Chagnon remained perfect with two innings of hitless relief against the Cubs after Glenn Spencer went the first nine. Pittsburgh plated a run in the bottom of the 11th to beat the Cubs, 6–5, giving Chagnon the victory.

Cy Blanton (photo courtesy of the Pittsburgh Pirates)

BEST PIRATES TO WEAR THE NUMBER: (W-L-ERA) (HR-RBI-AVE)

Cy Blanton (58–51-3.28)

One of the top pitchers for the Pirates in the 1930s, Cy Blanton could have been one of the best in the history of the franchise, if not for the fact he had issues with alcohol. The right-hander, who had a breaking pitch that dazzled hitters with its sharp drop at the end, won the NL ERA title his rookie season in 1935, with a 2.58 mark. He went on to pitch well with the Bucs until 1939. The following spring training, he tore ligaments in his elbow and was dealt to the Phils, where he ended his career two years later. After failing an Army physical, Blanton sadly died at the age of thirty-seven, in 1945, at an Oklahoma hospital due to the effects of his alcoholism. According to his biography on the SABR bio project by Gregory H Wolf, the cause of death was toxic psychosis from "multiple internal hemorrhages caused by cirrhosis of the liver."

Garrett Jones (100–325-.256)

No one thought much of it when the Pirates signed Garrett Jones in December of 2008; it appeared to be yet another reclamation project of a failed prospect who would end up a failure here as well. Luckily, this one worked, as Jones went back and forth between first base and right field, hitting 100 home runs over five seasons, including a banner campaign in 2012 when he hit 27 and knocked in 86. It was a prelude of things to come: Pittsburgh has become a place where reclamation projects go to succeed.

Jermaine Allensworth (10–98-.272)

Jermaine Allensworth possessed little power, but the former first-round pick seemed to be coming into his own during his third major league season, when he was hitting .309 mid-way through the 1998 campaign. The first baseball All-American in Purdue University history became yet another Pirates casualty in the late '90s. He was dealt to the Royals for virtually no return, a minor league pitcher named Manuel Bernal who never played in the show.

WORST PIRATES TO WEAR THE NUMBER: (W-L-ERA) (HR-RBI-AVE)

Tom Prince (4–44-.177)

Usually, a .177 hitter wouldn't last seven seasons with a team, but in the case of backup catcher Tom Prince, he was so good defensively that's exactly what happened. Prince went on to play seventeen years in the majors even though his average barely made it above the Mendoza line, at .202. Prince went on to become a good minor league manager in the Bucs' organization, that included a stint with their AA team in Altoona.

Ray Krawczyk (0–3-8.65)

Ray Krawczyk was a Roy Face clone in the minor leagues; his forkball made him a minor league all-star. Unfortunately, throughout his three seasons in a Pirates uniform his forkball resembled a batting practice toss, as his 2.462 WHIP would attest to.

Hector Fajardo (0–0-9.95)

Hector Fajardo's velocity went up almost 10 MPH after bone chips were removed from his arm, but unfortunately it didn't result in success in the big leagues. He struggled in his brief Pirates career before doing the same with the Rangers over four seasons.

Reggie Walton (0–0-.200)

A top prospect in the Mariners system, who hit .302 with the Bucs' AAA team with Portland in 1982, Reggie Walton had an abbreviated major league career that ended with 15 unproductive at bats in a Pirates uniform after a call-up during his banner season with Portland.

OTHER NOTABLE PIRATES TO WEAR THE NUMBER

Leon Chagnon

A struggling reliever for most of his five seasons in a Pirates uniform, where he went 19–14 with a 4.61 ERA, Leon Chagnon was at his best when he first donned a number on his back, winning 15 of his 19 career games in 1932 and '33.

Orlando Pena

Cuban Orlando Pena was a junkballer who had the distinction of losing 20 games in a season, which he did in 1963 with the Kansas City A's. He would eventually spend fourteen seasons in the majors, but his original run ended in 1967. Three years later, in 1970, after he had served as a batting practice pitcher with the Royals, the Bucs inked the thirty-six-year-old. Pena had a 4.78 ERA in 23 appearances that year. He stayed in the majors until 1975, retiring at forty-one after a brief stint with the Angels.

Tony Armas

He would eventually go on to become a two-time American League home run champion, the second coming in 1984 with a career-high 43 and AL-best 123 RBIs, but in 1976 Tony Armas was a young player with Pittsburgh in his first major league season. He had two hits in six at bats before being dealt to the A's as part of the Phil Garner deal.

Steve Brye

A decent outfielder with the Twins for seven seasons, averaging .261, Steve Brye ended his nine-year major league career in Pittsburgh, hitting .235 in 115 at bats during the 1978 campaign.

Doug Bair

Over fifteen seasons, Doug Bair was a good reliever who saved 44 games for the Reds in 1978 and '79. He ended his big league career with the Bucs in 1989 and '90, when he went out in a bang posting a 3.12 ERA in the Black and Gold.

Pete Schourek

He pitched in eleven major league campaigns, but in reality Pete Schourek's career comes down to one season, 1995, when he ran up an 18–7 record for the Reds and was the Cy Young runner-up. He was only 48–70 the rest of his career, including a 4–7 mark with the Bucs in 1999.

Brian Meadows

A struggling starter in his first five seasons with the Marlins, Padres, and Royals, Brian Meadows continued his issues with the Bucs in his first year with a 1–6 record in 2002. The Bucs turned him into a middle reliever; he appeared in 160 games in three campaigns and had decent success, with a 1.319 WHIP and 4.28 ERA.

Tony Armas Jr.

Tony Armas Jr. pitched one season with the Bucs, in the latter part of his major league career, where he was 4–5 with a 6.03 ERA . With Pittsburgh he chose to wear his dad's Pirates number. He had actually been a good starter with the Expos early on, but arm injuries in 2003 curtailed his success.

Vance Worley

Once called the best pitching prospect in Northern California, the "Vanimal" came to Pittsburgh a broken hurler who had once been 11–3 with the Phillies; he was fixed by the great Ray Searage and became an important member of the 2014 Bucs, with an 8–4 mark and 2.85 ERA.

#47: PAPA FRANCISCO

ALL TIME NO. 47 ROSTER	YEAR
Francisco Liriano	(2013–2015)
Evan Meek	(2009–2012)
John Van Benschoten	(2004–2005, 2007–2008)
Scott Sauerbeck	(1999–2003)
Jon Lieber	(1994–1998)
Scott Bullett	(1991, 1993)
Jeff Schulz	(1991)
Jerry Reuss	(1990)
Scott Little	(1989)
Randy Milligan	(1988)
Tommy Gregg	(1987–1988)
Cecilio Guante	(1982–1986)
Ernie Camacho	(1981)
Ed Whitson	(1977)
Dave Parker	(1973)
Jim Nelson	(1972)
Mudcat Grant	(1970)
Earl Francis	(1960)
Bill Clemensen	(1946)
Mace Brown	(1936–1939)
Bud Hafey	(1935)
Harold Smith	(1932–1935)
Glenn Spencer	(1932)

NUMBER RETIRED: None

HALL OF FAMERS TO WEAR THE NUMBER: None

FIRST PERFORMANCE WITH THE NUMBER

7/4/1932- In the second game of a July 4 double header, Glenn Spencer went nine innings, allowing ten hits and four runs in a 6–5 victory over the Cubs, Unfortunately, the game went 11 innings, so Spencer did not get the decision.

FIRST HOME RUN WITH THE NUMBER

8/6/1935- the Cubs' Roy Henshaw limited the Pirates to one run on this day, in a 2–1 Chicago win; that one run was Bud Hafey's first Bucco homer, a seventh-inning solo shot.

FIRST VICTORY BY A PITCHER WITH THE NUMBER

9/21/1932- Pitching the last four innings of relief for Bill Swift, Glenn Spencer gave up three hits and a run as the Pirates rebounded with six runs in the final three innings for a 9–6 victory over the Cubs, giving Spencer his fourth win of the season.

BEST PIRATES TO WEAR THE NUMBER: (W-L-ERA)

Francisco Liriano (35–25-3.26)

After the twentieth consecutive disappointing season, 2012, one couldn't blame the Pirates Nation for not being too excited when

GM Neal Huntington signed former golden boy Francisco Liriano to a contract. When he broke his arm in a Christmas Day household accident trying to playfully scare his children, the signing became almost comical. Liriano got together with Ray Searage, and magic was made. He went on to win 16 games, capturing *The Sporting News* Comeback Player of the Year Award, and was masterful

Francisco Liriano (photo courtesy of the author)

in the wild card game against the Reds. Signing a three-year contract with the club before 2015, Liriano continued to be strong, and hopefully in the future will make what was once considered a comical signing one of the best for the franchise in its long, storied history.

Mace Brown (55–45-3.67)

A pioneer of sorts as one of the game's first great relievers, Mace Brown was at his best in 1938 when the Bucs were about to win their seventh National League crown, only to falter the final week of the season. That year Brown pitched in a NL high 51 games, all but two in relief, while going 15–9. The World War II vet and two-time senior circuit saves leader became a longtime coach and scout for the Red Sox after he retired from the game.

Cecilio Guante (13–17-3.06)

There wasn't much to get excited about with the Pirates in the mid-1980s, but right-handed reliever Cecilio Guante was certainly one positive note for the Bucco Nation. A native of the Dominican Republic, Guante was very effective over his five Pittsburgh seasons, with a 3.06 ERA and 1.223 WHIP, allowing only 7.6 hits per nine innings. He was also a treasure for the franchise, because he left town as part of the deal with the New York Yankees that brought the Pirates Doug Drabek.

WORST PIRATES TO WEAR THE NUMBER: (W-L-ERA) (HR-RBI-AVE)

John Van Benschoten (2–13-9.20)

The first-round pick by the Pirates in 2001, John Van Benschoten was a powerful hitter for Kent State who led the nation with 31 long balls as well as being a dominant pitcher. The Bucs chose him as a pitcher, which was a move they would regret. He only won two games as a Pirate, with a 9.20 ERA, a major league high for any player with at least 17 starts. He also holds the dubious mark for most innings pitched while giving up more runs than innings pitched (90 innings, 92 runs). To be fair, he had major shoulder surgery in 2005, but with the way he had pitched for Pittsburgh before the surgery, it's not sure it would have mattered much.

Bud Hafey (10–29-.222)

There was Hall of Fame blood cursing through Bud Hafey; unfortunately, his cousin Chick got the motherlode of it, as this Hafey hit only .222 in 1935 and '36.

Scott Bullett (0–4-.186)

An eighteen-year professional baseball veteran who became a world traveler, also playing in Mexico and Japan, Scott Bullett's long career unfortunately included only four seasons in the big leagues, the first two with the Bucs, where he hit .186 in 59 at bats.

OTHER NOTABLE PIRATES TO WEAR THE NUMBER

Glenn Spencer

Pitching for four of his five seasons in a Pirates uniform, Glenn Spencer won 23 times during that time period, almost half of them in 1931 when he had 11 victories. Spencer also led the senior circuit in games finished in 1931 with 22. His time in the show came to an end in 1933, with 17 appearances for the Giants.

Hal Smith

The question that begs to be asked is, how many Hal Smiths played major league baseball? The answer is three, all playing a portion of their careers in Pittsburgh. This particular Hal Smith, or Harold if you want to be technical, was the only one to spend his whole time in the show with the Bucs, and who tossed a shutout in his first start, a 7–0 win against the Cubs on September 22, 1932. He pitched between 1932 and '35, when he was 12–11 with a 3.77 ERA.

Dave Parker and Jerry Reuss

Dave Parker wore 47 for his first major league season in 1973. Jerry Reuss wore it as he returned to Pittsburgh in 1990, in his last of 22 years in the show.

Ernie Camacho

Longtime reliever Ernie Camacho, who spent ten years in the show, mostly with the Indians, was in his second season when he came to the Steel City in 1981. A twelfth-round draft pick by Pittsburgh in 1975 who chose not to sign with the team, Camacho was 0–1 with a 4.98 ERA in seven appearances.

Tommy Gregg

A top prospect with the Bucs, who hit .371 in Harrisburg before being called up in 1987, Tommy Gregg hit only .217 in 23 at bats for Pittsburgh in two seasons before being dealt to Atlanta for Ken Oberkfell in 1988. He went on to play for the hated Braves through 1992, and eventually became a longtime minor league coach, the last five years with the Omaha Storm Chasers.

Randy Milligan

The Pirates traded Mackey Sasser for the Mets' slugging first-base prospect, Randy Milligan, in 1988. They didn't give him much of a chance, sending him to Baltimore a year later after only 103 at bats.

He eventually became that anticipated slugger in an Orioles uniform, smacking 20 home runs in 1990 and 70 over his career.

Jon Lieber

A top prospect with the Royals who was supposed to be one of the pieces of the Pirates rotation that would keep the franchise winning through the 1990s, Jon Lieber never lived up to those lofty hopes; he and his savage slider won 38 games for the Bucs over five years. Just like so many others had in the 1990s, Lieber transitioned into a star only after he left Pittsburgh, becoming a 20-game winner with the Cubs in 2001, a season that saw him finish fourth in the Cy Young chase. He was their last 20-game winner until Pirate slayer Jake Arrieta turned the trick fourteen years later.

Scott Sauerbeck

Southpaws are always an important part of a bullpen, and in the early years of the twenty-first century Scott Sauerbeck was that person for the Pirates. He tossed 341 games in five seasons for the team, winning 19 games with a 3.56 ERA.

Evan Meek

Evan Meek pitched for six major league seasons but, let's be honest, his career can be defined by one, 2010, when he was selected to pitch in his one and only All-Star Game. He had a 2.14 ERA that year, and an impressive 1.050 WHIP. It was a great campaign for the former Rule V draft pick, as injuries would limit his success to that one season.

#48: THE TINKERER

ALL TIME NO. 48 ROSTER	YEAR
Jared Hughes	(2012–2015)
Jose Veras	(2011)
Tim Wood	(2011)
Matt Pagnozzi	(2011)
Javier Lopez	(2010)
Joe Martinez	(2010)
Delwyn Young	(2009)
T.J. Beam	(2008)
Oliver Perez	(2003–2005)
Jim Mann	(2003)
Sean Lowe	(2002)
Todd Ritchie	(1999–2001)
Sean Lawrence	(1998)
Abraham Nunez	(1997)
Rich Aude	(1993, 1995–1996)
Dave Otto	(1993)
Roger Mason	(1991–1992)
Ted Power	(1990)
Rick Reuschel	(1985–1987)
Clay Carroll	(1978)
Timothy Jones	(1977)
Jim Minshall	(1975)
Sam McDowell	(1975)
Omar Moreno	(1974–1975)
John Lamb	(1973)
Chuck Goggin	(1972)
Rimp Lanier	(1971)
Dick Barone	(1960)
Tom Cheney	(1960)
Ron Blackburn	(1958)
Ken Hamlin	(1957, 1959)
Joe Bowman	(1938–1939)
Ray Berres	(1937)
Waite Hoyt	(1933–1937)
Erv Brame	(1932)
COACHES	
Bob Skinner	(1979–1985)
Jim Colborn	(2006–2007)

NUMBER RETIRED: None

HALL OF FAMERS TO WEAR THE NUMBER: WAITE HOYT (1969)

FIRST PERFORMANCE WITH THE NUMBER

7/2/1932- In a 5–4 loss to the Cardinals, Erv Brame was the last of four pitchers, allowing three hits and a run in two innings.

FIRST HOME RUN WITH THE NUMBER

8/25/1985- Rick Reuschel led off the top of the eighth with his only home run in a Pirate uniform during a 9–3 victory over the Cubs. Reuschel also had a double and two RBIs in the rout.

FIRST VICTORY BY A PITCHER WITH THE NUMBER

7/23/1932- With the Pirates and Cubs tied at six after five innings, Erv Brame came into the contest for Bill Swift. He went two innings, surrendering a run on two hits as the Bucs rebounded for an 11–8 win, with Brame picking up his second win of the year.

Omar Moreno (photo courtesy of the Pittsburgh Pirates)

BEST PIRATES TO WEAR THE NUMBER: (W-L-ERA)

Waite Hoyt (35–31-3.08)

Waite Hoyt was a Hall of Fame hurler with the New York Yankees during the Babe Ruth era, winning a league-high 22 games for the famed Murderers Row team in 1927. In 21 seasons, Hoyt won 237 games and came to the Bucs in 1933 at the age of thirty-three. He won 35 games over five seasons, including a fantastic 15–6 campaign in 1934. A fine announcer with Cincinnati after he retired, Hoyt was elected to the Hall of Fame in 1969.

Rick Reuschel (31–30-3.04)

Rick Reuschel was a thirty-six-year-old hurler when the Pirates signed him before the 1985 campaign. He was more than worth the money, winning 14 games his first season, going on to a third-place finish in the Cy Young race in 1987. That year, the Bucs would deal their veteran hurler in August to the Giants. He went on to pitch nineteen major league seasons, winning 214 games.

Erv Brame (52–37-4.76)

Spending his entire five-year career in a Pirates uniform, Erv Brame showed that, despite the fact that he was a top pitcher with the Bucs and won 17 games in 1930, he pitched in a hitting era that caused two pitching maladies associated with such great hitting periods: high ERAs and WHIPs. In Brame's case, his ERA was close to 5 and his WHIP stood at 1.488. Besides being a good pitcher, he was also a great hitter with a career .306 average, and was used many times as a pinch-hitter. Even though others in franchise history may have had loftier stats, when they needed a win during his time, Brame would find a way to get it.

WORST PIRATES TO WEAR THE NUMBER: (W-L-ERA) (HR-RBI-AVE)

Jim Colborn (2006–2007)

An All-Star hurler who pitched a no-hitter in 1977 with the Royals, Jim Colborn came to the Bucs as a pitching coach for manager Jim Tracy. Tracy proved not to be the man for the job, and neither was

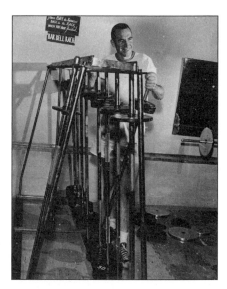

Bob Skinner (photo courtesy of the Pittsburgh Pirates)

Colborn. He reportedly took one of the team's great prospects, Zach Duke, who was coming off an incredible rookie year, and tried to change Duke's mechanics. He changed them to the point that the future ace couldn't even make it as a number five hurler. Reliever Josh Sharpless also had the same complaints. Fixing pitchers who don't need fixing is what gets you on a "worst of" list, and this legendary tinkerer is right where he belongs.

Dick Barone (0–0–.000)

It was 1960, and the Pirates were in the midst of an exciting pennant chase when future MVP Dick Groat went down with a broken wrist. Dick Schofield took over at short and did well, but the team needed a backup at the position, so they called up Dick Barone. Barone only came up six times and was hitless. While it would be the only six at bats in his major league career, he had them with the world champions and won himself a ring.

Sean Lawrence (2–1-7.32)-

Despite the fact that he went 2–1 in his rookie year as a late season call-up in 1998, southpaw Sean Lawrence had a huge 7.02 ERA, which precluded any future call-ups to the majors.

OTHER NOTABLE PIRATES TO WEAR THE NUMBER

Joe Bowman

A 20-game loser with the Phillies, who was the starting pitcher for Philadelphia at Cincinnati in the first night game ever, in 1935, Joe Bowman finally stopped losing when he played for a team that wasn't bad. He was 33–38 for the Bucs over five seasons, before ending his Pirates career in 1941.

Sam McDowell

"Sudden Sam" McDowell was one of the great forces in the American League in the 1970s. He led the American League in strikeouts with the Indians five times, twice surpassing 300 Ks. McDowell also was a 20-game winner, and captured the ERA title in 1965 at 2.18. He was a Pittsburgh native who could have been a Hall of Famer if not for his bouts with alcoholism. In 1975 he ended his time in the show with his hometown team, going 2–1 with a 2.86 ERA. He eventually overcame his demons, and went on to be a substance abuse counselor with the Bucs.

Timothy Jones

It was a brief career for Timothy Jones, lasting all of ten innings in 1977, but while short, it was a spectacular ten innings, allowing only four hits and no runs while winning his only major league decision, a 5–1 victory against the Cubs on October 2.

Clay Carroll

For fourteen seasons Clay Carroll was one of the best relievers in the game, mostly for the Cincinnati Reds, saving 143 games while winning

96. He spent year number fifteen, his final big league season, in the Steel City, where he pitched twice, allowing a run in four innings of work.

Ted Power

Thirteen-year vet Ted Power was a reliever who became a starter, then returned to the pen when he came to Pittsburgh in 1990. He was effective in 40 games for the eastern division champs, with a 3.66 ERA before heading back from whence he came, the Reds.

Roger Mason

For two seasons, Roger Mason was a good reliever for the Pittsburgh Pirates during their eastern division championship run in the 1990s. Mason was 8–9 with a 3.82 ERA and 11 saves, over two seasons.

Rich Aude

A second-round pick by the Bucs in 1989, Rich Aude was a top prospect with the Pirates who never made it big in the show. Playing in three abbreviated seasons, he hit .225 in 151 at bats. After he retired he became a longtime scout for Tampa Bay.

Todd Richie

After coming over from the Twins, Todd Richie became the best pitcher in the Pirates rotation during the 1999 campaign, with a career-best 15–9 mark. But he wasn't able to duplicate that success, and was sent to the White Sox in 2002 for Kip Wells, Sean Lowe, and Josh Fogg.

Oliver Perez

While his career still continues as a reliever after thirteen seasons, there was a time in 2004 when Oliver Perez looked as if he was going to be one of the best starters in the league. He went 12–10 that year, with a 2.98 ERA. Perez never replicated 2004 with Pittsburgh, but did rebound with the Mets in 2007 and '08, winning 25 games before being banished to the pen.

Delwyn Young

A utility man extraordinaire for the Bucs in 2009 and '10, Delwyn Young was never able to secure a starting spot; he batted .255 in 545 at bats. The highlight of his career was hitting the first home run given up by Washington superstar Steven Strasberg.

Javier Lopez

In 2010 the Pittsburgh Pirates signed reliever Javier Lopez to a free-agent contract. In his six previous seasons he had mixed success, but was decent in 50 appearances for the Bucs. Unfortunately, they dealt him to the Giants before the season ended. He has since been an important cog for the unhittable San Francisco bullpen, with a 2.29 ERA in six years, helping the Giants to three world championships.

Jared Hughes

While the Pirates let Lopez go before he had a chance to contribute to winning baseball in Pittsburgh, they did hold on to Jared Hughes who has been a fine middle reliever for the Pirates with 14 wins and a 2.77 ERA over his five seasons. He best year was 2014, when he had a sub-2 ERA at 1.96, and an impressive 1.088 WHIP.

Omar Moreno

The former Pirate speedster wore 48 in his first two seasons in the majors in 1974 and 1975.

Bob Skinner

Popular Pirate outfielder for the 1960 world championship squad donned #48 as a hitting coach with the club between 1979 and 1985, when he won another ring as a member of the famed '79 "Fam-a-lee" team.

#49: THE KNUCKLEBALL

ALL TIME NO. 49 ROSTER	YEAR
Jeff Locke	(2012–2015)
Ross Ohlendorf	(2008–2011)
Bryan Bullington	(2007)
Nate McLouth	(2006–2007)
Jose Mesa	(2004–2005)
Jeff Reboulet	(2003)
Josias Manzanillo	(2000–2002)
Jeff Tabaka	(1998)
Matt Ruebel	(1996–1997)
Ross Powell	(1995)
Tim Wakefield	(1992–1993)
Jerry Don Gleaton	(1992)
Jeff Robinson	(1987–1989)
Mark Ross	(1987)
Hipolito Pena	(1987)
Larry McWilliams	(1982–1986)
Victor Cruz	(1981)
Vance Law	(1980)
Dave Roberts	(1979–1980)
Dave May	(1978)
Steve Nicosia	(1978)
Tony Armas	(1975–1976)
Juan Pizarro	(1974)
Jim McKee	(1972)
Ben Guintini	(1946)
Ed Brandt	(1937–1938)
Ralph Birkofer	(1933–1936)

NUMBER RETIRED: None

HALL OF FAMERS TO WEAR THE NUMBER: None

FIRST PERFORMANCE WITH THE NUMBER

4/25/1933- In a 10–3 rout by the Cardinals, Ralph Birkofer was one of the lone bright spots of a bad day, pitching two hitless inning of relief.

FIRST HOME RUN WITH THE NUMBER

7/7/1993- It was a tough season for Tim Wakefield in 1993, but on this day, while he pitched poorly and was pulled after 3 2/3 innings, having given up five hits and two runs, he hit his first home run, a fourth-inning solo shot.

FIRST VICTORY BY A PITCHER WITH THE NUMBER

8/26/1933- In his first major league start Ralph Birkofer went five innings, allowing three hits and a run during a 7–2 win over the Giants for his initial victory in the show.

BEST PIRATES TO WEAR THE NUMBER: (W-L-ERA)
Larry McWilliams (43–33-3.64)

Larry McWilliams was a first-round pick by the Braves in 1974 who didn't find true success in the majors until he came to the Steel City

Juan Pizzaro (photo courtesy of the
Pittsburgh Pirates)

in 1982. A year later he had his best
season in the show, with a 15–8 mark
and fifth-place finish in the race for
the Cy Young. McWilliams continued to roll a year later, with 12 wins
and a 2.93 ERA. After the 1987 campaign, he was released by the club
with 43 wins in hand.

Jose Mesa (7–10-3.93)

Jose Mesa was the shutdown closer
for the Cleveland Indians during
their championship run in the mid-
1990s, and then for the Mariners and
Phillies before he became a Pirate
in 2004. While he was thirty-eight at
the time, he saved 70 games for the
Pirates in two seasons, including 43 during his first campaign. After
leaving Pittsburgh in 2006, he stayed in the big leagues for two more
seasons. Mesa had 321 saves over the course of his nineteen-year major league career, which still stands as the seventeenth most of all time.

Tim Wakefield (14–12-4.17)

Tim Wakefield came out on the mound in 1992 for his first big league
game, against the Cardinals, a former first baseman who learned how
to throw a knuckleball and got a chance to pitch in the majors. No one
knew what to make of him at the time, but by the end of the year he
was 8–1 with a 2.15 ERA, and had a spectacular performance against
the Braves in the NLCS. The knuckleball didn't knuckle the next season as his Pirates' career ended, and it looked as though his time in
the majors would be over. Luckily, he went to Boston, where the magic
pitch regained its effectiveness. Seventeen years later, he had racked
up 200 wins and became a Red Sox legend with two world championships. Had Pirates management only known to trust the knuckleball.

WORST PIRATES TO WEAR THE NUMBER: (W-L-ERA)

Bryan Bullington (0–3-5.89)

When GM David Littlefield selected Bryan Bullington with the first pick of the 2002 draft and promptly stated he'd be a great number three pitcher in the Pirate rotation, red sirens should have gone off warning that this was a bad pick. Going winless in three decisions for the Bucs, leading to a 1–9 major league career, would have confirmed that assumption. He eventually found his way . . . in Japan, where he has won 45 games for Hiroshima and Orix, making Bullington a pretty damn good number three pitcher for them. Who knew David Littlefield would finally be proved correct.

Ben Guintini (0–0-.000)

An athletic player who had some success in the Pacific Coast League, Ben Guintini was perfect in his short-lived major league career; he went hitless in four at bats for the Bucs in 1946 after serving in the Army during World War II. Guintini matched that mark four years later with a zero-for-four performance with the A's.

Ross Powell (0–2-5.23)

After a career at Michigan singing "Hail to the Victors," Ross Powell pitched three less-than-stellar seasons out of the pen, ending with the Bucs in 1995.

OTHER NOTABLE PIRATES TO WEAR THE NUMBER

Ralph Birkofer

A tough southpaw for the Pirates in the mid-1930s, Ralph Birkofer was 31–26 for the Bucs over his four-year career in the Steel City.

Ed Brandt

After a successful nine-year career with the Braves and Dodgers, where he won 105 games, Ed Brandt came to the Bucs in 1937 for his final two years in the show. The southpaw went 16–14, including 11 wins his first season.

Juan Pizarro

The eighteen-year vet spent his final season in a Pirates uniform in 1974 wearing the number 49.

Dave May

Dave May was a slugging outfielder for twelve seasons, ending his career in a Pirates uniform in 1978. His best year was 1973, when he hit 25 home runs and knocked in 93 for the Brewers. With the Bucs he was hitless in four at bats, with a walk and a stolen base.

Dave Roberts

A former top prospect with the Bucs in the late 1960s, pitcher Dave Roberts returned to the Pirates for the pennant drive run in 1979 after having success in San Diego, Houston, and Detroit. He pitched well for the Bucs that season in 21 appearances, going 5–2 with a save. Roberts was at his best in 1979, when he had a memorable clutch relief performance in a 19-inning affair against the Padres on August 25 garnering a win. He was sent to the Mariners early in 1980, where he ended his thirteen-year career with 103 wins.

Jeff Robinson

For the better part of three seasons, Jeff Robinson was a fine reliever for the Bucs before starting 19 games in 1989. His best year came during the team's surprising 1988 campaign, when he won 11 games in relief, with 75 appearances.

Jerry Don Gleaton

Over a period of twelve years, Texas alum Jerry Don Gleaton not only had a great flowing name, but was a decent reliever for six major league teams. His time in the majors ended in 1992, when he won his only decision in 23 appearances with the eastern division champion Pirates.

Jeff Tabaka

Kent State University southpaw Jeff Tabaka had two stints with the Bucs in his six years in the big leagues. The first was in 1994, when he gave up eight runs in four innings; the second was four years later, when he was much better with a 2–2 mark and 3.02 ERA in 37 appearances. With the future of the thirty-four-year-old hurler looking up, injuries ended his career in 2001, with the Cardinals.

Josaias Manzanillo

A decent reliever with the Bucs in the early seasons of the twenty-first century, Josaias Manzanillo's career was defined in a most unsavory manner. He was mentioned in the Mitchell Report for steroid use.

Jeff Reboulet

A teammate of Albert Belle at LSU, Jeff Reboulet played twelve seasons in the show with five teams as a utility infielder; it all ended in Pittsburgh, in 2003, with a .241 average in 261 at bats.

Ross Ohlendorf

It was a tale of two seasons for Princeton alum Ross Ohlendorf: 2009, when he was labeled a star of the future after an 11–10 campaign for the Bucs, and a year later when a 1–11 record ended those expectations. He still remains in the majors, though, most recently pitching in relief for the Rangers in 2015.

Jeff Locke

Following a tremendous first half of the 2013 campaign, when Jeff Locke was named to his first and only All-Star Game, the southpaw has been a much maligned number-five hurler. At times he looks dominant, while at others appears to be a batting practice pitcher. Locke remains in the rotation despite complaints from the Pirates Nation, but despite all the criticisms he has decent stats when compared to other major league number five hurlers.

#50-#59: THINGS GET BETTER IN THE 50s?

ALL TIME NO. 50–59 ROSTER	YEAR
#50	
Charlie Morton	(2011–2015)
Brian Bass	(2010)
Dave Davidson	(2007)
Tom Gorzelanny	(2006)
Matt Lawton	(2005)
Jason Boyd	(2004)
Jose Bautista	(2004)
Julian Tavarez	(2003)
Andy Barkett	(2001)
Marc Wilkins	(2001)
Dennis Konuszewski	(1995)
Mark Dewey	(1993–1994)
Stan Belinda	(1991–1993)
Dave LaPoint	(1988)
Barry Jones	(1986–1988)
Eddie Vargas	(1982, 1984)
Odell Jones	(1975)
Kent Tekulve	(1974)
Frank Taveras	(1971)
Jim Tobin	(1937–1939)
Mace Brown	(1935)
Lloyd Johnson	(1934)
Clise Dudley	(1933)
COACHES	
Pete Vuckovich	(1997–2000)

HALL OF FAMERS TO WEAR THE NUMBER: None

FIRST PERFORMANCE WITH THE NUMBER

9/15/1933- The former Dodger and Phillie pitched only one-third of an inning in his Pittsburgh Pirates career, but make no mistake for Clise Dudley it was a very bad third of an inning. Starter Hal Smith allowed five runs in 2 2/3 innings and gave way to Dudley, who matched Smith with five runs allowed of his own, along with six hits and a walk, all packed into that third of an inning.

BEST PIRATE TO WEAR THE NUMBER: (W-L-ERA)

Stan Belinda (19–15-3.52)

Even though he broke our hearts in game seven of the 1992 NLCS, Stan Belinda was a pretty good closer. He saved 61 games during the team's championship era in the 1990s, and went on to pitch twelve seasons for six teams. The side-arm hurler was diagnosed with multiple sclerosis in 1998, but pitched two more seasons. While we may remember him for that unfortunate loss, Belinda was a class act and good closer for the team.

Antonio Bastardo (photo courtesy of Christina Bortak)

OTHER NOTABLE PIRATES TO WEAR THE NUMBER

Jim Tobin

For a pitcher Jim Tobin was a hell of a hitter, smacking 17 home runs in his career, along with 102 RBIs. It's not to say he wasn't a good pitcher; he was, with a 29–24 mark in three years as a Pirate, while throwing two no-hitters in 1944, as well as back-to-back one-hitters while with the Braves, all after he learned the knuckleball. But there aren't many pitchers who had that kind of power at the plate.

Doug Frobel (photo courtesy of the Pittsburgh Pirates)

#51

HALL OF FAMERS TO WEAR THE NUMBER: None

FIRST PERFORMANCE WITH THE NUMBER

4/16/1936- In the second game of the 1936 season, pitcher Johnny Welch tossed a complete game, allowing ten hits and three runs in a 10–4 victory over the Phillies.

BEST PIRATE TO WEAR THE NUMBER: (W-L-ERA)

Rich Loiselle (9–18-4.38)

He may not have been the greatest reliever in the history of the game, and he is perhaps the most controversial "best of" pick in the book — choosing him over Tony Womack, Carlos Garcia, and Russ Bauers — but in 1997, when the team was in financial straits with a payroll less than what Albert Belle was making on his own — Loiselle was the Pirates' awesome closer with 29 saves for the surprising Freak Show that helped save the franchise. For that reason, he's a perfect fit for the "best of," as all who help save a franchise should be.

OTHER NOTABLE PIRATE TO WEAR THE NUMBER

Doug Frobel

He was the future power hitter extraordinaire of the franchise in the 1980s; the Canadian-born Doug Frobel was supposed to help the Bucs reach the promised land once again. Replacing Willie Stargell as a pinch-runner in the legend's last game was supposed to be the ceremonial passing of the torch. Unfortunately, .201 hitters don't usually help franchises do that; he was lucky he didn't burn down Three Rivers Stadium when he quickly dropped that torch. Frobel, who is currently a scout for the franchise, was the ultimate bust. While a forgettable figure in Pittsburgh history, he is still honored in his native Canada: a park in Nepean, Ontario, is named after him; proof positive that .201 hitters can still be remembered.

#52

HALL OF FAMERS TO WEAR THE NUMBER: None

FIRST PERFORMANCE WITH THE NUMBER

4/18/1935- During a 9–4 loss to the Reds, manager Pie Traynor called on Wayne Osborne with two outs in the sixth inning to be his fourth pitcher of the day. In his first major league game, Osborne retired the only batter he faced.

BEST PIRATE TO WEAR THE NUMBER: (W-L-ERA)
Joel Hanrahan (10–8-2.59)

Joel Hanrahan was a great closer for the Pirates as the last moments of their record-setting twenty-year losing streak came to an end. He saved a total of 76 games in 2011 and 2012. Hanrahan has turned out to be the ultimate giving tree for the new era of winning baseball, as a trade to the Red Sox before 2013 brought the Bucs Mark Melancon. An injury in Boston that seems to have ended Hanrahan's career, as added to the fact that Melancon had arguably the best season by a reliever in Pittsburgh's franchise history, tells us that he's very generous.

OTHER NOTABLE PIRATE TO WEAR THE NUMBER
Moises Alou

A descendant of the famous Alou brothers, Moises was a great prospect in the Pirates system who had only five at bats for the team. He was sent to the Expos in 1990 in exchange for Zane Smith, the missing piece in the rotation during the Pirates' pennant chase. Alou went on to become a fine player with a seventeen-year career that included 332 home runs. The one memorable moment in his career was yelling at poor Steve Bartman in the infamous game six of the 2003 NLCS, when the Cubs imploded.

#53

HALL OF FAMERS TO WEAR THE NUMBER: None

FIRST PERFORMANCE WITH THE NUMBER

5/6/1938- In his only game of the season, Ken Heintzelman was the last of four pitchers in an 11–7 loss to the Giants; he gave up two runs, a hit, and three walks in two innings of work.

BEST PIRATE TO WEAR THE NUMBER: (W-L-ERA)

James McDonald (27–24-4.21)

Son of a former tight end for the Los Angeles Rams by the same name, James McDonald had a tantalizing talent that at times made him look like a Cy Young winner, and at other times resembled a slow pitch softball hurler. He showed enough talent to win 12 games in 2012, but looked like that softball player a year late, when his Pirates' and major league careers came to an end.

OTHER NOTABLE PIRATE TO WEAR THE NUMBER

John Axford

John Axford could dial up a fastball that at times made him one of the most dangerous closers in the league. Proof came in 2011, when he saved a league-high 46 games for the Brewers, with a 1.95 ERA. Unfortunately, he also had a wildness that led to 4.5 walks per nine innings. He came to Pittsburgh late in the 2014 campaign, with the Bucs hoping they were getting that dominant closer. He did okay, but his 4.09 ERA led to him being released after the season.

#54

HALL OF FAMERS TO WEAR THE NUMBER: RICH GOSSAGE (2008)

FIRST PERFORMANCE WITH THE NUMBER

4/7/1977- On opening day, 1977, Rich Gossage came into the contest in the seventh inning of what would be a 12–6 loss to the Cardinals. He went two-thirds of an inning, walking Jerry DaVanon in the process.

BEST PIRATE TO WEAR THE NUMBER: (W-L-ERA)

Rich Gossage (11–9-1.62)

Rich Gossage spent only one of his twenty-two major league seasons in a Pirates uniform, but in 1977 that one season would be one of the most dominant in franchise history. He was 11–9 with 26 saves, a 1.62 ERA, and a phenomenal 0.955 WHIP, and he was named to the All-Star team. Gossage would eventually be given baseball's highest honor, with election to the Hall of Fame in 2008.

OTHER NOTABLE PIRATE TO WEAR THE NUMBER

Ray Searage

The West Liberty State College alum was an unspectacular reliever for seven seasons in the show, ending his big league career in 1990 with an 11–13 mark. Somehow that unspectacular guy became arguably the most important cog of the Pirate turnaround. Ray Searage has become a Mound Whisperer, turning rotted veterans into valuable MLB commodities. Doubt his abilities? Just ask Vance Worley,

A.J. Burnett, Joe Blanton, Francisco Liriano, and Edinson Volquez, and they will vouch for his brilliance. As the Pirates continue their quest for a world championship, they should forget about high-priced free agents, instead paying Searage whatever they must to keep him in tow.

#55

HALL OF FAMERS TO WEAR THE NUMBER: None

FIRST PERFORMANCE WITH THE NUMBER:

9/5/1982- During a 2–1 loss to the Dodgers, Doug Frobel ran for Richie Hebner in the eighth and then went into his right field spot, striking out in his first major league at bat in the 10th inning.

BEST PIRATE TO WEAR THE NUMBER: (HR-RBI-AVE)

Russell Martin (26–122-.256)

A former All-Star catcher, who appeared to be ending his major league career when the Pirates rescued him from the Yankees, Russell Martin became an integral part of their magnificent turnaround. He not only got his offensive game in gear with a .293 average in 2014, but gave them a defensive presence behind the plate they hadn't had in over twenty years. When he left for the Blue Jays, a Pirates Nation was understandably depressed when he went on to help lead Toronto to greatness, too.

OTHER NOTABLE PIRATE TO WEAR THE NUMBER

Jimmy Anderson

After a fine minor league career that saw him go 11–2 with Nashville in 1999, heavy-set Jimmy Anderson embarked on his Pirates odyssey hoping to be the lynchpin in their starting rotation. Instead, he went 24–42 with a 5.17 ERA, and was only a lynchpin on the grenade that was the Pirates pitching staff at that point in time.

#56

HALL OF FAMERS TO WEAR THE NUMBER: None

FIRST PERFORMANCE WITH THE NUMBER

9/9/1974- In the eighth inning of a 9–4 win against the Cubs, rookie Jose Jimenez came into the game for his first major league appearance. He allowed two hits and a run in his initial performance.

BEST PIRATE TO WEAR THE NUMBER: (W-L-ERA)

Jose Silva (24–28-5.41)

The Pirates had hoped that Jose Silva would be one of the answers for the pitching staff, either in their bullpen or starting rotation. Despite the fact that he won 11 games in 2000, his ERA was below 5 only once in the five years he spent in a Pirates uniform, and that was 4.40 in 1998. Still, he was the winningest number 56 in Pirate history.

OTHER NOTABLE PIRATE TO WEAR THE NUMBER

Rich Renteria

Rich Renteria had only a small cup of coffee with the Bucs in 1986, with three hits in 12 at bats. While his playing career wasn't impressive, the former first round-pick by the Bucs in 1980 became a manager with the Cubs in 2014. Unfortunately, while he did a fine job leading them to 73 wins, Joe Maddon became available and Renteria lost his job. Fair or not, Maddon took a young team to the playoffs with 24 more wins, so it probably was the right call.

#57

HALL OF FAMERS TO WEAR THE NUMBER: None

FIRST PERFORMANCE WITH THE NUMBER

6/16/1953- Starting his first major league game, catcher Pete Naton was hitless in three at bats during a 3–2 loss to the Cubs.

BEST PIRATE TO WEAR THE NUMBER: (W-L-ERA)

John Smiley (60–42-3.57)

Twenty-game winner John Smiley gets the nod here as the unabashed best player ever to wear 57. After Smiley struggled in the bullpen in 1987, Jim Leyland put him in the starting rotation a year later with wonderful results. His last season in Pittsburgh, in 1991, saw him lead the league in wins with 20, and winning percentage at .714. Traded after the season to Minnesota at the beginning of the Bucs' salary purge, Smiley went on to win a total of 126 major league games.

OTHER NOTABLE PIRATE TO WEAR THE NUMBER

Daniel Moskos

He was one of the fathers of winning baseball in Pittsburgh, although at the time Daniel Moskos had no way of knowing that. Picking Moskos, a reliever, as the fourth pick in the first round in 2007 (along with the trade of Matt Morris) was probably the straw that broke the camel's back for general manager David Littlefield. He would soon be replaced by Neal Huntington as the revival began. Who knows, had

Littlefield picked Matt Wieters, whom the Orioles chose right after Moskos, he may have survived a little longer and the new winning era may never have come. This is why, despite a brief career that lasted all of 31 games in 2011, Daniel Moskos is the official father of winning baseball in Pittsburgh.

#58

HALL OF FAMERS TO WEAR THE NUMBER: None

FIRST PERFORMANCE WITH THE NUMBER

9/21/1973- On September 21, 1973, Steve Blass started the game and was continuing his legendary 1973 troubles. By the time Jim Foor made his Bucco debut in the seventh inning, the team was down 7–2 against the great Tom Seaver and the Mets. Foor pitched well, allowing only a hit while striking out a batter in his inning of work. New York went on to score three in the bottom of the eighth to put the nail in the Pirates' coffin, 10–2.

BEST PIRATE TO WEAR THE NUMBER: (W-L-ERA)

David Williams (17–26-4.25)

Just as David Williams finally seemed to be breaking out and becoming a key member of the Pirates' starting rotation in 2005, David Littlefield pulled the plug and sent him to Cincinnati. The Anchorage, Alaska, native was having a wonderful 10–11 campaign on yet another bad Pirates team. Feeling the need to continually dump potential pitching talent, Littlefield got an aging Sean Casey in return for Williams. While Littlefield then turned around and dumped Casey, Williams on the other hand was never able to capitalize on the momentum of 2005 and went 5–5 in his final two years in the show, although in his defense an operation on a herniated disk in his neck didn't help. Williams pitched one season in Japan, and currently is a pitching coach in the Gulf Coast League.

OTHER NOTABLE PIRATE TO WEAR THE NUMBER

Romulo Sanchez

Romulo Sanchez didn't have much of a major league career, playing two seasons with the Bucs in 2006 and '07 with a 1–0 mark and 4.60 ERA, but the Venezuelan was a hard-throwing reliever who could hurl his fastball in the upper 1990s. Unfortunately, his fastball didn't miss bats, and Sanchez never struck out as many as he probably should have. Despite that fact, when pitching for the Bucs' Venezuelan league team in 2004 he tossed a no-hitter for San Joaquin and was lights out for Altoona in '07. *Baseball America* felt, in 2008, that he could turn into a great late-inning pitcher out of the bullpen if he could only work on his curveball. He never did, and turned into another proud Pirates prospect during that time period who never became an effective major league player.

#59

HALL OF FAMERS TO WEAR THE NUMBER: None

FIRST PERFORMANCE WITH THE NUMBER

4/11/1986- Starting in his first game for the Pirates, Mike Diaz played first base and went hitless in two at bats before being pinch-hit for in the seventh inning by Sid Bream. The Pirates would go on to lose, 5–4, to the Cubs.

BEST PIRATE TO WEAR THE NUMBER: (HR-RBI-AVE)

Rob Mackowiak (52–221-.258)

A solid hitter who not only showed power — twice hitting more than 16 homers for the Bucs — but was able to play anywhere in the infield and outfield, Rob Mackowiak was a popular Pirate among the Bucco Nation. On August 28, 2004, he had a day for the ages as he celebrated the birth of his first kid in a memorable doubleheader. In the first game he had only one hit in five at bats, but that hit was a walk-off grand slam in the bottom of the ninth to defeat the Cubs, 9–5. In game two he slammed a two-run, bottom-of-the-ninth homer that erased a 4–2 Chicago lead, and the Bucs won an inning later, 5–4.

OTHER NOTABLE PIRATE TO WEAR THE NUMBER

Tony Sanchez

Tony Sanchez is player liked by Pirates fans and players, who all hoped that former first-round pick would be able to take over the starting spot behind the plate for the Bucs. To this point he hasn't come close, so the team has had to find the likes of Martin and Cervelli instead. Even Elias Diaz seems to have usurped Sanchez on the organizational depth chart, and Reese McGuire looks to be ahead of him, too. Stranger things have happened, but a .259 average in his brief Pirates career with substandard defense, coupled with the fact he hit a mere .235 in Indianapolis in 2015, as well as the fact he was DFA'd in January of 2016 makes the odds even longer for Sanchez.

#60-#97: FROM INFINITY AND BEYOND

#60

ALL TIME NO. 60 ROSTER	YEAR
Keon Broxton	(2015)
Bobby LaFromboise	(2014)
Kris Johnson	(2013)
Kyle McPherson	(2012)
Michael Crotta	(2011)
Aaron Thompson	(2011)
Bryan Bullington	(2005)
Jose Parra	(2000)
Jason Boyd	(1999)
Mike Maddux	(1995)
Stan Belinda	(1989–1990)
Randy Kramer	(1988)
COACHES	
Luis Dorante	(2008–2010)

#61

ALL TIME NO. 61 ROSTER	YEAR
Duke Welker	(2013)
Justin Wilson	(2012)
Jeff Locke	(2011)
Chan Ho Park	(2010)
Anthony Claggett	(2009)
Sean Burnett	(2004, 2008)
Tom Gorzelanny	(2005)
Alex Ramirez	(2000)
Darrell May	(1996)
Freddie Toliver	(1993)
Victor Cole	(1992)
Dorn Taylor	(1989)
Moises Alou	(1987)
Ray Krawczyk	(1984)
Joe Orsulak	(1983)
Dick Anderson	(1972)

#62

ALL TIME NO. 62 ROSTER	YEAR
Gorkys Hernandez	(2012)
Josh Harrison	(2011)

BEST OF THE 60s

Francisco Cordova (42–47-3.96)

Veracruz, Mexico, native Francisco Cordova burst onto the scene in 1996, first as a reliever his rookie season when he saved 12 games, then as a starter the next year as he combined with Ricardo Rincon to throw the last no-hitter in franchise history, an exciting 3–0, ten-inning victory over Houston. Unfortunately, as stardom was about to come for Cordova, injuries would end his big league career in 2000.

BEST OF THE 70s

Ricardo Rincon (4–10-3.17)

Famous in the movie, *Moneyball,* for the trade Brad Pitt AKA Billy Beane made with Cleveland toward the end of the movie, southpaw reliever Ricardo Rincon started his eleven-year career in 1997 with the Pirates. That season he combined with fellow Veracruz native Francisco Cordova for the last no-hitter a Pirate has thrown. He pitched two seasons with the Bucs before being the trade bait that got the Pirates Brian Giles from the Indians . . . the team that allowed him to be famous in the motion pictures!

Hayden Penn	(2010)
Daniel McCutchen	(2009)
Matt Capps	(2005)
Steve Bieser	(1998)
Marc Wilkins	(1996)
Mike Dyer	(1994–1995)
Chris Green	(1984)

#63

ALL TIME NO. 63 ROSTER	YEAR
Chris Leroux	(2011–2013)
Luis Cruz	(2008)
Tim Laker	(1999)
Clint Sodowsky	(1997)
Keith Osik	(1996)
Rich Robertson	(1994)
Jeff Tabaka	(1994)
Rich Sauveur	(1986)

#64

ALL TIME NO. 64 ROSTER	YEAR
Deolis Guerra	(2015)
Matt Skrmetta	(2000)
Mike Garcia	(1999–2000)
Mike Williams	(1998)
Joel Johnston	(1993–1994)
Paul Miller	(1991–1992)
Houston Jimenez	(1987)
John Candelaria	(1975)

#65

ALL TIME NO. 65 ROSTER	YEAR
Casey Sadler	(2014–2015)
Matt Hague	(2012)
Tony Watson	(2011)
Justin Thomas	(2010)
Mark Petkovsek	(1993)
Armando Moreno	(1990–1991)

#66

ALL TIME NO. 66 ROSTER	YEAR
Elias Diaz	(2015)
Justin Morneau	(2013)

Jared Hughes (photo courtesy of Christina Bortak)

BEST OF THE 80s

Heberto Andrade

Twelve seasons with a number above 59 makes him the granddaddy of high numbers in Pirates history. He has been the bullpen catcher in his time here, after spending three seasons as a catcher in the Cubs organization. He is the link between what was bad and what is now good, which puts him above any player in the 80s.

BEST OF THE 90s

Joe Beimel (11–20-5.03)

He is the only choice for the best player to wear a number in the 90s; literally, he is the only player to have worn a number in the 90s. Joe Beimel has a Pittsburgh back-

J.J. Furmaniak	(2005)
Chris Tremie	(1999)
Jeff Ballard	(1994)
Ben Shelton	(1993)
Blas Minor	(1992–1993)
Rafael Belliard	(1982)

#67

ALL TIME NO. 67 ROSTER YEAR

Francisco Cordova	(1996–2000)
Tony Menendez	(1993)
Sam McDowell	(1975)

#68

ALL TIME NO. 68 ROSTER YEAR

Vic Black	(2013)
Wyatt Toregas	(2011)
Jim Dougherty	(1999)
Dave Clark	(1992)
Benny DiStefano	(1984)

#69

ALL TIME NO. 69 ROSTER YEAR

Jordy Mercer	(2012)
Eric Fryer	(2011)
Bronson Arroyo	(2000–2002)
Jeff Schulz	(1991)

#70

ALL TIME NO. 70 ROSTER YEAR

Jared Hughes	(2011)

#71

ALL TIME NO. 71 ROSTER YEAR

Brian Burres	(2010–2011)
Brian Boehringer	(2002–2003)
Elmer Dessens	(1996–1998)

#73

ALL TIME NO. 73 ROSTER YEAR

Argenis Diaz	(2010)
Ricardo Rincon	(1997–1998)

#75

ALL TIME NO. 75 ROSTER YEAR

Alex Presley	(2010)
Rich Loiselle	(1996)
Joe Redfield	(1991)

COACHES

Jeff Livesey	(2014–2015)

#77

ALL TIME NO. 77 ROSTER YEAR

D.J. Carrasco	(2010)
Brian Burres	(2011)

#85

ALL TIME NO. 85 ROSTER YEAR

Lastings Milledge	(2009–2010)

COACHES

Dave Jauss	(2013–2015)

#86

ALL TIME NO. 86 ROSTER YEAR

Heberto Andrade	(2004–2014)

#87

ALL TIME NO. 87 ROSTER YEAR

Jeff Branson	(2013)

#88

ALL TIME NO 88 ROSTER YEAR

Rick White	(2005)

#97

ALL TIME NO. 97 ROSTER YEAR

Joe Beimel	(2011)

ground; he is an alum of Duquesne University. He started his career in 2001 in the Steel City, staying three seasons; then, after playing elsewhere for eight years, Beimel returned in 2011 and donned the highest number in franchise history. After being out of the majors for two seasons, he joined the Seattle Mariners in 2014 and has pitched effectively for the past two seasons. He continues to wear the high number he fell in love with in 2011.

BLANK BACKS

Before 1932 Pirates uniforms appeared blank on the back—no numbers on them—so some of the greatest players in franchise history have no numbers with which to associate themselves. When the New York Yankees became the first team to make numbers a permanent part of their uniforms, they did so by giving each player a number based on his position in the batting order. While there is no explanation for pitchers, it appears that the team gave its best pitcher the number 11 and went forward from there (except for the unlucky number 13, which apparently wasn't given out). On the basis of this theory, we're going to have a little fun here and see what numbers the old Bucs would have had. If a player eventually wore a number as a player with the Bucs, such as the Waners, he will be excluded. Since this is a fun encounter, we will use the box scores from the various World Series games to come up with a guesstimate. For pitchers we will use a similar system, excluding 13 of course.

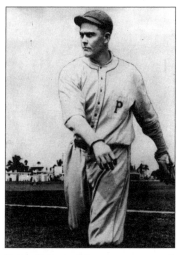

Babe Adams (photo courtesy of the Pittsburgh Pirates)

Fred Clarke (photo courtesy of the Pittsburgh Pirates)

NUMBER	PLAYER
1	Ginger Beaumont
1	Bobby Byrne
2	Max Carey
2	Fred Clarke
3	Tommy Leach
3	Kiki Cuyler
4	Honus Wagner
5	Dots Miller
6	Claude Ritchey
6	Glenn Wright
7	Chief Wilson
7	George Grantham
8	George Gibson

11	Jack Chesbro
11	Vic Willis
11	Wilbur Cooper
11	Lee Meadows
12	Deacon Phillippe-*
12	Ray Kremer
14	Jesse Tannehill
14	Ed Doheny
14	Nick Maddox
14	Vic Aldridge
15	Sam Leever-*
16	Babe Adams
16	Johnny Miljus

*- allowed to keep number from 1902, even though they weren't top performers by 1909

ACKNOWLEDGMENTS

Projects such of this are never complete without the incredible support of many, most importantly my wonderful family that includes my wife, Vivian, as well as my children Matthew, Tony, and Cara.

My extended family has always been a source of support over the years, no matter where I've been and what I've accomplished. My father Domenic, brother Jamie, his wife Cindy, my nieces Brianna and Marissa, my sister Mary, her husband Matthew, my aunts Maryanne, and Betty, my cousins Fran, Luci, Flo, Beth, Tom, Gary, Linda, Amy, Amanda, Claudia, Ginny Lynn, Pam, Debbie, Diane, Vince, and Richard, as well as the memories of my mother Eleanor, my cousins Tom Aikens and Eddie DiLello, my Uncle Vince, my grandparents, and my aunts Louise, Norma, Jeannie, Libby, Mary, and Evie, have all been essential in any success I've enjoyed in my life. A thank-you also has to go to my in-laws, Vivian and Salvatore Pansino, as well as their daughters Sondra, Cindy, and Nancy, and my nephew Nathaniel, and niece Teresa for their continual support.

The bullpen of Bill Ranier, Chris Fletcher, Dan Russell, Bob O'Brien, Matt O'Brotka, and Rich Boyer have always been available to bounce whatever ideas or thoughts I've had with my projects, as have the fine people of the Society of American Baseball Research, without whom I would never have the incredible research opportunities that they have made available to me.

Finally, a thank-you to Jim Trdinich of the Pittsburgh Pirates for contributing the wonderful photos in the book, Christina Bortak, who also contributed photos, as well as Niels Aaboe and the fine people at Sports Publishing, Inc., who have made this project a wonderful experience.

ABOUT THE AUTHOR

David Finoli is a sports historian and author who has written nineteen books, mostly dealing with the rich history of sports in Western Pennsylvania. A member of the Society of American Baseball research since 1999, Finoli has also contributed to two books, *The Cambridge Companion to Baseball,* for which he wrote a chapter on the history of baseball's expansion and franchise movement, and *Who's on First: Replacement Players in World War II,* a SABR publication, for which he wrote chapters on Pirates players who were there during the time period, plus a synopsis of the franchise during the war.

A veteran of thirty-two years in retail management, Finoli graduated from Duquesne University with a BA in journalism, and currently lives in a suburb of Pittsburgh with his wife, Vivian, and children Tony, Matthew, and Cara.